FRANK
O'HARA
POET
AMONG
PAINTERS

FRANK O'HARA

POET AMONG PAINTERS

Marjorie Perloff

University of Texas Press, Austin and London

To
MAUREEN GRANVILLE-SMITH
and DONALD ALLEN

Note: Since the original publication of this book, all manuscripts cited on pages 36–38, 41–42, 44–45, 52–53 and in
notes 1, 3, 4, 8, 17, 18, and 20 for Chapter Two have been
published in two volumes edited by Donald Allen: *Early
Writing* and *Poems Retrieved* by Frank O'Hara (Bolinas,
Calif.: Grey Fox Press, 1977). Copyright © 1977 by Maureen Granville-Smith, Administratrix of the Estate of Frank
O'Hara. I am grateful to Donald Allen and Grey Fox Press
for permission to include material published in these two
books.

International Standard Book Number 0-292-72429-2
Library of Congress Catalog Card Number 78-71567

Designed by MaryJane DiMassi
Typeset by York Graphic Services, Inc.
Printed in the United States of America

First Paperback Edition, 1979

PREFACE

A DECADE AFTER HIS death, Frank O'Hara remains a controversial figure. Among New York poets and artists, he has been well-known since the mid-fifties, and by the early sixties he had become a kind of culture hero. Yet precisely because of his close association with the "New York School," O'Hara was—and continues to be—considered an "art world" figure rather than a serious poet. Because he wrote his poems very quickly—often on the run and during his lunch hour at the Museum of Modern Art—it has been assumed that his poetry is trivial and frivolous. Because his life was so colorful and his accidental death on Fire Island when he was only forty such a dramatic, indeed a tragic event, interest has centered on the man rather than on the work.

The purpose of my book is to right this balance. Like many students of contemporary poetry, I first read Frank O'Hara in Donald Allen's pivotal anthology, *The New American Poetry* (New York: Grove, 1960), but it was not until 1972, when the editors of *Contemporary Literature* asked me to write a review essay on the volumes of poetry that had appeared within the preceding two years, that I began to understand O'Hara's poetic world. The occasion was the publication

OH is central to Postwar poetry

of Ron Padgett and David Shapiro's *Anthology of New York Poets* (New York: Random House, 1970). This anthology was dedicated to Frank O'Hara; the preface pays special tribute to him and reprints the entire text of "Personism: A Manifesto," written in 1959. There are twenty-two pages of poems by O'Hara and an interesting biographical/bibliographical note.

The more O'Hara I read, the more enthusiastic I became about his work. Here, I felt, was a writer who made poetry look like a delightful game but who also had an uncanny way of getting what John Ashbery has called, with reference to Picabia, "the perishable fragrance of tradition" into his work, a tradition he sometimes extended, sometimes subverted. It was this combination of seeming artlessness and an acute awareness of poetic tradition that aroused my interest and curiosity, and when I came to write my review-essay, O'Hara became its center.

The present study thus reflects my growing conviction that O'Hara is one of the central poets of the postwar period, and that his influence will continue to grow in the years to come. He is also an important art critic, his improvisatory but incisive essays and reviews recalling those of an earlier poet-art critic whom he loved—Apollinaire. And his collaborations with painters, composers, playwrights, and film-makers have given us some of the most delightful mixed-media works of the fifties and sixties.

The chapters that follow treat O'Hara's poetry chronologically. The focus is critical rather than biographical, but whenever it seems useful, I relate the poetry to the life. I begin with the poetry scene of the early fifties as a context for O'Hara's poetic, as that poetic can be deduced from his practical criticism and casual commentary, for O'Hara disliked theory for its own sake. The second chapter deals with the early period (1946–53), when O'Hara was beginning to invent a style. Access to the unpublished manuscripts of the Harvard years (1946–50) has shown me how learned and sophisticated this "playful" poet really was, and in discussing the early New York period I try to demonstrate how O'Hara's interest in Dada and Surrealist poetry, in Abstract Expressionist painting, and in the colloquial speech of poets like William Carlos Williams came together to produce a body of exciting experimental poetry, quite unlike the established neo-Symbolist verse of the fifties.

The third chapter breaks the chronological development and takes up O'Hara's relationship to the visual artists of his time, including the various ways in which painting affected his poetry, his collaborations with Larry Rivers and Norman Bluhm, and his prolific art criticism. Chapter Four is the longest and perhaps the central chapter. Here I submit the poems of the "great period" (1954–61) to close inspection, discussing their style, genre, and use of convention. The problem of influence is a major topic, for O'Hara assimilated an astonishing variety of styles. His best poems fuse what he called the "charming artifice" of Apollinaire (and of a host of other French poets from Rimbaud to the Surrealists) with the bardic voice of Mayakovsky, the colloquial speech of Williams or the late Auden, the documentary precision of Pound's *Cantos,* and the Rilkean notion of being "needed by things." *Model + Technique* O'Hara's equivocal response to the English Romantics is especially interesting. Generically, his major poems follow Romantic models, but he almost always injects a note of parody, turning the conventions he uses inside out. Aside from literary models, O'Hara's poetry also incorporates specific film techniques, phonetic and rhythmic devices modeled on the music of John Cage and Eric Satie, and such concepts of Action Painting as "push and pull," the "all-over," and the notion of the canvas as a field which the artist enters. The result of assimilating such varied influences is the creation of a new kind of lyric poem.

The final chapter considers the work of the sixties—smaller in output and rather different in kind—and takes up the difficult question of O'Hara's role as a New York poet. After discussing some of the astonishing elegies written for him by his friends and followers (a whole book could be compiled of these), I consider the relationship of O'Hara's poetry to that of John Ashbery and Allen Ginsberg, the two poets perhaps most immediately comparable, although in very different ways. I conclude that these poets have taken the contemporary lyric down parallel courses that never quite meet. And this is only natural: "schools" or movements always recede into the background as the permanently interesting artists emerge from their ranks.

Throughout this book I have tried to keep in mind O'Hara's own strictures on literary criticism, so charmingly put forward in the little poem, "The Critic" (1951), cited at the beginning of the Preface. I hope that if O'Hara were alive today, he would not consider me "the assassin of [his] orchards." I have tried, on the contrary, to respect his wish: "Do not / frighten me more than you / have to! I must live forever."

Many people have helped me to write this book. The following granted interviews: Joe LeSueur, John Ashbery, Grace Hartigan, Norman Bluhm, David Shapiro, and Patsy Southgate. These writers and artists helped to make the poetry milieu of the fifties and sixties come alive. They provided indispensable information about specific poems, collaborations, and events in O'Hara's life. They also persuaded me, I might add, that the time is not yet ripe for a biography, because their versions of specific incidents did not always coincide. I have had helpful conversation and/or correspondence about O'Hara with Bill Berkson, Paul Schmidt, and Allen Ginsberg. Kenneth Koch offered his assistance by mail but could not be interviewed because he was out of the country during the year in which this book was written.

I have profited from discussion of O'Hara's poetry with the following persons: Charles Altieri, James Breslin, Gerda Blumenthal, Stuart Curran, Frederick Garber, Lawrence Kramer, William McPherson, Diane Middlebrook, Norma Procopiow, David St. John, and Catharine R. Stimpson. Emily Mitchell Wallace deserves special mention: friend and fellow scholar, she was always ready to take up a difficult point, to help me track down a possible influence or reference, or to advise me on handling controversial biographical material tactfully. Doris Grumbach invited me, in January 1975, to review *Art Chronicles* for the *New Republic;* it was this review (1 March 1975) that brought my work on O'Hara to the attention of Michael Braziller of George Braziller, Inc., and initiated what has been a happy association between author and publisher, especially with my patient and discerning editor, James Hoekema. I should also like to thank Julia Strand for helping to bring the manuscript to completion. I owe a particular debt to the students in my seminar, "The Poetics of the Contemporary Lyric," given at the University of Maryland in the fall of 1975, especially to Douglas Messerli and Donald Duncan.

The following persons read portions of the manuscript and gave sound advice: Joe LeSueur, Sandra Earl Mintz, Claude Rawson, David Shapiro, William Spanos, Minda Tessler, and my two college-age daughters, Nancy and Carey—both keen O'Hara fans. My husband, Joseph K. Perloff, took time off from his heavy schedule at the

Hospital of the University of Pennsylvania, and time away from his own writings, to read every page (at every stage) and to help me organize the material and present it as clearly as possible. His suggestions—the suggestions of someone outside "the field"—were especially helpful. I am happy to add that, unlike many spouses, he had nothing to do with typing the manuscript; that unpleasant task was entirely my own.

I come finally to the two people to whom this book is dedicated and without whom it could not have been written. Frank O'Hara's sister, Maureen O'Hara Granville-Smith, the executrix of the Frank O'Hara Estate, has made available to me many unpublished manuscripts and letters as well as published items I might have missed: newspaper clippings, articles, photographs, reproductions of art works, recordings, etc. More important, she has encouraged the project from its inception, discussing the book with me at every stage of development and helping me to make crucial decisions. She has made me feel that I too "knew" Frank O'Hara. Her generosity and kindness can never be repaid.

Donald Allen, O'Hara's literary executor, has provided me with many copies of the manuscripts—letters, poems, essays, journals—he is currently editing. He has read my book from an editorial standpoint, providing missing or additional information, correcting errors of fact, expression, or taste, and detailing the necessary background. In conversation and correspondence, he has led me to many important sources I might otherwise have missed. I feel very fortunate to have had the help of the person who probably knows more about Frank O'Hara's poetry than anyone else.

MARJORIE G. PERLOFF

University of Southern California
Los Angeles, California

1
THE AESTHETIC OF ATTENTION

—Don't be bored, don't be lazy, don't be trivial, and don't be proud. The slightest loss of attention leads to death.[1]

MYTHOLOGIES

IN THE FALL OF 1975, at the Frumkin Gallery on 57th Street, Alfred Leslie exhibited a startling group of neo-realist—or as he calls them, "confrontational"—paintings, consciously modeled on the art of David, Caravaggio, and Rubens, and "meant to influence the conduct of people."[2] The most controversial, if not the best, painting in the Leslie show was a large (9-by-6-foot) canvas called *The Killing of Frank O'Hara*. O'Hara was only forty years old when he was fatally injured, having been struck by a beach buggy on Fire Island in the early morning hours of 24 July 1966; he died the next evening in Bayview Hospital at Mastic Beach, Long Island. Leslie chose to dismiss the facts, which I shall detail in a moment, and depicted the accident as if it were an heroic myth. The dead poet, dressed in a plain white T-shirt and tan trousers, lies serenely on a rectangular plank, his body showing no signs of injury. Four teen-age girls, wearing cut-off jeans and bathing suits, are carefully lowering the body from a raised platform, which floats ambiguously in midair against an empty background painted in thick browns and blacks. A young bearded man, standing toward the rear of the platform, is pulling a rope, his movements suggesting the tolling of a mourning bell. "The painting," wrote

David Bourdon in the *Village Voice,* "is in effect a modern-dress apotheosis which Leslie paints with as much drama as Renaissance painters gave to the lowering of Christ from the cross."[3] Another reviewer, John Perreault, commented, "This painting redeems Frank O'Hara from the sordidness of his death."[4]

But why should Frank O'Hara be depicted as Christ descending from the Cross? Why the teen-age girls (Perreault calls them the "furies") as if O'Hara had been some sort of pop idol or rock star? And why the title, which implies that the poet was somehow tracked down and murdered by his enemies? It is, to say the least, a strange conception of the accident,[5] and O'Hara himself, who disliked all forms of apotheosis, hero worship, the making of "monuments," who loved to debunk those he called "the farters of our country," whose own poetry leans heavily toward parody, would surely have been amused and embarrassed by the painting's implications.

Yet we cannot simply dismiss *The Killing of Frank O'Hara* as a bad mistake or a piece of hackwork. Leslie is a highly accomplished, intelligent artist; he and O'Hara were friends and collaborated on films together; he had, moreover, thought about the subject for a long time, having already painted two versions—both more realistic images of the accident itself—in 1968 and 1972.[6] What Leslie's painting suggests to me is that, within a decade of the poet's death, an elaborate myth had been built up, a myth centering on O'Hara as the "laureate of the New York art scene"—the minor artist, memorable less for his actual achievement than for his colorful life and his influence on others. "From his posts as critic for *Art News* and curator at the Museum of Modern Art," writes Herbert A. Leibowitz, "he moved as a mercurial presence through the galleries and the studios of such painters as de Kooning and Larry Rivers, writing monographs about the new masters, encouraging the young, amusing with his talk—and dashing off his poems at odd moments with an insouciance that was legendary."[7]

It is easy to see how this legend of O'Hara as "aesthetic courtier" arose. In the course of his brief career, he experimented with every literary genre as well as with mixed-media works—poem-paintings, musical comedies, films, ballets, operas. His wide circle of devoted friends seems to have adored him for his great personal charm, his humor, his startling insight, and his extraordinary generosity. A poet who could refer to himself jestingly as having been "made in the image of a sissy truck-driver" (*CP*, 338), he had romantic attachments to any number of artist friends. He was a tireless partygoer, a heavy drinker, a restless, inexhaustible, eclectic, and wildly energetic genius. Pater's famous credo: "To burn always with this hard, gemlike flame, to maintain this ecstasy, is success in life," might well have been his motto.[8] Accordingly, his premature death—a death caused by such a freak accident—was quickly mythologized. "The loss of the man," wrote the young Ted Berrigan in his obituary essay, "makes the air more difficult to breathe in."[9] And Allen Ginsberg, in an elegy written just four days after O'Hara's death, declared:

> Deep philosophical terms dear Edwin Denby serious as Herbert Read
>   with silvery hair   announcing your dead gift
> to the grave crowd   whose historic op art   frisson was
> the new sculpture your big blue wounded body made in the
>   Universe. . . .[10]

The artist, in short, became a work of art, and attention was deflected from O'Hara's real achievement, which was his poetry. The myth has two variants. The first, seen in Leslie's painting, is that of the artist as victim of a cruel, uncaring society, a man too good for this world. The second also views the artist as outsider but stresses his self-destructive bent. According to this myth, the poet who lives too hard and fast, burning the candle at both ends, finds his fulfillment only in death.[11] Thus, in an essay called "The New York School," written for the San Francisco *Advocate*, James M. Saslow writes: "Many of the lives [of the New York artists] tell us as much or more about their real purpose as did their paintings and poems. By their own admission, many remained frustrated in their work, and turned to other parts of their lives for fulfillment. Booze, fast cars and a feverish creativity took their toll. Many, like Jackson Pollock, Mark Rothko, and Frank O'Hara died violently or committed suicide." After describing, with dubious accuracy, the wild drinking parties of the New York artists, Saslow writes: "The pivotal figure in the cross-fertilization [between the poets and the painters] was the still unsung gay poet Frank O'Hara. Frail, thin, with a capacity for alcohol described as 'truly monumental,' O'Hara was at once poet laureate, guru, art critic and associate curator of painting at the Museum of Modern Art." The heavy drinking of O'Hara and his friends, Saslow explains, reflected "an overriding group obsession with *machismo*" at a time when Gay Liberation had not yet occurred. Drinking was a show of prowess, "a way of parodying Western movies." Within this false "macho framework," "the artists chose the most violent and extreme aspects of life, as if to dramatize their credo that *all* feeling, *all* experience is precious—regardless of its place in traditional good and evil. And ultimately, they deliberately courted death—at once the most taboo and most sublime experience."

Here is where the myth becomes dangerous: "When Frank O'Hara died it was officially termed an accident. But Elaine de Kooning felt deeper, more primeval forces were at work:

> And Frank O'Hara, getting killed on Fire Island, standing next to a beach buggy at three in the morning with 30 people standing around, and a car was coming with headlights on. Everyone saw it. How can you be hit by a car with headlights which everyone saw?

"The whole New York art scene," Saslow concludes, "was shattered by this mystery, which seemed to touch so many chords in their collective struggle."[12]

But the "mystery" Saslow speaks of so ominously has very little to do with what really happened on Fire Island on the evening in question. The facts, very briefly, are these. On Saturday, 23 July 1966, O'Hara and his friend J. J. Mitchell were houseguests at the home of Morris Golde on Water Island, Fire Island. That evening, O'Hara and Mitchell went to the Fire Island Pines, a bar-discotheque. At approximately 2 A.M., they set out to return to Golde's house in a beach taxi. About seven other people, who were also at the discotheque, but whom they did not know, were fellow passengers. A few minutes after reaching the beach, the taxi (a covered jeep) damaged a rear wheel and stopped. All the passengers descended and assembled near the left side of the taxi, away from the ocean, while the driver tried to repair the wheel. The headlights remained on because there was no other source of illumination; the beach was very dark. The driver radioed for another taxi, and the passengers milled about, waiting. O'Hara, who had been standing next to Mitchell, wandered toward the rear of the taxi. After a few minutes, another beach buggy came from the opposite direction. This buggy (an open jeep) appeared to be coming quite close to the disabled car at a speed of 15–20 m.p.h. The passengers standing in front of the taxi got out of the way, and Mitchell shouted "Frank!" At that moment, O'Hara emerged from the rear of the taxi, facing the headlights of the oncoming jeep. The young driver said he was blinded by the headlights of the stalled taxi, shining up into the air. O'Hara was struck by the right front fender, evidently in the abdomen; the jeep continued on for another ten feet or so and came to a stop. A policeman was on the scene within four or five minutes and a doctor was called. Arrangements were made to take O'Hara by ambulance and police launch to Bayview General Hospital in Mastic Beach. Mitchell accompanied O'Hara, who was in great pain. Later that day, July 24, he underwent exploratory abdominal surgery, but he died on the evening of July 25, of traumatic internal abdominal injury. According to a friend who was at his bedside, even during these last terrible days of his life, O'Hara "had the courtesy to notice his nurse's accent, and he insisted on speaking to her in French. He even made jokes for her."[13]

I cite these facts only to show how careful we must be not to mythologize the death of the poet. No one can know, of course, what was going on inside O'Hara's mind during the night of July 24, but it seems safe to say that if he had wanted to commit suicide, if he had "courted death" as the myth has it, there would have been a much surer way of doing it. Being hit by a beach buggy is hardly a guarantee of instant—or certain—death, and indeed, as we have seen, O'Hara did not die immediately and remained conscious until the end. I cannot even regard the poet's act as an unconscious death wish—what Yeats called "a lonely impulse of delight." The circumstances were too trivial, too fortuitous—one might say, too ridiculous. Who would think that one could be killed by a beach buggy? If, moreover, O'Hara had somehow survived the accident, what shape would the myth take then?

I think, accordingly, that it is time to forget all about Fire Island and the so-called "killing"—or instinctive suicide—of Frank O'Hara. For what really matters is not the myth of the *poète maudit* but his work. As his friend, the composer Morton Feldman, recalls: "I know if Frank could give me one message from the grave as I write he would say, 'Don't tell them the kind of man I was. *Did I do it?* Never mind the rest.'"[14]

"Did I do it?" A decade after O'Hara's death this question remains largely unanswered, partly because interest in the legend—our inveterate love of gossip—has deflected attention from the poet's accomplishment. By the early sixties, O'Hara had acquired a large underground reputation, appearing in such avant-garde periodicals as *Evergreen Review, Kulchur, Big Table, Floating Bear,* and *Locus Solus,* as well as in Donald Allen's pivotal anthology *The New American Poetry* (1960).[15] But the more established Little Magazines—*Poetry,* the *Kenyon Review,* the *Hudson*—regarded O'Hara as little more than a New York dilettante, an art-world figure who dashed off occasional poems mainly to amuse his friends. In a typical response Marius Bewley, reviewing *Love Poems* (1965) for the *New York Review of Books,* called O'Hara's lyrics "amiable and gay, like streamers of crêpe paper, fluttering before an electric fan."[16]

The posthumous publication in 1971 of the *Collected Poems,* meticulously edited by Donald Allen and beautifully produced by Alfred A. Knopf, should have exploded this image. For one thing, no one suspected that O'Hara had written so much: as John Ashbery says in his Introduction, "That *The Collected Poems of Frank O'Hara* should turn out to be a volume of the present dimensions will surprise those who knew him, and would have surprised Frank even more" (*CP,* vii). But although the *Collected Poems* won the National Book Award, its amazing size (over five hundred pages) turned out to be something of a handicap. Critics immediately complained that the book was too monumental. Thus William Dickey remarks that it is "pretentious" to "enshrine" a poet as delicate, charming, and evanescent as O'Hara "in a volume that rivals the Variorum Yeats, in size if not in seriousness. Surely that solemnity would have amused Frank."[17] And Helen Vendler begins her review by saying: "Now that Knopf has given us O'Hara's *Collected Poems,* they had better rapidly produce a *Selected Poems,* a book that wouldn't drown O'Hara in his own fluency. For the record, we need this new edition; for the sake of fame and poetry, we need a massively reduced version, showing O'Hara at his best. His charms are inseparable from his overproduction."[18]

In theory, Vendler is quite right. Many of the poems in the volume are negligible—impromptu notes to friends, in-jokes, birthday or Christmas greetings—and it may well be the case that O'Hara himself would not have reproduced them all in a *Collected Poems.* Yet the editor of a posthumous collection is in a difficult position, especially when the poet in question is, as Donald Allen points out in his Editor's Note, both "diffident and tentative" about the publication of his work. O'Hara always found it difficult to assemble poems for a volume, to meet deadlines or editorial demands. Indeed, he used to stuff some of his best poems into desk drawers or coat pockets and then forget all about them. Since the poet's precise wishes were thus impossible to determine, Allen decided "to provide a reliable text for all the poems Frank O'Hara published during his lifetime—in individual volumes and in anthologies and periodicals—together with all the unpublished poems he conceivably would have wanted to see in print."[19]

There are, I think, two justifications for this procedure. First, it can be argued that no editor can determine, especially so soon after a poet's death, which of his poems are important, which expendable. The burden of choice is too great, and so Allen rightly includes all those poems that O'Hara would have been willing to publish separately. Secondly, and more important, as both Allen and Ashbery note, O'Hara did tend to think of his work as a whole, an ongoing record of his life. The sum of the *Collected Poems* is, in fact, much greater than its parts, and the more one reads even the slight poems, the more one sees their place in the total pattern. Future readers will not, I think, be satisfied with an abbreviated text. Indeed, although the *Selected Poems,* issued in 1973, is still a large volume (over two hundred pages), I find that, despite my concurrence with most of Allen's choices, there are too many poems missing. In his review of the *Collected Poems* for *The New Republic,* Kenneth Koch explains why this is the case:

> It is a great experience to read it all. I have known Frank O'Hara's work for about twenty years, and I had read a great many of the poems before. One reaction I had to this book, though, was astonishment. All those "moments," all the momentary enthusiasms and despairs which I had been moved by when I first read them when they were here altogether made something I had never imagined. It is not all one great poem, but something in some ways better: a collection of created moments that illuminate a whole life.[20]

Others were less convinced that "this huge tombstone of a book," as Thomas Shapcott calls the *Collected Poems* in his review for *Poetry,* represents an important poetic achievement. Neither the major anthologies nor the standard surveys of the poetry of the fifties and sixties have paid much attention to O'Hara. M. L. Rosenthal's well-known *The Modern Poets, American and British Poetry After World War II,* published in 1967, still provides the norm. Rosenthal devotes two long chapters to the Confessional Poets, Robert Lowell having the place of honor, followed by Sylvia Plath, John Berryman, W. D. Snodgrass, Anne Sexton, and, rather oddly, Theodore Roethke and Allen Ginsberg. Another chapter called "The 'Projectivist' Movement" discusses Charles Olson, Robert Creeley, and Robert Duncan, with briefer commentary on Denise Levertov, Paul Blackburn, and LeRoi Jones (now Imamu Baraka). The epilogue, "American Crosscurrents," refers briefly to such diverse poets as Theodore Weiss, Paul Goodman, Galway Kinnell, Louis Simpson, Robert Bly, and James Wright. O'Hara is not mentioned a single time; neither, it is only fair to say, are such other New York poets as John Ashbery and Kenneth Koch, or West Coast poets like Edward Dorn and Philip Whalen.[21]

A slightly later survey, *Salmagundi's* special double issue devoted to Contemporary Poetry (Spring–Summer 1973), adds to the names in Rosenthal's book those of Adrienne Rich, A. R. Ammons, and John Ashbery. Each of these poets is the subject of a long sympathetic essay; O'Hara is mentioned only in passing in Paul Zweig's essay on "The New Surrealism." Again, *The Norton Introduction to Literature: Poetry* (1973) includes poems by Lowell, Plath, Olson, Ginsberg, Kinnell, Ammons, and Baraka, as well as a special thirty-page section on Adrienne Rich as a representative contemporary poet. The *Norton* contains one poem by Ashbery and one by Koch—there are no poems by O'Hara.[22]

This, then, is the current situation. On the one side, we have O'Hara's devoted admirers, generally themselves artists, who regard the poet as their Lost Leader. On the other, there is the Academy, which remains largely indifferent to the poetry. There are now signs that the gap is narrowing as a new generation of students and younger poet-critics are discovering O'Hara's poetry.[23] But O'Hara continues to be a controversial figure, a poet who elicits curiously contradictory responses from readers who otherwise tend to agree about the poetry they admire. To understand why this is the case, we must begin by looking at the poetry climate of the early fifties, when O'Hara first arrived in New York, fresh from a year of study at Ann Arbor (1950–51), and got a job at the front desk of the Museum of Modern Art. It was a chance move that turned out to be decisive in shaping his aesthetic.

THE "RAW" AND THE "COOKED"

In *The Poem in its Skin* (1968), which contains one of the first useful discussions of O'Hara's poetry, Paul Carroll writes:

> To a young poet the scene in American verse in the late 1940s and early 1950s seemed much like walking down 59th Street in New York for the first time. Elegant and sturdy hotels and apartment buildings stand in the enveloping dusk, mysterious in their power, sophistication, wealth and inaccessibility. One of the most magnificent buildings houses Eliot, his heirs and their sons; other tall, graceful buildings contain e.e. cummings, Marianne Moore, Ezra Pound, Wallace Stevens, William Carlos Williams. The doormen look past you but you are noted if you walk too near. No Admission.
>
> Civilized, verbally excellent, ironic, cerebral and clearly bearers of the Tradition, the poems admired as models included: the Eliot of "The Love Song of J. Alfred Prufrock" and *Poems 1920* and "The Waste Land," the Ransom of "The Equilibrists" and "Bells for John Whiteside's Daughter," the Tate of "Sonnets at Christmas," . . . the Warren of "Bearded Oaks," and of course the Auden of "In Memory of W. B. Yeats," "September 1, 1939," and "Musée des Beaux Arts." Then came the sons: the Lowell of *Lord Weary's Castle,* the Delmore Schwartz of "For Rhoda" and "In the Naked Bed, in Plato's Cave," the Shapiro of *Person, Place and Thing* and *V-Letter,* the Wilbur of "A Black November Turkey" and "Love Calls us to the Things of This World." [24]

Or, as O'Hara himself was to sum it up in *US,* the first of the lithograph stones he made with Larry Rivers,[25] "poetry was declining / Painting advancing / we were complaining / it was '50." Eliot, he declared in 1952, had had a "deadening and obscuring and precious effect" on his "respective followers." [26] It is important to note that the Eliot described by O'Hara is not at all the *real* poet, the self-doubting, struggling revolutionary of the early twenties. Rather, the Eliot venerated by the generation brought up on Brooks and Warren's *Understanding Poetry* was the magisterial Elder Statesman, no longer writing lyric poetry (*Four Quartets* was published in 1944) but making important public pronouncements about its nature and function. James Breslin points out, quite rightly I think, that Williams's well-known attack on "The Waste Land" in his *Autobiography* (a book O'Hara knew well) as the poem that "returned us to the classroom just at the moment when . . . we were on the point of escape . . . to the essence of a new art form" reflects Eliot's position at the time the statement was made (1951) rather than the time about which it was ostensibly made (1922).[27]

What troubled Williams, in short, was less "The Waste Land" itself than that Eliot had become, in the words of Delmore Schwartz, an "international hero," the age's "literary dictator," at a time when Williams's own poetry was not yet widely appreciated.[28] Wallace Stevens represents a related case. By 1950, Stevens had many admirers, but he was still considered something of a coterie poet whose later work seemed to defy the New Critical demand for precision and complexity. In *Poetry and the Age* (1953), for example, Randall Jarrell complained of Stevens's tendency to use philosophical abstractions, declaring: "But surely a poet *has* to treat the concrete as primary. . . . for him it is always the generalization whose life is derived."[29] As for Pound, although the *Pisan Cantos* won the Bollingen Prize for 1949, the poet who wrote those Cantos was, after all, a mental patient at St. Elizabeth's until 1958, and thus relatively inaccessible to most younger poets.

Eliot thus reigned supreme, and the prevailing mode was that of neo-Symbolism—a poetry, in Paul Carroll's words, "civilized, verbally excellent, ironic, cerebral"—and traditional. Even *Lord Weary's Castle* (1947), a book thoroughly disliked by O'Hara and his circle, was, of course, still squarely in the Eliot tradition that Lowell had absorbed from Tate, Ransom, and Jarrell at Kenyon College. Although everyone called it a "difficult" book, full of recondite symbols, *Lord Weary's Castle* was an instant success. Eliot himself, who rarely commended younger poets, singled out Lowell for praise.[30] The reason for the book's success is quite simple: whereas *Prufrock and Other Observa-*

tions, published in a limited edition of five hundred copies, was at first wholly misunderstood, and Eliot had to create his own audience, Lowell, as Breslin notes, "received [an audience] ready-made—the one created (in the main) by Eliot."[31]

It is a nice irony. Looking back at *Lord Weary's Castle* some ten years later, Lowell admitted that he now found its formalism oppressive, that he longed for a more "open," less "Alexandrian" poetry. "Any number of people," he said, "are guilty of writing a complicated poem that has a certain amount of Symbolism in it and really difficult meaning, a wonderful poem to teach. Then you unwind it and you feel that the intelligence, the experience, whatever goes into it, is skin deep."[32] And W. D. Snodgrass similarly recalls:

> . . . in school, we had been taught to write a very difficult and very intellectual poem. We tried to achieve the obscure and dense texture of the French Symbolists (very intuitive and often deranged poets), but by using methods similar to those of the very intellectual and conscious poets of the English Renaissance, especially the Metaphysical poets. . . .[33]

This demand for the tightly structured lyric, distinguished by its complex network of symbols, its metaphysical wit, and its adaptation of traditional meters, lasted well into the sixties. A perfect emblem of the time is Anthony Ostroff's *The Contemporary Poet as Artist and Critic* (1964), a popular collection of symposia in each of which three poets comment on a poem by a fourth poet who then comments on their comments. Thus Richard Wilbur's "Love Calls Us to the Things of this World" is submitted to close analysis by Richard Eberhart, May Swenson, and Robert Horan. The three poet-critics concur on Wilbur's central theme but disagree about such details as the use of Biblical allusions—for example, the line "Let there be clean linen for the backs of thieves." In his reply, Wilbur notes that, given his natural bent toward indirection and ambiguity, "it is good to be so thoroughly understood."[34] It is as if the dismemberment of Orpheus had become, by a curious inversion, the favorite pastime of Orpheus himself.

Yet all this time, as Carroll puts it, "the barbarians were already inside the gates of the city." By "barbarian," Carroll means simply "the alien or enemy of prevailing contemporary standards of correctness or purity of taste." More specifically, the "barbarians" were those who "shared a concern with trying to write types of poems either alien or hostile to the poem as defined and explored by Eliot and his heirs" (pp. 206–07). And Carroll suggests that one might appropriately date "the invasion of the barbarians" as taking place in 1956 "when Lawrence Ferlinghetti published in his City Lights Pocket Poet Series the small hardboiled-looking, funeral-black bordered edition of *Howl and Other Poems* by young Allen Ginsberg."

The challenge Ginsberg and the Beats presented to the Establishment has often been chronicled, as has the parallel revolt of the Black Mountain poets.[35] O'Hara's role in the ongoing battle between Redskin and Paleface, between the "raw" and the "cooked," is more difficult to assess. Indeed, as Ashbery argues in a remarkable obituary essay,[36] O'Hara was caught between "opposing power blocs":

> "Too hip for the squares and too square for the hips" is a category of oblivion which increasingly threatens any artist who dares to take his own way, regardless of mass public and journalistic approval. And how could it be otherwise in a supremely tribal civilization like ours, where even artists feel compelled to band together in marauding packs, where the loyalty-oath mentality has pervaded outer Bohemia, and where Grove Press subway posters invite the lumpenproletariat to "join the Underground Generation" as though this were as simple a matter as joining the Pepsi Generation which it probably is.

In such a setting, O'Hara's "Lunch Poems," with their recreation of everyday experience, could only confound their audience. For

> O'Hara's poetry has no program and therefore cannot be joined. It does not advocate sex and dope as a panacea for the ills of modern society; it does not speak out against the war in Viet Nam or in favor of civil rights; it does not paint gothic vignettes of the post-Atomic Age: in a word, it does not attack the establishment. It merely ignores its right to exist, and is thus a source of annoyance for partisans of every stripe.

Here Ashbery seems to be thinking not only of O'Hara's poetry but of his own. He too had no "program," and his highly original lyric mode did not gain wide recognition until the seventies. In a sense, Ashbery speaks for the whole New York School—Kenneth Koch,

James Schuyler, Barbara Guest, Edwin Denby, and their followers—although, as I shall argue later, the differences between these poets finally make the group label (derived from their shared allegiance to the New York painters) largely irrelevant. O'Hara's sense of what a poem should be, for that matter, turns out to be rather different from Ashbery's poetic.

But it is quite right to point out, as Ashbery does, that O'Hara was caught between the "opposing power blocs" of "hip" and "square." On the one hand, although his own poetry stems directly from his personal experience, he disliked Confessionalism, the baring of the recesses of the soul. Of Lowell's famed "Skunk Hour," he remarked:

> I don't think that anyone has to get themselves to go and watch lovers in a parking lot necking in order to write a poem, and I don't see why it's admirable if they feel guilty about it. They should feel guilty. Why are they snooping? What's so wonderful about a Peeping Tom? And then if you liken them to skunks putting their noses into garbage pails, you've just done something perfectly revolting. No matter what the metrics are. And the metrics aren't all that unusual. Every other person in any university in the United States could put that thing into metrics.

Lowell's "confessional manner," O'Hara feels, lets him "get away with things that are just plain bad but you're supposed to be interested because he's supposed to be so upset." [37]

Such severe judgment is unusual for O'Hara, who generally refused to attack other poets, because, as he put it, "It'll slip into oblivion without my help." But Lowell's poetic sensibility was peculiarly alien to his. Joe LeSueur, one of O'Hara's closest friends, tells an amusing anecdote about a poetry reading given by O'Hara and Lowell at Wagner College on Staten Island in 1962. O'Hara, who read first, introduced his work by saying, "On the ferry coming over here, I wrote a poem," and proceeded to read "Lana Turner has collapsed!" (*CP*, 449), much to the amusement of the audience. When it was Lowell's turn, he said something to the effect: "Well, I'm sorry *I* didn't write a poem on the way over here," the implication being that poetry is a *serious* business and that O'Hara was trivializing it and camping it up. [38]

From then on, the two poets kept their distance. But O'Hara had his reasons for rejecting the Lowell mode. When he says of "Skunk Hour": "I really dislike dishonesty [more] than bad lines" (*SS*, 13), he means, I think, that the reputed "openness" of *Life Studies* is only a surface gesture; that "Skunk Hour" is still a conventional poem in its reliance on Biblical and literary allusions (e.g., John of the Cross's "One dark night," Satan's "I myself am hell"), its double meanings ("the chalk-dry and spar spire / of the Trinitarian Church"), and its pervasive symbolism. Rightly or wrongly, O'Hara regarded such poetry as extending the New Critical, academic tradition.[39]

O'Hara's attitude to what Lucie-Smith calls "the raw" (*SS*, 12) is more complicated. Allen Ginsberg, who wrote one of the first elegies for O'Hara, was a good friend, and O'Hara always spoke of his poetry with love and admiration. There are frequent references to Ginsberg in the poems, for example:

> so they repair the street in the middle of the night
> and Allen and Peter can once again walk forth to visit friends
>
> (*CP*, 346)

or

> . . . and Allen and I getting depressed and angry
> becoming again the male version of wallflower or wallpaper
>
> (*CP*, 400)

He was also very fond of Gregory Corso's *Gasoline* and *Bomb* (both 1958), calling the latter a "superb and praiseful poem."[40] Between 1958 and 1962, in the pages of *Yūgen, Kulchur,* and the *Evergreen Review,* O'Hara's work appeared side by side with that of Ginsberg, Corso, Michael McClure, Gary Snyder, and Philip Whalen—all poets whose work he praised.[41] During these years he was especially close—both personally and in his attitudes toward poetry—to LeRoi Jones (Imamu Baraka), who edited first *Yūgen* and was later one of the editors of *Kulchur.*

Yet O'Hara had none of the revolutionary fervor, the prophetic zeal of the Beats. Unlike Ginsberg, he neither attacked "the narcotic / tobacco haze of Capitalism" nor believed that poetry was closely related to mysticism and could *change* one's life. Unlike Jack Kerouac, whose prose style he admired,[42] he cared nothing for the mystique of "saintly motorcyclists" on the Open Road. Unlike Gary Snyder, he was not enchanted by Zen or Japanese culture. While others journeyed to the Himalayas, Kyoto, or Tangier, O'Hara preferred to walk the streets of Manhattan with its rush-hour frenzy and warring taxicabs, the "luminous humidity" of the Seagram Building, the "gusts of water" spraying in the Plaza fountain.

O'Hara's relationship to the Black Mountain poets was more remote. Like the Beats, these poets appeared side by side with him in the Little Magazines: *Yūgen* 6 (1960), for example, contains O'Hara's "Personal Poem" and Charles Olson's famed "The Distances." But O'Hara had few personal ties to Black Mountain, the main connection being John Wieners, who was a devoted student and friend of Olson's but was never really considered a member of the Black Mountain group. O'Hara first met Wieners in Cambridge in 1956, and the two remained friends, often exchanging poems. When Wieners's *Hotel Wentley Poems* appeared in 1958, O'Hara called it "a beautiful sequence of things,"[43] and in "Les Luths" (1959), he remarks: "everybody here is running around after dull pleasantries and / wondering if *The Hotel Wentley Poems* is as great as I say it is" (*CP*, 343). From the vantage point of the mid-seventies, one can see many similarities between Wieners and O'Hara. Both loved to parody established genres; both wrote bittersweet lyrics, at once formal and colloquial, about homosexual love; both regarded all Movements and Manifestos with some suspicion.

Such instinctive distrust of dogma must have colored O'Hara's view of Charles Olson. When he gave Jasper Johns a list of the "poets [who] interested [him] most," he said, "I don't know if you like Charles Olson but I always find him interesting if sometimes rather cold and echoey of Ezra Pound, but I like the Maximus poems and IN COLD HELL IN THICKET . . . very much."[44] "Olson," he told Lucie-Smith, "is—a great spirit. I don't think that he is willing to be as delicate as his sensibility may be emotionally and he's extremely conscious of the Pound heritage and of saying the important utterance, which one cannot always summon up and indeed is not particularly desirable most of the time" (*SS*, 13).

What O'Hara implies here is that Olson's poetry is perhaps too *willed*, too consciously "significant." Poetry need not have palpable design on us; the "important utterance," indeed, "is not particularly desirable most of the time." Again, O'Hara was skeptical about Olson's epic ambitions (his allegiance to the form of the *Cantos*) even though Pound was, as we shall see, one of O'Hara's own models. As for Creeley and Levertov, O'Hara told Lucie-Smith that their limitation was "making *control* practically the subject matter of the poem": "*control* of the language ... *control* of the experiences and ... *control* of your thought." "The amazing thing," he added, "is that where they've pared down the diction so that the experience presumably will come through as strongly as possible, it's the experience of their paring it down that comes through ... and not the experience that is the subject (*SS*, 23).

This is another way of saying that the Black Mountain poets were too theoretical, too self-consciously programmatic—one might even say, despite their protests to the contrary, too "academic." Or at least so it would appear to O'Hara who, as Bill Berkson observes in one of the best essays on the poet, regarded "ideas as inseparable from the people who had them. Theory and experience had to jell, and the varieties of experience around made dogma appear pointless."[45] Indeed, O'Hara's now notorious "Personism: a Manifesto," first written for Donald Allen's *New American Poetry* (1960), but then retracted and published in *Yūgen*,[46] is probably a sly parody of Black Mountain manifestos, particularly Olson's "Projective Verse," that Sacred Text of 1950, revered by Creeley, Duncan, Levertov, Dorn, and a score of other poets.[47] For Olson's complex network of "principles" and "rules"—his talk of kinetics, energy discharges, field composition, and logos—O'Hara substitutes an air of innocent bonhommie about versecraft:

> Everything is in the poems. . . . I don't believe in god, so I don't have to make elaborately sounded structures. I hate Vachel Lindsay, always have; I don't even like rhythm, assonance, all that stuff. You just go on your nerve. If someone's chasing you down the street with a knife you just run, you don't turn around and shout, "Give it up! I was a track star for Mineola Prep." (*CP*, 498)

The witty insouciance displayed in this passage is, of course, something of a pose. For, as we shall see, O'Hara cared very much indeed about the creation of "elaborately sounded structures." In a lecture on "Design" given at The Club in 1952, he discussed, with great insight, the relative merits of the stanza forms and linear patterns of such poets as George Herbert, Apollinaire, and e.e. cummings.[48] Thus, the insistence that "You just go on your nerve" must be seen as O'Hara's reaction to the endless pomposities of the poetry manifestos of the fifties and sixties. In 1961, for example, when the Paterson Society asked him to submit a statement on his poetic, O'Hara wrote a letter explaining why he couldn't formulate such a statement—and then never sent the letter. Reprinted at the back of the *Collected Poems,* this letter expresses O'Hara's life-long conviction that one cannot theorize about poetry, at least not in a formal way:

> I don't want to make up a lot of prose about something that is perfectly clear in the poems. If you cover someone with earth and grass grows, you don't know what they looked like any more. Critical prose makes too much grass grow, and I don't want to help hide my own poems, much less kill them. (*CP,* 510)

To understand O'Hara's conviction that "critical prose makes too much grass grow," we need merely read the first few "Statements on Poetics" at the back of Donald Allen's *New American Poetry.* Olson's "Projective Verse" is followed by his "Letter to Elaine Feinstein," which contains commentary like the following:

> Image, therefore, is vector. It carries the trinity via the double to the single form which one makes oneself able, if so, to issue from the "content" (multiplicity: originally, and repetitively, chaos—Tiamat: wot the Hindo-Europeans knocked out by giving the Old Man (Juice himself) all the lightning. (p. 399)

Or take this passage from Robert Duncan's "Pages from a Notebook" in the same anthology: "I study what I write as I study out any mystery. A poem, mine or anothers, is an occult document, a body awaiting vivisection, analysis, X-rays" (p. 400).

In the same period, Robert Bly and his followers were publishing manifestos in *The Fifties* (later *The Sixties*), advocating the liberation of the unconscious and the use of "deep images,"[49] while the Objectivists, dormant for a few decades, were being recalled to life and reformulating their doctrines. In an interview for *Contemporary Literature,* George Oppen explains the meaning of *Discrete Series,* the title of a book of poems he had published in 1934, as follows:

> That's a phrase in mathematics. A pure mathematical series would be one in which each term is derived from the preceding term by a rule. A discrete series is a series of terms each of which is empirically derived, each of which is empirically true. And this is the reason for the fragmentary character of those poems. I was attempting to construct a meaning by empirical statements, by imagist statements.[50]

O'Hara's response to what must have seemed to him unnecessarily labored accounts of the poetic process was to assume the role of Poetic Innocent:

> . . . how can you really care if anybody gets it, or gets what it means, or if it improves them? Improves them for what? For death? Why hurry them along? Too many poets act like a middle-aged mother trying to get her kids to eat too much cooked meat, and potatoes with drippings (tears). I don't give a damn whether they eat or not. Forced feeding leads to excessive thinness (effete). Nobody should experience anything they don't need to, if they don't need poetry bully for them. I like the movies too. And after all, only Whitman and Crane and Williams, of the American poets, are better than the movies. (*CP,* 498)

If these comments sound unnecessarily frivolous, we should remember that O'Hara consistently rebelled against the notion of poetry as an Institution precisely because he personally cared about it so much. In a 1957 letter to John Ashbery, he wrote: "It seems that my life has been very empty due to work [i.e., at the Museum of Modern Art] and that I am padding this letter with all sorts of boring things. I've been very depressed lately but now that I've done a few poems, however bad, I feel much better. Sometimes when I don't have the chance to spill the beans into a few deaf lines I think I'm losing my mind."[51] And a few years later, he wrote to Bill Berkson, "poetry is the highest art, everything else, however gratifying . . . moving, and grand, is less demanding, more indulgent, more casual, more gratuitous, more instantly apprehensible, which I assume is not exactly what we are after."[52]

What, then, was O'Hara after? If none of the existing movements of the fifties could provide a model for what he considered *poetry,* what were its roots? In one of his rare formal statements on aesthetics, written at the request of Donald Allen for the appendix of *The New American Poetry,* O'Hara said: "It may be that poetry makes life's nebulous events tangible to me and restores their detail; or conversely, that poetry brings forth the intangible quality of incidents which are all too concrete and circumstantial."[53] Here the poet oddly echoes the great Russian Formalist critic Viktor Shklovsky, who said in a famous essay of 1917: "Art exists that one may recover the sensation of life; it exists to make one feel things, to make the stone *stony*—art removes objects from the automatism of perception." It *defamiliarizes* objects by presenting them as if seen for the first time or by distorting their form "so as to make the act of perception more difficult and to prolong its duration."[54]

In his drive to "defamiliarize" the ordinary—even the "sheer ugliness in America"[55]—the artist must be as *attentive* as possible to the world around him. As O'Hara puts it in "Meditations in an Emergency":

> My eyes are vague blue, like the sky, and change all the time; they are indiscriminate but fleeting, entirely specific and disloyal, so that no one trusts me. I am always looking away. Or again at something after it has given me up. It makes me restless and that makes me unhappy, but I cannot keep them still. . . . It's not that I'm curious. On the contrary, I am bored but it's my duty to be attentive, I am needed by things as the sky must be above the earth. And lately so great has *their* anxiety become, I can spare myself little sleep. (*CP,* 197)

The notion of being "needed by things," playful as O'Hara makes it sound in this context, is a central feature of his poetic. It derives, quite possibly, from Rilke, whose poetry O'Hara knew well and loved.[56] In the first of the *Duino Elegies,* the poet reminds himself:

> Yes, the seasons of spring needed you. Some of the stars
> made claims on you, so that you would feel them. In the past,
> a wave rose up to reach you, or

> as you walked by an open window
> a violin gave itself to you. All this was your task.[57]

For both Rilke and O'Hara, it is the artist's "duty to be attentive" to the world of process in which he finds himself. And such attention requires a peculiar self-discipline, the ability to look at something and, paraphrasing Ezra Pound, to "See It New!" In the interview with Lucie-Smith, O'Hara explains de Kooning's attitude to the great painters of the past in this way: "if de Kooning says that what he really is interested in is Poussin; that's his way of not being bored with Kandinsky when all the world is looking at Kandinsky. That attitude may only work for two years, but that doesn't matter in the life of the artist as long as it energizes him to produce more works that are beautiful" (*SS*, 35).

To be "influenced" by another artist, then, is to find new means of evading monotony, boredom, sameness—to force oneself to "see" in new ways, to *defamiliarize* the object. The painting of Larry Rivers, says O'Hara, "has taught me to be more keenly interested while I'm still alive. And perhaps this is the most important thing art can say."[58]

One way of avoiding boredom, of keeping oneself and one's reader "more keenly interested," is to create a poetic structure that is always changing, shifting, becoming. In an early lyric called "Poetry" (1951), O'Hara declares:

> The only way to be quiet
> is to be quick, so I scare
> you clumsily, or surprise
> you with a stab.   (*CP*, 49)

The poet's desire is "to deepen you by my quickness," or, as he puts it in "My Heart" (1955):

> I'm not going to cry all the time
> nor shall I laugh all the time,
> I don't prefer one "strain" to another.
> I'd have the immediacy of a bad movie,
> not just a sleeper, but also the big,
> over-produced first-run kind. I want to be
> at least as alive as the vulgar.   (*CP*, 231)

And he concludes: "you can't plan on the heart, but / the better part of it, my poetry, is open."

Openness, quickening, immediacy—these are the qualities O'Hara wants to capture in his poetry. In "Music" (1954), for example, the poet-speaker is "naked as a tablecloth," and his door "is *open* to the evenings of midwinter's / lightly falling snow." Or again, in "Digression on Number 1, 1948," the poet says:

> I am ill today, but I am not
> too ill. I am not ill at all.
> It is a perfect day, warm
> for winter, cold for fall.
>
> A fine day for seeing.   (*CP*, 260)

"A fine day for seeing" is thus a quirky day, "warm / for winter, cold for fall." Contradiction becomes the proper condition for "seeing." Sameness, monotony, evenness of surface—these create boredom. This is why the poet exclaims in "To Hell With It":

> (How I hate subject matter! melancholy,
>   intruding on the vigorous heart,
>   the soul telling itself
> you haven't suffered enough ((Hyalomiel))
>   and all things that don't change,
> photographs,
>   monuments,
>   memories of Bunny and Gregory and me in /
>   costume. . . .
>   (*CP*, 275)

Photographs, monuments, static memories—"all things that don't change"—these have no place in the poet's world. We can now understand why O'Hara loves the *motion* picture, *action* painting, and all forms of dance—art forms that capture the *present* rather than the past, the present in all its chaotic splendor. And New York is therefore the very center of being, quite simply because it is the place where more is happening at once than anywhere else in the world: "I can't even enjoy a blade of grass unless I know there's a subway handy, or a record store or some other sign that people do not totally *regret* life" (*CP*, 197).

But how does one create a poetic structure that has immediacy, openness, "quickness," a structure that avoids the monotony and stasis of monuments and photographs? An important hint is provided in a letter O'Hara wrote to Larry Rivers in 1957, enclosing a group of poems, a letter Rivers then incorporated into a collage:[59]

> Now please tell me if you think these poems are filled with disgusting self-pity, if there are "holes" in them, if the surface isn't kept "up," if there are recognizable images, if they show nostalgia for the avant-garde, or if they don't have "push" and "pull," and I'll keep working on them until each is a foot high.
>
> Yours in action art,
> Frank

Although O'Hara is partly joking here, teasing Rivers who had accused his poems of being filled with "gorgeous self-pity," this letter is surely a key document for any student of O'Hara's work. The notion that, as in the case of abstract painting, the "surface" must be kept "up," is a recurrent theme in his writings. In "Notes on *Second Avenue*" (1953), for example, he talks of wanting "to keep the surface of the poem high and dry, not wet, reflective and self-conscious. . . . I hope the poem to *be* the subject, not just about it."[60] Again, the terms "push" and "pull" derive from theoretical discussions of Abstract Expressionism, specifically to Hans Hofmann's discussion of the successful relationship of planes in Cubist and abstract art. "Pictorial space," wrote Hofmann, "exists two-dimensionally. . . . Depth . . . is not created by the arrangement of objects, one after another, toward a vanishing point, in the sense of Renaissance perspective, but on the contrary . . . by the creation of forces in the sense of *push and pull.*"[61]

O'Hara's understanding of Jackson Pollock's sense of *scale* sheds further light on the terminology used in the letter to Larry Rivers:

> In the past, an artist by means of scale could create a vast panorama on a few feet of canvas or wall, relating this scale both to the visual reality of known images . . . and to the real setting. . . . Pollock, choosing to use no images with real visual equivalents . . . struck upon a use of scale which was to have a revolutionary effect on contemporary painting and sculpture. The scale of the painting became that of the painter's body, not the image of a body, and the setting for the scale, which would include all

referents, would be the canvas surface itself. Upon this field the physical energies of the artist operate in actual detail, in full scale. . . . It is the physical reality of the artist and his activity of expressing it, united with the spiritual reality of the artist in a oneness which has no need for the mediation of metaphor or symbol. It is Action Painting.[62]

The *surface* of the painting, and by analogy the *surface* of the poem, must, then, be regarded as a field upon which the physical energies of the artist can operate, without mediation of metaphor or symbol. The poet's images—for example, the "hum-colored / cabs," the "yellow helmets" worn by the laborers, or the "glass of papaya juice" in "A Step Away From Them" (*CP,* 257–58)—are not symbolic properties; there is nothing *behind* these surfaces. Rather, their positioning in the poet's field, their *push and pull* interaction, function metonymically to create a microcosm of the poet's New York world—a world verifiable on any city map yet also fictive in its fantastic configurations:

> now it is dark on 2d Street near the abattoir
> and a smell as of hair comes up the dovecotes
> as the gentleman poles a pounce of pigeons
> in the lower East Sideness rippling river. . . .   (*CP,* 324)

This distrust of symbolism is a central tenet of O'Hara's poetic. In a 1962 essay on Philip Guston, he praises the late oils and gouaches in which there is "no symbolic aura. . . . There are no figures, the images are material presences like Druidic spirits." In works like *North* and *The Scale,* "the marvelous burgeoning into life of their surfaces [note again the stress on surface], the visual velocity of the painter's unerring hand make of Guston's self-imposed demands simultaneous triumphs."[63] Again, in his first "Art Chronicle" for *Kulchur* (Summer 1962), O'Hara admires Jasper Johns's "meticulously and sensually painted rituals of imagery" which "express a profound boredom, in the Baudelairean sense, with the symbols of an over-symbolic society."[64] Similarly, he writes enthusiastically of the "found objects" in Claes Oldenburg's first exhibit at *The Store* (1962) where "you find cakes your mother never baked, letters you never received, jackets you never stole when you broke into that apartment." Oldenburg succeeds because he manages to "transform his materials into something magical and strange."[65] The following year, O'Hara again praises Oldenburg's ability to make "the very objects and symbols themselves, with the help of papiêr-maché, cloth, wood, glue, paint and whatever other mysterious materials are inside and on them, *into* art. . . . There is no hint of mysticism, no 'significance,' no commentary, in the work."[66]

The aesthetic of *presence* rather than transcendence is formulated with particular force in O'Hara's first essay on David Smith, which appeared in *Art News* in 1961. The stainless steel and painted sculptures standing on the lawn at Bolton's Landing, New York, near Smith's house, are not so much formal constructs as they are live presences. They remind the poet of "people who are awaiting admittance to a formal reception and, while they wait, are thinking about their roles when they join the rest of the guests already in the meadow."[67] Smith's sculptures, O'Hara argues, defy all our traditional notions of organic oneness and unity. "This is no longer the Constructivist intersection of colored planes, nor is the color used as a means of unifying the surface. Unification is approached by inviting the eye to travel over the complicated surface exhaustively, rather than inviting it to settle on the whole first and then explore details. It is the esthetic of culmination rather than examination."

The esthetic of culmination rather than examination—this formulation applies nicely to O'Hara's own poetry. As in the case of Smith's sculptures, O'Hara's poems reject the dense network of symbolic images one finds in, say, Richard Wilbur's "Love Calls Us To The Things Of This World" or John Crowe Ransom's "The Equilibrists." Rather, the reader's eye and ear must "travel over the complicated surface exhaustively," participating in the ongoing process of discovery and continually revising his sense of what the poem is "saying." The observer can no longer be detached. "The best of the current sculptures," says O'Hara, "didn't make me feel I wanted to *have* one, they made me feel I wanted to *be* one" (p. 125). If the art work has *presence* and if the beholder is as *attentive* as possible, the process of identification thus becomes complete.

I have drawn the above examples from O'Hara's art criticism rather than from his commentary on poetry simply because it is so much more plentiful. But in his rare literary essays, he makes precisely the same points. In his review of John Rechy's *City of Night,* for example, he argues that the novel's real forte is its naturalistic surface, its concrete embodiment of scenes and moods. "What comes out in the *Mardi Gras* section of the book is that atrocious fanfare which Rimbaud celebrated; it is to my mind the finest and most compelling prose realization of derangement through social confrontation in American letters . . . since *Day of the Locust.*" In such explorations of "the distinctive and odd quality of a city or a quarter or a milieu," Rechy follows William Carlos Williams's prescription that "the objective in writing is to reveal. It is not to teach, not to advertise, not to see, not even to communicate . . . but to reveal." Rechy's book is a "quest novel," an attempt to escape from Hell, but "it is no paradigm of Dante. It would be boring if it were . . . since that aspect of the Joycean-Eliotean idea . . . has been pretty much exhausted by Harvard and Yale students. (Lord! spare us from any more Fisher kings!)."[68]

Here, as generally in O'Hara's criticism, Williams clearly takes precedence over Eliot as a model; indeed, as we shall see, Williams's influence is seminal.[69] As always for O'Hara, the Enemy is the Great Insight or the Mythic-Symbolic Analogue—being excessively solemn about oneself. "Life," as he says in his essay on Pasternak, "is not a landscape before which the poet postures, but the very condition of his inspiration in a deeply personal way: 'My sister, life, is in flood today. . . .' This is not the nineteenth-century Romantic identification, but a recognition."[70]

The notion that *recognition* is central to art is the cornerstone of O'Hara's "Personism." The background of this "manifesto" is interesting. Allen Ginsberg had argued in an essay called "Abstraction in Poetry" that poems like O'Hara's *Second Avenue* were experiments in writing "long meaningless poems," "bulling along page after page" so as to learn "freedom of composition," and that from such "freedom of composition," in which the poet tries to avoid personal considerations, a new poetry comparable to abstract art would emerge.[71]

O'Hara found Ginsberg's argument "intriguing" but felt that it didn't quite define what he was trying to do:

> Personism, a movement which I recently founded and which nobody knows about, interests me a great deal, being so totally opposed to this kind of abstract removal [i.e., the kind Ginsberg describes] that it is verging on true abstraction for the first time, really, in the history of

poetry. . . . Personism has nothing to do with philosophy, it's all art. It does not have to do with personality or intimacy, far from it! But to give you a vague idea, one of its minimal aspects is to address itself to one person (other than the poet himself), thus evoking overtones of love without destroying love's life-giving vulgarity, and sustaining the poet's feelings toward the poem while preventing love from distracting him into feeling about the person. That's part of Personism. It was founded by me after lunch with LeRoi Jones on August 27, 1959, a day in which I was in love with someone (not Roy, by the way, a blond). I went back to work and wrote a poem for this person. While I was writing it I was realizing that if I wanted to I could use the telephone instead of writing the poem, and so Personism was born. It's a very exciting movement which will undoubtedly have lots of adherents. It puts the poem squarely between the poet and the person, Lucky Pierre style, and the poem is correspondingly gratified. The poem is at last between two persons instead of two pages. (*CP,* 498–99)

Much of this "manifesto" is, of course tongue-in-cheek: the reference to the "founding" of the movement, its arcane quality (nobody knows about it!), the comical reference to Lucky Pierre, the insistence that he could have used the telephone "instead of writing the poem"—an insistence most reviewers have taken all too seriously.

But beneath the bravado, O'Hara is quite serious. He implies, for example, that the dramatic monologue has become a dead convention, its use assuming that the poet can penetrate the experience of a fictional narrator, can distance himself from that experience and define its meaning.[72] Always a skeptic, O'Hara recognizes that the only mind he can wholly penetrate is his own, but he sees that this need not be a loss if he can project a lyric "I" engaged in what looks like live talk—intimate, familiar, expressive; "real" conversation that seems purely personal and yet avoids what he calls in the letter to Larry Rivers "disgusting self-pity."

"Personism," says O'Hara, "does not have to do with personality, or intimacy, far from it!" What he means is that the poet does not use the poem as a vehicle to lay bare his soul, to reveal his secret anxieties or provide autobiographical information. Indeed, O'Hara's personal pronouns shift so disarmingly and confusingly that we are never quite sure who's who, and accordingly, we don't take the text as a personal testament. Rather, "Personism" means the *illusion* of intimate talk between an "I" and a "you" (or sometimes "we," "he," "they," or "one"), giving us the sense that we are eavesdropping on an ongoing conversation, that we are *present*. But this is not to say, as critics often have, that an O'Hara poem is just good casual talk. Here is a passage from a letter to Joe LeSueur from Belgrade in 1963:

> As for the smokey dark lights of Belgrade, I do hope that Prague isn't *more* like Kafka than this! In the daytime it's very nice and pleasant and even rather pretty in a wrong-headed sort of way (the parks don't fit right somehow, and the squares appear to be in the wrong places, and there is all of a sudden a hill or an abutment where there shouldn't be—as if the building of the city had stubbornly resisted taking cognizance of the site), but as soon as dusk falls, about 5:30 it is really quite dark, these peculiar ghostly iridescent lightings come on here and there making very bright places and leaving very dark ominous ones, and a dry smokey mist appears, like in the back of a pool hall ... and all the places (or Trgs, as they're called here) fill with people and many of the streets too, all of them looking dark and sort of ominous in the light, strolling and windowshopping and realshopping and talking, and the cars disappear entirely from whole streets in the center of the city (they couldn't get through them anyway), and it is all rather subduedly noisy and noncheerful, as if Orson Welles in one of his more malevolent moments had taken over the Galleria Umberta from the Milanese.[73]

Compare this description of Belgrade to the image of New York found in "Rhapsody" (1959), a poem which begins:

> 515 Madison Avenue
> door to heaven? portal
> stopped realities and eternal licentiousness
> or at least the jungle of impossible eagerness
> your marble is bronze and your lianas elevator cables
> swinging from the myth of ascending
> I would join
> or declining the challenge of racial attractions
> they zing on (into the lynch, dear friends)
> while everywhere love is breathing draftily
> like a doorway linking 53rd with 54th
> the east-bound with the west-bound traffic by 8,000,000s
> o midtown tunnels and the tunnels, too, of Holland[74]

The letter, although charming, witty, and graphic, is perfectly straightforward, its syntax loosely paratactic, with a piling up of qualifiers, parenthetical clauses, and prepositional phrases like "from whole streets in the center of the city" or "like in the back of the pool hall." Everything is given more or less the same emphasis: this is what I saw (or did), and then this and then this. The description of Belgrade is highly subjective but still essentially realistic: this is how the city looks to the poet at different times of day. In "Rhapsody," on the other hand, we begin with juxtaposition and ellipsis:

> 515 Madison Avenue
> door to heaven? portal
> stopped realities and eternal licentiousness

Here phrases and clauses are much shorter, and the connectives are often missing or confusing. The "eternal licentiousness" of the "portal" of 515 Madison Avenue immediately modulates into the fantasy of the jungle, the elevator cables turning into lianas and the elevator ride itself into a wonderful journey to *Schlaraffenland,* and then into an East-West joyride through "midtown tunnels and the tunnels, too, of Holland" so that the whole world is absorbed into the fabric of the voyage. Thus, although the letter is allusive—note the references to Kafka and Orson Welles—it does not transform names into something wholly other, as O'Hara does in the case of the dreary Holland Tunnel.

Lineation, of course, is a major factor in making the poem seem so different from the letter. For when word groups are set off in line units, we respond to them quite differently than we would if we met them in a paragraph. The words "I would join," for example, stand out as particularly emphatic, as if the poet were *joining* the "Rhapsody" (the title alludes to an Elizabeth Taylor movie) of the elevator trip. And the three monosyllabic words seem to float in space, suspended between the preceding line ("swinging from the myth of ascending") and the following one ("or declining the challenge of racial attractions"). Between "ascending" and "declining," the poet's consciousness floats for a brief moment at heaven's gate.

The letter from Belgrade is much less structured; it has none of the defamiliarization we meet everywhere in the poem. In terms of O'Hara's own aesthetic, it has too many "holes" in it, too many phrases and sentences that are entertaining but could obviously be eliminated (for example, "it is all rather subduedly noisy and non-cheerful"). It lacks the "push and pull" of "Rhapsody," whose "surface" is "kept up" and peculiarly tight. Despite its air of casual talk, the poem displays careful sound patterning: take the short i's in "impossible," "lianas," "swinging from the myth of ascending," "they zing on (into the lynch, dear friends)." Again, the witty reverberations of "the challenge of racial attractions," a phrase that originally refers to the jungle imagery of the elevator cables, is transformed, in stanza after stanza, as we shift from the anecdote in which "the Negro driver tells me about a $120 apartment / where you can't walk across the floor after 10 at night / not even to pee, cause it keeps them awake downstairs," to the "Niger" which "joins the Gulf of Guinea near the Menemsha Bar," and then to the "hammock on St. Mark's Place . . . in the rancid nourishment of this mountain island"—Manhattan. The poem, moreover, shifts back and forth from present to past in a series of rapid dissolves, thus creating "push and pull," and, by shifting address regularly (the "you" is alternately "515 Madison Avenue" and the "you who were there always," the "you [who] know[s] all about these things"), O'Hara distances his emotions, thus avoiding "disgusting self-pity."

There is, therefore, a real difference between the "verse letter" or "verse telephone call" we find in the *Collected Poems* and an actual letter or phone call. The letter moves from one item to another just as we all put down our thoughts (even if we don't all write such charming and amusing letters); the poem *looks* improvisatory but invites "the eye [or ear] to travel over the complicated surface exhaustively," tracing the process whereby the poet's consciousness moves from perception to perception until he comes to the awareness that he belongs "to the enormous bliss of American death." Only when we reach the last line of "Rhapsody" do we understand how its seemingly unrelated images have led up to this conclusion. Here, then, is what O'Hara called "the esthetic of culmination."

In the poetry of postwar America, it is difficult to find precise models or analogues for an "action poem" like "Rhapsody." Painting, sculpture, film, music—these provide much more useful analogues, and I shall discuss the role they play in O'Hara's development. But for literary models we must turn to France—to the poetry of Rimbaud and Apollinaire, to Tristan Tzara and the Dadaists, to such Surrealists as Robert Desnos and Benjamin Péret. Indeed, much of what O'Hara admired in the visual arts of his own time came out of this tradition.

Russian literature—the poetry of Mayakovsky and the prose of Pasternak—also finds its way into the *Collected Poems,* as does, in a more oblique way, the poetry and poetic of Rilke. But it is the French influence that sets O'Hara apart from Black Mountain and the Beats, not to speak of the Confessional Poets like Lowell and Berryman, or the oracular "deep image" school associated with Robert Bly, James Wright, and Galway Kinnell.

How that French influence was gradually adapted to an American idiom, how O'Hara came to fuse the "charming artifice" of Apollinaire with the vernacular toughness he admired in the poetry of Williams, Pound, and the later Auden, and in the prose of Joyce and Gertrude Stein, is a central concern of the chapters that follow. It is a fascinating study in "tradition and the individual talent." In that insistently documentary New York poem, "A Step Away from Them" (1957), O'Hara declares:

> My heart is in my
> pocket. It is Poems by Pierre Reverdy.   (*CP,* 258)

2
THE EARLY
YEARS (1946-53)

THE POET WHO WAS TO declare in "Personism" (1959) that "Nobody should experience anything they don't need to, if they don't need poetry bully for them" (*CP*, 498), began his writing career with a very different point of view. In a journal kept during his junior year at Harvard (from October 1948 through January 1949), O'Hara writes: "No matter what, I am romantic enough or sentimental enough to wish to contribute something to life's fabric, to the world's beauty. . . . Simply to live does not justify existence, for life is a mere gesture on the surface of the earth, and death a return to that from which we had never been wholly separated; but oh to leave a trace, no matter how faint, of that brief gesture! For someone, some day, may find it beautiful!"[1]

These words recall Stephen Dedalus in Joyce's *Portrait of the Artist*, longing to forge "out of the sluggish matter of the earth a new soaring impalpable being,"[2] and indeed the young Frank O'Hara regarded Joyce as his hero. In "Lament and Chastisement," an account of his Navy days (1944-46), written for Albert Guérard's Advanced Composition course in 1948, O'Hara notes that during the trying days of basic training at Key West, "I carried *Ulysses* with me for luck. I read it in high school because a friend who was preping [*sic*] for West Point sent it to me because it was so dirty. Then I read it from beginning and it was about something else entirely. In my locker: *Ulysses* for luck, and oh my god didn't *Portrait of the Artist as a Young Man* say everything? Should I send it to all my friends so they'd understand me?" Later, during heavy fighting in the Pacific, he recalls that "I reread *Ulysses,* needing to throw up my sensibility and Joyce's art into the face of my surroundings; I found that Joyce was more than a match. I was reassured that what was important to me would always be important to me. . . . I found that I myself was my life."[3]

O'Hara's juvenilia are particularly interesting because they immediately dispel the myth of the poet as charming pop artist or spontaneous scribbler, which grew up in his later years. Surely he was one of the best read and most learned poets of his time. In this respect—and in this respect only—he recalls his Harvard predecessor T. S. Eliot. Even before he entered college, as "Lament and Chastisement" makes clear, O'Hara was quite familiar with Whitman and Stevens, with *Swann's Way* and *The Counterfeiters,* as well as with the music of Stravinsky and Schoenberg.

At Harvard, O'Hara took the standard courses required of English majors between 1946 and 1950.[4] Aside from six courses in English Composition (some of these were, in fact, advanced writing courses), he took Chaucer, a one-year survey of "English Literature from the Beginning to 1700," and period courses on the Renaissance, the Restoration, the Eighteenth Century, and the Romantics. Only in his senior year could he "branch out" somewhat: he elected to take John Ciardi's "Poetry Workshop," Albert Guérard's "Forms of the Modern Novel," Edwin Honig's "Allegory," Walter Jackson Bate's "English Critics," and—perhaps most important for his future development— Renato Poggioli's "The Symbolist Movement."

Yet the Commonplace Book that O'Hara kept during these years reveals a breadth of reading that goes far beyond the classroom. Interestingly, the writers he cites least frequently are the great English classics: Shakespeare, Spenser, Milton, Wordsworth, Keats, Tennyson, Browning, and, among novelists, Richardson, Austen, Eliot, Dickens, James, and Lawrence. From the first, then, his literary predilections reflect a highly personal note. Thus he prefers Anglo-Saxon charms and *Beowulf* to Chaucer; the Jacobean dramatists, especially Webster, to Shakespeare; he considers Donne's sermons and the *Devotions upon Emergent Occasions* superior to the lyric poems; he admires the plays of Dryden and Otway, the poems of the Earl of Rochester and Christopher Smart;[5] Fielding's *Jonathan Wild* (*Tom Jones* and *Joseph Andrews* are not mentioned), and Gothic Romances, especially Maturin's *Melmoth the Wanderer.*

The Commonplace Book frequently cites Dostoyevsky, Strindberg, and Kierkegaard, but never mentions Tolstoy or Chekhov, perhaps because these writers were too "realistic" for O'Hara's taste. Again, although his amusing accounts of Manhattan cocktail parties have been compared to those of Scott Fitzgerald, O'Hara makes no mention of Fitzgerald's novels and disparages Hemingway. "I can learn little from him [Hemingway]," he writes in the Harvard Journal, "I'm tired of the current fad for short stories which clack along like a sewing machine dispensing pertinent information in stitches and stopping only when the garment is finished. . . . I want to move toward a complexity which makes life within the work and which does not resemble life as most people seem to think it is lived. . . ."[6]

Because his imagination was essentially lyric rather than narrative, O'Hara was always drawn to novels that are nonmimetic and stylized, novels that subordinate plot and characterization to linguistic innovation: Djuna Barnes's *Nightwood*, Virginia Woolf's *Between the Acts* and *The Waves*, Ronald Firbank's *Vainglory* and *The Flower beneath the Foot*, Beckett's *Murphy* and *More Pricks than Kicks*, the fiction of Gertrude Stein and Jean Rhys. Yet despite his love for these writers, it is no exaggeration to say that O'Hara's heart was, from the very beginning, French. Baudelaire and Rimbaud were early favorites. In his moving memoir of the writer Bunny Lang, one of his closest friends in Cambridge, who was to die tragically of cancer in 1956 at the age of thirty-two, O'Hara typically recalls: "We both loved Rimbaud and Auden: she thought I loved Rimbaud too much and I thought the same about Auden and her."[7]

In the Harvard Journal, he talks enthusiastically of Camus, Cocteau, and Stendhal's *Red and the Black* in the Scott-Moncrieff translation. In 1948–49, his command of the French language was evidently still limited; in the Commonplace Book, he cites Corneille and Racine, Voltaire and Laclos, Baudelaire and Nerval, Rimbaud and Lautréamont (a particular favorite) in translation. Yet in the same notebook, he copies out whole sonnets by Ronsard and Desportes and begins to write playful French poems of his own, for example, "L'Ennui," which ends with the lines:

> notre pain quotidien
> de l'angoisse s'efface.
> Quelle mélasse.[8]

A reading list compiled toward the end of the Harvard period[9] adds the names of later French poets from Villiers de l'Isle Adam and Mallarmé to Breton and Char, this time referring to all titles in French. Here Dada and Surrealist texts begin to assume importance: the list contains ten poems by Apollinaire, Reverdy's *Les Epaves du ciel,* Jarry's *Les Minutes de sable mémorial,* Aragon's *Le Paysan de Paris,* Desnos's *Deuil pour deuil,* Max Ernst's *La Femme 100 têtes,* and Péret's *Le Grand jeu.* Whether or not O'Hara knew enough French to read these texts with relative ease,[10] it is remarkable that he turned to these poets rather than to what were then the "acceptable" models—Yeats, Hopkins, Eliot, Frost, Tate, Ransom—for inspiration. For that matter, despite all his later travels abroad in connection with Museum of Modern Art traveling exhibitions, O'Hara never visited England and never expressed any particular desire to see London.[11] With the exception of Auden, whom he considered an American poet anyway,[12] and the early Dylan Thomas, the poetic landscape of modern Britain struck O'Hara as excessively conventional and tame; it could not, in any case, compete with the Germany of Rilke, the Russia of Mayakovksy and Pasternak, the Spain of Lorca—and certainly not with France.

From the first, then, O'Hara emerges as a highly sophisticated poet with strong tastes of his own. Having studied music all his life—he originally wanted to be a concert pianist—he could relate poetry to developments in contemporary music: it was he who was to introduce Ashbery to the work of Schoenberg and Cage.[13] Yet, as in the case of literature, his musical tastes were eclectic: if he admired Cage, he also loved Rachmaninoff, *La Bohème* and the Weill-Brecht operas. John Ciardi, whose Freshman Composition course O'Hara took in 1946–47, and who recalls that "aside from picking and probing at his papers I could teach him nothing but only hope to stir him a little closer to his questions," comments in a letter to Donald Allen:

> His talent was obvious, even when he was a Freshman. He also had a lovely sardonic sense of fun. When my wife and I were fixing an attic apartment in Medford, Frank and Ted Gorey [Edward St. John Gorey]—they were inseparable in college and took all my courses to-gether—and George Rinehart (who showed high promise in his short stories but who left Harvard in disgust at the end of his junior year and who never went on to write)—these three, as students needing some extra money made a crew to steam the weird wall paper from the apartment. They were at it for days as they played a game of killing insults. They were beautiful and bright and I have never come on three students as a group who seemed to have such unlimited prospects.[14]

Yet the winter of 1948–49 seems to have been a time of crisis in O'Hara's life. "I often wish," he writes in a journal entry of 17 October, "I had the strength to commit suicide, but on the other hand, if I had, I probably wouldn't feel the need." Here we already see the poet's characteristic self-deprecatory humor, his refusal to take himself too seriously. And despite these moments of despair, near the end of the journal the tone changes: "If life were merely a habit, I should commit suicide; but even now, more or less desperate, I cannot but think, 'Something wonderful may happen.' It is not optimism, it is a rejection of self-pity (I hope) which leaves a loophole for life. . . . I merely choose to remain living out of respect for possibility. And possibility is the great good."[15]

These words turned out to be oddly prophetic. A few months after he made this journal entry, O'Hara met John Ashbery, who was to become a life-long poet friend and fellow art critic, and who later wrote so movingly about O'Hara's poetry.[16] Ashbery was then an editor of the *Advocate;* he admired a group of poems O'Hara submitted and sent them on to Kenneth Koch who had recently graduated and was living in New York. A friendship between O'Hara and Koch was thus formed. Within the next year, O'Hara was to achieve what he probably most longed for at this point in his life—a circle of exciting artist friends, among them Bunny Lang and George Montgomery, whom he knew at Harvard, and three painters whom he met on visits to New York: Fairfield Porter, Jane Freilicher, and Larry Rivers. All would play an important part in his life and his poetry.

What sort of poetry was O'Hara writing as an undergraduate? The first surviving poems, dating from the fall of 1946, are generally imitations or parodies—what Ashbery has aptly called, with reference to the early work in general, "muscle-flexing" (*CP*, viii). Thus "Portrait of James Joyce" plays with the diction and themes of *Finnegans Wake:*

> riverrun, said jute, oh why the enterrential
> faggus?
> discolum in ionic, doric or sabbatic
> juicecum? [17]

The same poem alludes to Leopold Bloom ("remind people to go to church. / does em good.") as well as to Molly ("syncopated menstruation"). A related poem from this period, "Dialogue for man, woman & chorus of frogs," is a Joycean parody of pastoral comedy, in which "george" and "mary" exchange obscenities in high style ("I sat, forzando / And william's lips, fructose / pursed levulously") and poke fun at the Church in Joycean tones: "Kiss the foot of the papal chamberpot," or "In nomine papyrus / Ab altare dei. / Hocus in hodie. Pocus in anus." [18]

O'Hara's interest in Gertrude Stein is reflected in the following imitation:

> He rode and rode continuously, inexpressibly continuously, and stopped for rest every now and then. Too often then and not often now but just often enough. Yes, sometimes. Yes, sometimes he fell off now and then when he had ridden too long but it was not serious it was gay yes it was not serious because it was him if it had not been him or if it had ceased to be him it would have become serious. . . .
>
> "Portrait of J. Charles Kiefe" (PR, 4)

"A Procession of Peacocks" is an example of a Wallace Stevens imitation, generally rare in O'Hara's early work:

> At night they carry me
> in a palanquin of twigs
> as if I were a bruisable pear,
> soft as the sunrise. . . .   (PR, 9)

And in "The Muse Considered as a Demon Lover," O'Hara parodies both Baudelaire and Rimbaud:

> The light went
>
> out. "Que manges-tu, belle sphinx?"
> came roaring through the dark; beau!
>
> I muttered and hid my head, but a
> wrenching kiss woke me again with a
>
> "Suis-je belle, ô nausée?" . . .
>
> The angel's voice called gaily: "There
> are faith, hope, and charity, and
>
> the greatest of these is homily. I
> am an angel. Trouvez Hortense!" [19]

Not only does O'Hara imitate and parody the styles of his early masters; he also experiments with a wide variety of verse forms. There are, for example, a number of early nature poems written in quatrains:

> Stars nod without
> they show their light
> glimmer about
> keep dark the night. . . .
>
> ("Solstice," Notebook A, p. 5)

"Portrait of Jean Marais" has both end-rhyme and internal rhyme:

> Coursing blood is all the flood
> The heart espies and then decries
> as flowing in the winter night
> it searches for a spring surmise.   (Notebook A, p. 26)

The early manuscripts contain parody ballads like the erotic "Hellshaft":

> Really, said the red-faced axe-layer
> you have such lovely hair.
> Janus, said the red-faced axe-layer
> your skin is so fair.

> Really, said the red-faced axe-layer
> you have flanks like a mare.
> Janus, said the red-faced axe-layer
> even clothed you look bare. . . . (PR, 12)

Or heroic couplets are used for parody effect as in "Virtú":

> Marble niches frame a virgin's grey decay
> as casually as rain clouds fill the day
> with not quite black foreboding. As the sun
> beams sickly on the desecrated fun. (Notebook A, p. 24)

The influence of music, so important throughout O'Hara's career, is evident in "Quintet for Quasimodo" (Notebook A, pp. 14–15), "Triolet" (p. 33), and especially the charming "Gavotte," which begins:

> Alack alack alay
> my ministrante has come to me
> to lead the dark away.
> Meetly she
> embraces me
> coolly, drily, tenderly. (Notebook A, p. 28)

I cite these texts, not because they are "finished" poems in their own right, but to emphasize O'Hara's familiarity with poetic convention. However "unformed" his later poetry may look, we should bear in mind that he tried his hand at sonnets, songs, ballads, eclogues, litanies, and dirges: "Marian's Mortality" (Notebook A, pp. 42–44) is a good example of a conventional dirge with strophe, antistrophe, and epode.

In 1949 (O'Hara's senior year), these imitations, parodies, and exercises in adapting traditional verse forms give way to two kinds of poems that will continue to appear side by side until 1954 or so. One is the clotted, somewhat mannered Surrealist mode of *Oranges: 12 Pastorals* (*CP*, 5); the other, the natural, colloquial, whimsical, light-hearted mode of "Les Etiquettes Jaunes" (*CP*, 21), a mode clearly derived from William Carlos Williams. I shall argue later that not until O'Hara learned to fuse these two modes—to adapt Surrealist images and forms to an American idiom—was he able to write the poems that we think of as his central achievements.

John Ashbery speaks quite rightly of the "posturing that mars 'Oranges'" (*CP*, ix), but it is still a very interesting sequence. In its first version, written in 1948, it contained nineteen pastorals. When O'Hara gave the series to Grace Hartigan in 1952, he reduced the nineteen to twelve, and it is these twelve poems that were published in 1953 by the Tibor de Nagy Gallery on the occasion of an exhibition of Hartigan's series of twelve paintings called *Oranges,* which incorporates O'Hara's pastorals.[20] If we compare the two versions, we note that O'Hara eliminated passages of three kinds: (1) those that attempt to describe heterosexual love in conventional terms, for example: "Walking by water, at the harp's disgrace / we shuddered; the young girl wrapped / in her yielding but echoed faintly / across our hearts' dawn-bandaged tremors" (Part 3); (2) those that are realistic and matter-of-fact: "I was twelve. / She was my first whore and I was too young" (Part 12); and those with anti-Catholic references like the attack on the "nada litany" of Franco's Spain (Part 12) or Part 15, which ends with the words, "Hail to our Savior! I bathe His feet in my tears and rest Them on my head. Let us each place a corn-flake on the center of his tongue and ejaculate!"[21]

In its final version, *Oranges* is a series of prose poems in which the poet never mentions or so much as alludes to the title word, thus endowing it with an aura of Dada inconsequentiality. O'Hara gives us a witty account of its composition in his famous poem, "Why I Am Not a Painter," written in 1956:

> One day I am thinking of
> a color: orange. I write a line
> about orange. Pretty soon it is a
> whole page of words, not lines.
> Then another page. There should be
> so much more, not of orange, of
> words, of how terrible orange is
> and life. Days go by. It is even in
> prose. I am a real poet. My poem
> is finished and I haven't mentioned
> orange yet. It's twelve poems, I call
> it ORANGES.
>
> (*CP,* 262)

The twelve prose poems are essentially antipastorals in which the usual conventions are slyly inverted, but which, nevertheless, celebrate erotic love in "pastoral" settings. Thus the poem begins with the line, "Black crows in the burnt mauve grass, as intimate as rotting rice, snot on a white linen field" (*CP,* 5). The polarity of images in this sentence—"mauve grass" / "rotting rice"; "snot" / "white linen field"— can be traced back at least to Rimbaud's "Ce qu'on dit au poète à propos des fleurs," but more immediately to collections of prose poems like Tristan Tzara's *Cher ami, l'Antitête,* Louis Aragon's *Pur Jeudi,* or André Breton's *Poisson soluble.* Throughout, O'Hara juxtaposes the beautiful and the ugly, the elegant and the "low" or obscene, to create new angles of vision: "O pastures dotted with excremental discs, wheeling in interplanetary green" (p. 5); "There is a little pile of excrement at my nape like a Japanese pillow" (p. 5); "the sun seemed empty, a counterfeit coin hung round the blue throat patched with leprosy" (p. 6); or "Gregorian frogs belch and masturbate" (p. 9).

Such juxtapositions could easily become tedious, but *Oranges* subsumes them into a larger design. The poem begins with images of "Tess amidst the thorny hay, her new-born shredded by the ravenous cutter-bar" (a snide reference to Hardy's Tess of the d'Urbervilles and her illegitimate child), and of the "village Ophelia," "floating by," who "loved none but the everyday lotus, and slept with none but the bull on the hill," and ends with the view of "the body of a blue girl, hair floating weedy in the room" (p. 8). Between these derogatory images of floating female corpses, the poet as seer appears, invoking *his* gods— Pan and Orpheus. In Part II, he declares, "Pan, your flesh alone has escaped. Promise me, god of the attainable and always perfecting fruit, when I lie . . . play into my rain-sweet canals your notes of love!" (p. 5). His erotic ecstasy reaches its climax in Part 7:

> Then in other fields I saw people walking dreamily in the black hay and golden cockleburs; from the firmament streamed the music of Orpheus! and on earth Pan made vivid the pink and white hunger of my senses!
> Snakes twined about my limbs to cool them, and springs cold and light sucked my tongue; bees brushed sweet from my eyelids; clouds

washed my skin; at the end of the day a horse squandered his love. The sun replenishes, mirror and magnifier, of my own beauty! and at night through dreams reminds me, moaning, of my daytime self. (p. 7)

And now, in Part 8, the figures of Pan, Orpheus, and the poet himself merge in a frenzied pagan dance. After this crescendo, the poet comes back down to earth; in Part 11 he says: "I make my passport / dossier: a portrait of the poet wrapped in jungle leaves airy on vines, skin tender to the tough wind. . . . Standing in the photograph, then, filthy and verminous but for my lavender shaving lotion, I must confess that the poor have me always with them, and I love no god. My food is caviar, I love only music, and my bed is sin" (p. 8).

But although the poet now regresses, saying petulantly: "Bring me my doll: I must make contact with something dead" (an echo from Rilke),[22] the memory of the vision remains, and *Oranges* ends on a Paterian note: "O my posterity! This is the miracle: that our elegant invention the natural world redeems by filth" (p. 9). These exclamatory phrases provide artful closure, for the poet *has,* all along, tried to submit his powers of "elegant invention" to the "filth" of actual experience, of the "natural world": his inverted pastoral is a subtly veiled paean to homosexual love. The corpses of legendary women float downstream; other women drop dead in laundry yards (see Part 5), leaving the poet-as-Pan, or as Orpheus, dancing in the sunlight on the crest of rocky mountains.

If *Oranges* strikes us as unnecessarily long and repetitious, it is probably because its central polarity between beauty and ugliness, landscape and machine, the masculine and the feminine, is rendered in excessively abstract, amorphous terms. The poem also suffers from certain coy intrusions like "I forgot to post your letter yesterday. What shall we have for lunch?" or "We are all brothers. You do not have tuberculosis. Kiss me" (p. 7). But O'Hara's pastoral sequence remains an important early attempt to inject a Surrealist note into the neo-Symbolist poetic landscape of postwar America.

O'Hara's other long Surrealist poem of this period is "Meditations on Max Ernst's *Histoire Naturelle,*" a set of seven prose poems written in 1949 (PR, 15–24). Ernst's series of collages (1926) exploits the techniques of *frottage* and *decalcomania,* that is, "the production of images in the first case by rubbing a chalk or some other medium across a rough or textured surface, in the second by blotting images onto paper from wet paint." "From the random forms Ernst produced," writes Kenneth Coutts-Smith, "he read and isolated images that his conscious mind was too inhibited or preconditioned to discover; he tried to create an irrational, or unconditional landscape of images."[23]

One can argue that O'Hara's prose poems do create a verbal equivalent of Ernst's "frottage" landscapes. If *Oranges* stressed the juxtaposition of polar images, which is one of the central characteristics of Surrealist poetry,[24] "Meditations" concentrates on a slightly different aspect of Surrealism: the attempt to render subconscious states, the psychic automatism defined in Breton's First Manifesto.[25] The Introduction to "Meditations" presents the reader with "ferocious lions" who "scent succulence lasciviously," while "lime trees grow tractably, especially on the boarded plains" (p. 15). This dream landscape, rather like a canvas by Henri Rousseau, gives way, in the second paragraph, to "washing-machines (those mirrors of apple blossoms) and looms (the progenitors of nudes) and airplanes (memorials to our fathers). In the same way the films have taught us how beautiful we really are from the anguish of our shadows and the accuracy of objects (the heart of Charlie Chaplin). All machines, similarly, enliven us" (p. 15).

This conjunction of opposites—nature versus the machine—is, of course, typically Surrealist; like *Oranges,* the above passage is perhaps too pure an imitation. The six prose poems that follow remain opaque. We can say that they are clearly love poems of some sort; there are references to a passionate affair, as well as to the fear of a mother who asks the poet, "Are you a cannibal?" (p. 18), and of a father who "warned of the consequences / how passion wells up like a tornado of spiralling blood so that the tongue barely can move its thickness into the mouth of another" (p. 19). But too many references in these prose poems remain wholly private; there is a kind of veil between poet and reader so that the experience of the former remains largely inaccessible. Perhaps O'Hara wanted to create this blurred effect in keeping with the notion of *frottage,* but since words inevitably have meanings, it is doubtful whether one can ultimately "translate" Ernst's visual effects into poetry. *Meditations* remains an interesting experiment rather than a finished poem.

The short Surrealist poems of the Harvard period are generally merely clever. Take "Homage to Rrose Sélavy," based on Duchamp and Desnos:

> Towards you like amphibious airplanes
> peacocks and pigeons seem to scoot![26]

Or "Today":

> Oh! kangaroos, sequins, chocolate sodas!
> You really are beautiful! Pearls,
> harmonicas, jujubes, aspirins! all
> the stuff they've always talked about
>
> still makes a poem a surprise!   (*CP,* 15)

Or "Concert Champêtre":

> The cow belched and invited me
> to breakfast. "Ah" I said "I
> haven't written a pastoral for
>
> ages! . . ."   (*CP,* 15)

Or "A Scene":

> Pie, tomatoes, eggs, coffee, spaghetti
> clobbered the dusty kitchen toward
> Mrs. Bennett Smith, teacher of pianoforte.   (*CP,* 19)

These poems seem to be modeled closely on those of Péret. Take the following examples, translated by Michael Benedikt in his anthology, *The Poetry of Surrealism:*[27]

> Who Is It (*Qui est-ce*)
>
> I term tobacco that which is ear
> and so maggots take advantage of this opportunity to
>   throw themselves on ham   (p. 224)

It Keeps Going On (*Ça continue*)

An old suitcase a sock and an endive
have arranged for a rendezvous between two blades of grass
sprouting on an altar draped in drooping bowels   (p. 225)

A Thousand Times (*Mille fois*)

Among the gilded debris of the gasworks
You will come upon a bar of chocolate which flies off as
     you approach
If you run as fast as an aspirin-bottle
you will find yourself somewhere far beyond the chocolate
which upsets the landscape so
Just like an open-toed sandal. . . .   (p. 226)

Péret develops these images according to a peculiar inner logic appropriate to a given poem. His use of pseudo *if-then* clauses, and of false analogies using the word "like" (*comme*), leads inexorably to the poem's conclusion. "A Thousand Times," for example, converts the kaleidoscopic landscape of chocolate bars and aspirin bottles into one where the poet is alone and happy "at the bottom of the sea," where "there would be a telephone-booth / from which nobody could ever complete a call" (p. 226). In such later Surrealist poems as "Easter," O'Hara manages the same feat, but in the poems cited above, he all too often merely piles up bizarre disjunctive images in exclamatory line units; the poem could start or stop almost anywhere. Then too, the third-person mode used in "Concert Champêtre" or "A Scene" is essentially alien to O'Hara's sensibility; he needs always to *be* in the poem.

Indeed, even while he was writing fanciful lyrics about chocolate sodas and jujubes, O'Hara was, as I noted above, experimenting with the more personal, direct style of Williams. From the first, he accepted Williams as a master, no doubt because he identified with Williams's struggle against convention, pretentiousness, conformity—the "going thing."[28] Thus, in an amusing little poem of 1952 called "WHAT SLEDGEHAMMER? Or W. C. WILLIAMS'S BEEN ATTACKED!" (PR, 111), O'Hara writes:

Yester the heat I walked my tiglon "Charles F"
around the Park, as three nuns in a stationwagon

(au Zoo) robbed the Elizabeth Arden Building.
In the University pistols were not shot off

because they aren't "clean precise expression." Ho
ho ho, kra, chuh chuh, tssk tssk tssk, tereu. . . .

And there's going to be a wedding! there's going to be a
We-Know-What-To-Do-In-The-Fall (a Ball!) between
the Metatheosophists with Italian bedbugs
swinging from their woolly nipples and *The Hudson Review*

(that Organ) . . .

This is obviously an attack on the school of Eliot and the New Critical orthodoxy that made "The Waste Land" with its scenes of Philo-
mela's rape ("tereu") its sacred text. O'Hara admires Williams's "liberation of language," his "attempt to find an honest, tough, hard,
beautiful thing."[29] He follows Williams in believing that "The objective in writing is to reveal," and in a letter to Jasper Johns, listing his
favorite poets, he says: "you said you liked PATERSON; all the books of
WCW have great great great things in them, I don't believe he ever
wrote an uninteresting poem; the prose poems KORA IN HELL have
recently been reprinted and are very good, interesting because very
early and ambitious."[30]

Yet O'Hara also recognized that Williams often had an unfortunate
influence on lesser poets. In his lecture on "The New Poets," given at
The Club on 14 May 1952, he refers disparagingly to the "WC Wil-
liams-ites" with their "I am the man your father was Americanism,"
their "Cleanness thinned down to jingoism," their cult of the "He-
Man."[31] His own debt to Williams, for that matter, is less to the complex epic poem *Paterson* than to the Dadesque prose poems of *Kora,*
and especially to the early shorter poems, whose unrhymed tercets or
quatrains are distinguished by their very short lines, broken at odd
junctures, and their use of colloquial speech.

The charming "Autobiographia Literaria," for example, with its
parody-Coleridge title, uses the four-line stanza of such famous Williams poems as "The Catholic Bells" and "The Last Words of my
English Grandmother" to invert, very delicately, the Romantic notion
of the child as blessed seer, "trailing clouds of glory" before "Shades of
the prison-house begin to close" upon him. O'Hara's child, unlike

Wordsworth's, is a pathetic little misfit, unloved, unwanted, unfriendly. Even the animals "were / not friendly and birds / flew away." But, by a humorous twist, this child grows up to be, of all things, a happy poet:

> And here I am, the
> center of all beauty!
> writing these poems!
> Imagine!   (*CP*, 11)

Here the exclamatory tone, the colloquial manner, the transformation theme, the sense of immediacy (we *witness* the writing of "these poems"), and the final humorous twist are reminiscent of Williams's "Invocation and Conclusion" (1935):

> January!
> The beginning of all things!
> Spring from the old burning nest
> upward in the flame!
>
> I was married at thirteen
> My parents had nine kids
> and we were on the street
> That's why the old bugger—
>
> He was twenty-six
> and I hadn't even had
> my changes yet. Now look at me![32]

Williams's conclusion is more equivocal than O'Hara's; we can take the final "Now look at me!" as an exclamation of resignation rather than hope. But in style and structure, the two poems are certainly similar.

"Les Etiquettes Jaunes," written shortly after O'Hara graduated from Harvard, is an even better example of his Williams mode:

> I picked up a leaf
> today from the sidewalk.
> This seems childish.
>
> Leaf! you are so big!
> How can you change your
> color, then just fall!

As if there were no
such thing as integrity!

You are too relaxed
to answer me. I am too
frightened to insist.

Leaf! don't be neurotic
like the small chameleon.   (*CP,* 21)

This playful poem brings to mind two poems by Williams about trees:

Trees [1917]

Crooked, black tree
on your little grey-black hillock,
ridiculously raised one step toward
the infinite summits of the night. . . .

                    you alone
warp yourself passionately to one side
in your eagerness.   (*Collected Earlier Poems,* p. 142)

The Trees [1934]

The trees—being trees
thrash and scream
guffaw and curse—
wholly abandoned
damning the race of men—

Christ, the bastards
haven't even sense enough
to stay out of the rain. . . .
                    (*Collected Earlier Poems,* p. 66)

The poetic device of all these poems is to personify a plant form and
then rebuke it for possessing certain human follies. But O'Hara's is
more comically absurd than the two Williams poems; its title is in itself
quite different from "Trees," implying that leaves choose to turn yellow and fall according to some sort of Emily Post code, the French
language adding a note of mock elegance. The conversation between
poet and leaf enlarges on this humorous notion: it is fickle of the leaf to
change color and then, what's worse, just to "fall" (double entendre),

"As if there were no / such thing as integrity!" Both literally and figuratively, the leaf is "too relaxed / to answer" the poet, who is, in an absurd reversal, so amazed by its transformation that he is "too frightened to insist." Thus a simple thing like a wet autumn leaf, found on one's path, becomes comically emblematic of neurotic behavior. The poet begs the leaf not to be "like the small chameleon."

Unlike the Surrealist poems I discussed earlier, there is not a word in this poem that cannot be readily understood; the diction is childlike, monosyllabic, purposely flat; the sentences short and exclamatory; the line breaks quirky as in "too / frightened" or "no / such thing." "Les Etiquettes Jaunes" is no more than a charming slight poem, but we can already see O'Hara's own aesthetic emerging: even the falling of a single leaf, the poem implies, is worthy of notice. "Don't be bored, don't be lazy, don't be trivial, and don't be proud. The slightest loss of attention leads to death."

There are a number of other poems in the Williams mode dating from the Harvard period, beginning with "Gamin" on the opening page of the *Collected Poems* and including "God" (PR, 11), "First Night" (PR, 26), and "A Walk on Sunday Afternoon" (*CP,* 20). But the outstanding poem of the Harvard years—and one of O'Hara's first great poems—is "Memorial Day 1950" (*CP,* 17), written in the spring of that year and not published during O'Hara's lifetime. The poet was, as his friends attest,[33] an uncertain judge of his own work, often preferring a slight poem which happened to allude to something that interested him at the moment to one that would later be considered on aesthetic grounds an important poem. Indeed, "Memorial Day 1950" survived purely by accident: John Ashbery copied it out and sent it in a letter to Kenneth Koch, who fortunately saved the letter.[34]

"Memorial Day 1950" is O'Hara's version of Rimbaud's "Les Poètes de sept ans," part autobiographical memoir, part artistic manifesto—a portrait of the young artist escaping from the restrictions of his narrowly bourgeois childhood world. But whereas Rimbaud's poem still observes the unities of time (the terrible long Sundays) and place (the poet's stifling childhood home with its polished mahogany break fronts), and relates stimulus (the smell of latrines) to response (the longing for succulent grass) in what is still an essentially realistic mode, O'Hara's poem is the verbal equivalent of a Dada collage—a bright, colorful, exuberant poem that juxtaposes disparate images in dreamlike sequences.

Whereas O'Hara's first Surrealist experiments like *Oranges* are partial failures because they present a hothouse world under glass, a world cleverly organized around a particular set of images but too remote from the reader, "Memorial Day" succeeds because it fuses the colloquialism and natural speech rhythms of Williams with the dialectic of polarized images characteristic of Dada and Surrealism. It is a fusion O'Hara would not quite achieve again for some years to come.

The poem's language is dynamic and immediate: "Picasso made me tough and quick," "Once he got his axe going everyone was upset," "Through all that surgery I thought / I had a lot to say, and named several last things Gertrude Stein hadn't had time for," "Guernica hollered look out!" "those of us who thought poetry / was crap were throttled by Auden or Rimbaud," "you must look things / in the belly, not in the eye," and so on. Such racy diction is very different from the frequently ornate style of *Oranges:* "My feet, tender with sight, wander the yellow grass in search of love" (*CP,* 7).

But, more important, "Memorial Day 1950" is one of O'Hara's first poems to resemble film, with its dissolves, cuts, its images at once concrete and hallucinatory, bleeding into one another. Take the opening:

> Picasso made me tough and quick, and the world;
> just as in a minute plane trees are knocked down
> outside my window by a crew of creators.
> Once he got his axe going everyone was upset
> enough to fight for the last ditch and heap
> of rubbish.

Here Picasso appears as dream surgeon, chopping through the debris of dead art ("the last ditch and heap / of rubbish") with his axe, as if he were a human bulldozer chopping down plane trees outside the poet's window.[35] Similarly, the scene in which the poet's parents take exception to their son's vocation is presented in Surrealistic terms:

> How many trees and frying pans
> I loved and lost! Guernica hollered look out!

> but we were all busy hoping our eyes were talking
> to Paul Klee. My mother and father asked me and
> I told them from my tight blue pants we should
> love only the stones, the sea, and heroic figures.
> Wasted child! I'll club you on the shins! I
> wasn't surprised when the older people entered
> my cheap hotel room and broke my guitar and my can
> of blue paint.

This passage is enormously suggestive: the tight blue pants and blue paint, logically quite unrelated, merge as emblems of the rebellious creative imagination. The reproof, "Wasted child! I'll club you on the shins," is not only spoken by the parents but, it seems, by the whole community of "older people—those "older people" who enter the poet's cheap hotel room and break his guitar and can of paint.

But the guitar cannot be broken. In the final sequence its strings are used to hold up pictures in the poet's atelier. And if the paintcan breaks, all the better for it must be spilled to be explored:

> At that time all of us began to think
> with our bare hands and even with blood all over
> them we knew vertical from horizontal, we never
> smeared anything except to find out how it lived.

This elliptical statement is an important reference to the doctrine of Action Painting (and, by implication, Action Poetry)—the belief that the materials used by the artist exist in their own right; they are not merely means to the creation of mimetic illusion. From his masters— Picasso, Stein, Ernst, Auden, Rimbaud, Apollinaire—the poet learns that "art is no dictionary"—that the Symbolist doctrine of correspondences between external world and higher reality is meaningless although one's stance toward art can "tell" one certain things: "Poetry didn't tell me not to play with toys / but alone I could never have figured out that dolls meant death." [36]

Rather, the poet learns that art is the creation of new patterns out of disparate objects; he invokes the "Fathers of Dada!": "You carried shining erector sets / in your rough bony pockets, you were generous / and they were lovely as chewing gum or flowers!" His predilection is for "collages or sprechstimme," for "airplanes," those "perfect mobiles . . . crashing in flames" and showing us "how to be prodigal" (*CP,* 18). For the new artist, all change, flux—the celebrated *vertige* of the Surrealists[37]—is valuable, even "the sewage singing / underneath my bright white toilet seat" which will eventually "reach the sea," where "gulls and swordfishes will find it richer than a river."

In the final verse paragraph, the supposedly "wasted child," pitied by his parents, has become a real poet. All broken objects are now reassembled:

> Look at my room.
> Guitar strings hold up pictures. I don't need
> a piano to sing, and naming things is only the intention
> to make things. A locomotive is more melodious
> than a cello. I dress in oilcloth and read music
> by Guillaume Apollinaire's clay candelabra. Now
> my father is dead and has found you must look things
> in the belly, not in the eye. If only he had listened
> to the men who made us, hollering like stuck pigs!

In this landscape of guitar strings and locomotives, the poet practices his craft. "Naming things is only the intention / to make things"; the key is to recognize things for what they are, to "look things in the belly, not in the eye"—a lesson the poet's father evidently never learned.

"Memorial Day 1950" thus ends on what looks like a harsh note, but in the context of the poem, even this image of the father takes on an unreal quality. Once dead, he too can become part of the landscape of erector sets and airplanes, the locomotive, the white toilet seat, and the can of blue paint. The poem is, in short, a memorial to the great artists who were O'Hara's early models—Apollinaire and Rilke, Picasso and Stein, Max Ernst and Rimbaud. It is a poem of great vitality and joy, a poem that shrewdly and humorously assesses what it means to make oneself an artist in a world that distrusts art.

ANN ARBOR INTERLUDE

After his graduation from Harvard, O'Hara spent a year at Ann Arbor and received an M.A. in English from the University of Michigan in the summer of 1951. It is during this year that he won the Hopwood

Award in Creative Writing (thus winning a contest that John Ciardi had urged him to enter)[38] for *A Byzantine Place,* a manuscript that contained such early poems as "Les Etiquettes Jaunes" and "The Muse Considered as a Demon Lover."

O'Hara wrote a good deal of poetry during his Michigan year, but it is a poetry of consolation rather than of notable innovation. One senses that, his student apprenticeship behind him, the poet now needed a city—specifically New York City—just as much as, say, Wordsworth needed the Lake District or Van Gogh the landscape of Provençe as a source of inspiration. Away from the excitement, the violence, the whirlwind social scene of New York, he languished. Thus he writes in "Ann Arbor Variations" (*CP,* 65):

> The wind blows towards us particularly
> the sobbing of our dear friends on both
> coasts. We are sick of living and afraid
> that death will not be by water, o sea.

And in "A Pathetic Note," he writes to a New York friend:[39] "When you go down West / Fourteenth Street think of Africa and me.... Keep photographing the instant, / so that in my hysteria I will know what / it is like there" (PR, 50).

The Christmas holidays of 1950, spent in the magical city, prompted the following light-hearted, Cole Porter-type song:

> I'm going to New York!
> (what a lark! what a song!)
> where the tough Rocky's eaves
> hit the sea. Where th'Acro-
> polis is functional, the trains
> that run and shout! the books
> that have trousers and sleeves!
>
> I'm going to New York!
> (quel voyage! jamais plus!)
> far from Ypsilanti and Flint!
> where Goodman rules the Empire
> and the sunlight's eschato-
> logy upon the wizard's bridges
> and the galleries of print!

I'm going to New York!
(to my friends! mes semblables!)
I suppose I'll walk back West.
But for now I'm gone forever!
The city's hung with flashlights!
the Ferry's unbuttoning its vest!   (PR, 49)

Back in Ann Arbor, away from "the trains / that run and shout!,"
"the books / that have trousers and sleeves," "the galleries of print,"
and especially from "my friends! mes semblables," O'Hara continued
to write parodies and imitations. Thus he mocks Eliot in "Mr. O'Hara's
Sunday Morning Service," which begins: "There is this to be said / for
Sunday morning: that if / I have been very bad the night / before . . .
Dick will pop into my room / and invite me out to the / high abandoned airfield" (PR, 66). He tries his hand at a Drydenesque "Ode on
Saint Cecelia's Day" (*CP*, 27–29), and at Petrarchan sonnets like
"Boston," "The Satyr," and "The Tomb of Arnold Schoenberg." These
experiments are generally merely playful; "After Wyatt" (*CP*, 68), for
example, has a first quatrain that rhymes "semen" with "simoon,"
"parachute" with "boot." A more interesting poem is the charming
"Variations on a Theme by Shelley," which opens with the lines:

We live in an opal or
crystal ball. The sun's
an eye, against it clouds
crowd like Spanish castles
on a mountain.   (PR, 46)

This is an allusion to the "Hymn to Apollo" ("I am the eye with which
the universe / Beholds itself and knows itself divine"), but O'Hara
now inverts Shelley's theme, concluding that "we become the eye and
defy / questions with our beauty."

The Surrealist poems of the Ann Arbor period are mostly negligible.
There are experimental *calligrammes* in the Apollinaire tradition—
"WHEEWHEE" (*CP*, 25) is a forerunner of concrete poems, its words and
letters spread all over the page—and coy presentations of the poet as

"Dada / baby," as in "Night Thoughts in Greenwich Village," which begins:

> O my coevals! embarrassing
> memories! pastiches! jokes!
> All your pleasaunces and
> the vividness of your ills
> are only fertilizer for
> the kids.

and ends on a bathetic note, with echoes of Hart Crane's "Chaplinesque":

> O my coevals! we cannot die
> too soon. Art is sad and
> life is vapid. Can we thumb
> our nose at the very sea?   (*CP*, 38)

The best poems of the Ann Arbor year are those in the Williams mode; indeed, some of O'Hara's finest short poems date from 1950–51, even if these are less complex, less interesting than "Memorial Day 1950" or than the longer poems that were to be written just a few years later. "A Pleasant Thought from Whitehead," for example, is a witty Ars Poetica poem that brilliantly debunks the convention itself—witness Dylan Thomas's famed "In my Craft or Sullen Art," which appeared just five years earlier. Unlike Thomas's posturing speaker who "labour[s] by singing light / Not for ambition or bread. . . . But for the lovers, their arms / Round the griefs of the ages, / Who pay no praise or wages / Nor heed my craft or art,"[40] O'Hara's "I" is droll and self-deprecating:

> Here I am at my desk. The
> light is bright enough
> to read by it is a warm
> friendly day I am feeling
> assertive. I slip a few
> poems into the pelican's
> bill and he is off! out
> the window into the blue!   (*CP*, 23–24)

The notion of the pelican as carrier pigeon, delivering poems to an editor who is immediately "delighted," is wonderfully absurd, as is the idea that only an "assertive" person would risk the action described. But the poem is more than funny because O'Hara does such interesting things with lineation. By breaking lines where he does, he creates verbal patterns whose meaning runs counter to the literal sense of the poem as a continuous statement. For example "friendly day I am feeling" becomes a semantic unit in its own right, running counter to "I am feeling / assertive." In the second stanza, we have the following lines:

> Ah!
> reader! you open the page
> my poems stare at you you
> stare back, do you not? my
> poems speak on the silver
> of your eyes your eyes repeat
> them to your lover's this
> very night.   (*CP*, 24)

Here form *is* meaning in a very real sense: the placement of "my," framing lines 3 and 4 and thus enclosing the word "you" (repeated three times) and "stare" (used twice), serves to draw the reader into the poet's situation. The same effect is created in the next line with "your eyes your eyes repeat / them to your lover's this / very night." Having established a kind of love union with his reader, the poet is momentarily ecstatic. Even the "improving stars" seem to be reading his poems over his reader's (or lover's) "naked / shoulder" and then "flash / them onward to a friend."

Fred Moramarco has argued that the verbal positioning used in this passage is a technique derived from Abstract Expressionist painting.[41] This may well be the case, although O'Hara could have learned the same thing from Williams, whose short poems—"As the cat ... " or "Nantucket" or "The Red Wheelbarrow"—hammer words into what Hugh Kenner has called "an audio-visual counterpoint, a kind of "suspension system."[42] The bravado of "improving stars" certainly recalls Williams, but the last three lines strike me as pure O'Hara:

> The eyes the poems of the
> world are changed! Pelican!
> you will read them too!   (*CP*, 24)

This coda picks up the key words—*eyes, poems*—of the preceding section, and the final comic twist has an inexorably absurd logic all its own: the pelican has done all the dirty work, what with carrying those poems to the editor, so now he gets his reward—he may read them too! And we can further relate this conclusion to the comic title of the poem. Whitehead, after all, insisted that all forms of human inquiry and experience are interrelated, and that the gulf between man and nature, value and fact, must be bridged. So the "pleasant thought from Whitehead" is the comic notion that in our "organicist" universe, the gulf between poet and pelican has been bridged. One can take this theme in two opposite ways: as a kind of triumph or as an admission of failure—an invention of a poetry fit only for pelicans.

"Morning" (*CP*, 30) is one of O'Hara's first important love poems. Its model may well be Williams's famous "Love Song" in its first version of 1915, especially the stanza:

> I am alone
> The weight of love
> Has buoyed me up
> Till my head
> Knocks against the sky.[43]

O'Hara's poem, with its flat four-line stanzas characterized by short choppy lines, monosyllabic diction, and repeated *i* and *o* sounds, begins in low key:

> I've got to tell you
> how I love you always
> I think of it on grey
> mornings with death
>
> in my mouth the tea
> is never hot enough
> then and the cigarette
> dry the maroon robe
>
> chills me I need you

What makes this disarmingly simple declaration of love a poem? Chiefly, I think, its innovative lineation and syntax. "Morning" is one of O'Hara's first poems to contain what I call "floating modifiers"—

that is, word groups that point two ways. Thus, "in my mouth" literally refers back to "death," but the lineation forces us to relate it to "the tea" as well. The position of "dry" has the same effect—it looks back to "cigarette" but also forward to "maroon robe."

The syntactic ambiguity of these ordinary words and phrases as well as the consistent enjambment, which makes one read on without pausing all the way to the end, give the poem its "push and pull"— the reader is kept busy trying to bring its shifting surfaces to a point of rest. Moreover, O'Hara chooses his images very carefully: "I miss you always / when I go to the beach / the sand is wet with / tears that seem mine" seems banal enough until one realizes that the poet has here carried the pathetic fallacy to an absurd extreme—even the wetness of the sand is a projection of his sorrow. Or again, in the case of the stanza, "the parking lot is / crowded and I stand / rattling my keys the car / is empty as a bicycle," the effect is gained by setting off "crowded and I stand" in one line and by the odd reference to the car as being "empty as a bicycle" (room for one person only!) while the keys, disconcertingly, rattle.

"Morning" reaches a crescendo of anxiety in the eighth stanza: "What are you doing now / where did you eat your lunch . . . ," and then decelerates again, ending on a note of nice understatement:

> if there is a
> place further from me
> I beg you do not go   (*CP*, 32)

These lines have a Chaplinesque quality, a mixture of drollness and abject self-distrust: clearly the poet has no hope of recapturing the past but if he can just prevent his lover from going to "a place further from me," he will have won a Pyrrhic victory.[44]

The charm, wry humor, and technical mastery of O'Hara's quatrain poems is impressive, but he could only go so far in this vein. To get beyond the Williams mode as well as the rather frozen Surrealism of "Dido" (*CP*, 74) and "Jane Awake" (p. 72), he had to make contact with the artistic milieu of New York. In the fall of 1951, he settled permanently in Manhattan, and within the year, he had met Joe Le-Sueur, James Schuyler, Barbara Guest, Helen Frankenthaler, Grace

Hartigan, Franz Kline, Elaine and Willem de Kooning, Jackson Pollock, and Ned Rorem. He began his career at the Museum of Modern Art by working in the lobby at the front desk, ostensibly so that he could see Alfred Barr's monumental retrospective of Matisse. He also began to review for *Art News* and published his first book of poems, *A City Winter* (1952), as well as the pamphlet *Oranges* (1953). His play *Try! Try!* was produced by the Artists' Theatre, and he acted in the Living Theatre's production of Picasso's *Desire Caught by the Tail* at the Cherry Lane. The time of apprenticeship was over.

THE CITY "HUNG WITH FLASHLIGHTS"

In "Four Apartments," Joe LeSueur recalls his first meeting with O'Hara: "We met on New Year's Eve, 1951, at a party John Ashbery gave in a one-room apartment in the Village. Paul Goodman said: 'There's a poet named Frank O'Hara I think you'll like,' and led me across the room to him. Tchaikowsky's Third Piano Concerto was playing full-volume on John's portable phonograph, and almost immediately Frank and I began dreaming up a frivolous ballet scenario" (p. 287).

A "frivolous ballet scenario" inspired by Tchaikowsky's Third Piano Concerto, composed in a crowded room at a New Year's Eve party— here, in a nutshell, is a portrait of the artist during his early New York years, years in which O'Hara was, as LeSueur recalls, "in high [gear] all the time, high on himself, and his every waking minute, regardless of what he was doing, was vital, supercharged, never boring if he could help it" (p. 289). And James Schuyler confirms this image of the poet: "The first time I dropped by to see him [at the Museum] I found him in the admissions booth, waiting to sell tickets to visitors and meanwhile, writing a poem on a yellow lined pad called 'It's the Blue!' He also had beside him a translation of André Breton's *Young Cherry Trees Secured Against Hares. . . .*"[45]

O'Hara himself has described "the milieu of those days" in his memoir of Larry Rivers:

> We were all in our early twenties. John Ashbery, Barbara Guest, Kenneth Koch and I, being poets, divided our time between the literary bar, the

San Remo, and the artists' bar, the Cedar Tavern. In the San Remo, we argued and gossiped: in the Cedar we often wrote poems while listening to the painters argue and gossip. . . . An interesting sidelight to these social activities was that for most of us non-Academic and indeed non-literary poets in the sense of the American scene at the time, the painters were the only generous audience for our poetry, and most of us read first publicly in art galleries or at The Club. The literary establishment cared about as much for our work as the Frick cared for Pollock and de Kooning, not that we cared any more about establishments than they did, all the disinterested parties being honorable men. (*CP*, 512)

While it is no doubt true that the painters were "the only generous audience" for O'Hara's poetry in the early New York years, his reference to himself as a "non-literary poet" must, like many of his self-deprecatory remarks, be taken with a grain of salt. We have seen throughout this chapter that O'Hara was very literary indeed, even if his models were not the usual ones. At The Club (the 39 East 8th Street Club), which O'Hara mentions above as the meeting place for poets and artists, he gave, for that matter, some surprisingly "literary" lectures.

In a valuable essay for *Artforum*,[46] Irving Sandler gives a brief history of The Club: its founding in 1949 when the young Abstract Expressionists needed a meeting place more private and comfortable than their wartime haunt, The Waldorf Cafeteria on 6th Avenue; its lecture series and panel discussions, its styles of debate and aesthetic principles, and its ultimate demise in the mid-fifties after the leading painters of the group had become more established and came to prefer the informality of the Cedar Street Tavern (whose neutral, colorless decor typified what de Kooning called a "no-environment") to the organized panel discussions of The Club (p. 31). Sandler lists a selection of events held at The Club in 1951–52; let me cite those in which O'Hara participated as well as a few others which provide a backdrop for his activities and interests at this time:

November 9: An evening with Max Ernst, introduced by Robert Motherwell.

January 18: The first of three Symposia on Abstract Expressionism, promoted by the publication of Thomas Hess's *Abstract Painting*. The first panel, entitled "Expressionism," consisted of Harold Rosenberg (moderator), William Baziotes, Philip Guston, Thomas Hess, Franz Kline, Ad Reinhardt, and Jack Tworkov.

February 20: A conversation between Philip Guston, Franz Kline, Willem de Kooning, George McNeil, and Jack Tworkov.

March 7: A group of younger artists: Jane Freilicher, Grace Hartigan, Alfred Leslie, Joan Mitchell, Frank O'Hara, and Larry Rivers, moderated by John Meyers, continuing their discussion of Abstract Expressionism.

March 14: John Cage speaking on "Contemporary Music."

April 11: "The Image in Poetry and Painting": Nicholas Calas (moderator), Edwin Denby, David Gascoyne, Frank O'Hara, Ruthven Todd.

May 14: "New Poets": Larry Rivers (chairman), John Ashbery, Barbara Guest, Frank O'Hara, James Schuyler.

O'Hara's lecture notes for the April 11 panel are surprisingly formal. He begins with a dictionary definition of *design* and proceeds to contrast *design* to *form:* "design" is the "exterior aspect" of poetry, "form" its "interior structure." Thus the *design* of a devotional poem by George Herbert may be a chalice or a diamond, but its *form* is "the traditional rhymed metaphysical meditation, with the favorite metaphysical rhetorical characteristics including the far-fetched images called 'conceits.'" The poet, O'Hara argues, must steer clear of the Scylla of conventional design and form on the one hand, and the Charybdis of his own private ideas and emotions on the other. Excessive reliance on the design of earlier poets breeds dullness and deadness; too little design, on the other hand, produces "muddy rantings."[47]

This is, of course, a perfectly traditional argument; O'Hara might be T. S. Eliot talking about the delicate balance between fixity and flux.[48] But in judging the poets of his own time, O'Hara reveals his own biases. Yeats and Hopkins, he suggests, while obviously poets of the Great Tradition, are too remote to influence writers of his own generation. He praises Dylan Thomas's early poetry for its "directness and intensity, a richness and compulsive passion which is akin to that of Lautréamont and Rimbaud in French," but remarks shrewdly that "unfortunately his growing public demanded an image of the poet as stormbattered heather-kicking bard from the wilds, and Thomas' latest poetry shows to my mind that his over-emotional and semi-hysterical readings have led his own diction to the verge of sentimentality and verbosity."[49]

O'Hara's view of Wallace Stevens is respectful but somewhat distant. "Stevens . . . has had very little influence when one considers his stature. More than any other living poet he has maintained poetry as high art. Never making concessions to styles or public sentiments he has remained austere without becoming cold or finicky; his work has grown steadily in beauty and wisdom while never thickening into mere fuss and elegance nor hardening into theory. The sensibility his poems reveal is one which other ages [may] well envy us for possessing" (p. 3).

A great poet, in short, but one who looks to the past rather than to the future and who is, in any case, inimitable, *sui generis.* Interestingly, O'Hara here anticipates a controversial distinction Hugh Kenner has recently made in *A Homemade World* (1975) between Stevens's still traditional, Symbolist language and Williams's bold experimentation with audio-visual structures.[50]

The April 11 lecture contains one of O'Hara's first references to Ezra Pound, whom he calls "the father of modern poets in English." "His influence is pervasive and especially so now: his influence is almost invariably healthy in that it seldom detracts from the individuality of the poet who admires him; rather, it points up, clarifies it" (p. 4). This is, I think, a very perceptive comment for it is quite true that poets as otherwise dissimilar as Lowell and Zukovsky, Berryman and Ginsberg, or O'Hara himself and Olson, all felt a special debt to the style and structure of the *Cantos.*

A second new favorite (not quite new since his name is already invoked in "Memorial Day 1950") is Auden. According to O'Hara, Auden is "an American poet" in "his use of the vernacular," just as Eliot's style characterizes him as insistently English. "Auden extended our ideas of what poetry could be; his poems saw clearly into obscure areas of modern life and they provided us with obscure and complex insights into areas which had hitherto been banal." O'Hara praises Auden's poetry for being "intimately based on . . . experiences and expressions of what had been looked down upon by the pretentious estheticism and mysticism of the Eliot school" (p. 2).

So far as I know, O'Hara never reversed these estimates. Of modern English and American poets, Williams, Pound, and Auden remained his favorites, and certainly he never came to trust the school of Eliot, or to have much interest in Yeats, Hopkins, or Stevens. But despite his advocacy of the poetry of immediate experience, of concrete particulars and contemporary vernacular, his theory remained ahead of his practice for another few years. The choice of poems for inclusion in *A City Winter* (1952) is itself indicative. O'Hara's first published book contains fourteen poems: "Poem (At night Chinamen jump . . .)," "Early Mondrian," "Poem (Let's take a walk . . .)," "The Argonauts," "The Lover," "The Young Christ," "Yet Another Fan," "A Pastoral Dialogue," "A Terrestial Cuckoo," "A Mexican Guitar," "Jane Awake," "Gli Amanti," "Jove," and the title poem, which is a sonnet cycle based on specific sonnets by Wyatt, Petrarch, and Shakespeare. Reading "At night Chinamen jump / on Asia with a thump" (*CP,* 13) or most of the other poems in the volume one would never guess that O'Hara had already written such wonderful lyrics as "A Pleasant Thought from Whitehead," or "Memorial Day 1950." Take the octave of the second sonnet in "A City Winter":

> My ship is flung upon the gutter's wrist
> and cries for help of storm to violate
> that flesh your curiosity too late
> has flushed. The stem your garter tongue would twist
> has sunk upon the waveless bosom's mist,
> thigh of the city, apparition, hate,
> and the tower whose doves have, delicate,
> fled into my blood where they are not kissed.   (*CP,* 76)

This version of Wyatt's "The Lover Compareth His State to a Ship in Perilous Storm at Sea" is neither a full-fledged parody, nor a reasonably good imitation, nor an interesting poem in its own right. The game becomes tiresome as when, in the third sonnet, O'Hara concludes with the Shakesperean couplet: "you are not how the gods refused to die, / and I am scarred forever neath the eye." Auden, reading these and related Surrealist poems of the early fifties, wrote to O'Hara: "I think you . . . must watch what is always the great danger with any 'surrealistic' style, namely of confusing authentic non-logical relations which arouse wonder with accidental ones which arouse mere surprise and in the end fatigue."[51]

This is an interesting observation. For curiously, the major poems of

O'Hara's early New York period—"Chez Jane," "Easter," and "Sec-
ond Avenue"—are not vernacular poems in the Pound-Williams-
Auden tradition but Surrealist lyrics that carry the mode of the earlier
Oranges to what is probably a point of no return. These are the poems
of what John Ashbery has aptly called Frank's "French Zen period"
(*CP,* ix)—fascinating, if not always successful, experiments.

"Chez Jane" (September. 1952), for example, could be considered—to paraphrase Henry James's famous comment on Ford Madox
Ford's *The Good Soldier*—one of the best French Surrealist poems in
English. "Much surrealist poetry," writes Mary Ann Caws, "instantly
brings to mind the art of film, since both are above all concerned with
the changing moment, with the metamorphosis of the instant." Thus in
the "game called *l'un dans l'autre* . . . one thing is seen as potentially
within the other (for instance a lion's mane within the flame of a
match), opposites are joined, and the distance between the present and
the future is annihilated. The presence of one element is in some way
seen as predictive of the opposite element[s] by a deliberate and yet
spontaneous stretching of vision." The poem becomes a "collage in
motion," holding "within itself the opposition of poles."[52]

These principles are entirely applicable to "Chez Jane," which is one
of O'Hara's first "painterly" poems, a kind of Surrealist still life, de-
pending upon intense visualization.

> The white chocolate jar full of petals
> swills odds and ends around in a dizzying eye
> of four o'clocks now and to come. The tiger,
> marvellously striped and irritable, leaps
> on the table and without disturbing a hair
> of the flowers' breathless attention, pisses
> into the pot, right down its delicate spout.   (*CP,* 102)

On one level, this passage is quite literal. The scene is Jane Freilicher's living room; the "white chocolate jar" is evidently one of those
white Dutch cocoa jars commonly used as vases; "four o'clocks" are
little flowers of variegated colors, and Jane Freilicher recalls that on
this particular occasion, her cat did piss down the spout of her teapot.
Near the end of the poem, when O'Hara talks of "dropped aspirin /
into this sunset of roses," the reference is again to the common practice

of putting aspirin in water so that the roses in the vase will last longer.[53]

But although "Chez Jane" may be read as an occasional poem, its particular conjunction of images is wholly fanciful, exemplifying the game of *l'un dans l'autre*. The "white chocolate jar" immediately brings together opposites—light and dark; it is further juxtaposed to the "petals swill[ing] odds and ends around in a dizzying eye," so that stasis is opposed to movement. Again, it is a particular moment in time—four o'clock (I take the phrase in its primary sense here)—but also the "four o'clocks now and to come," so that the distance between present and future is annihilated. The static world of the white chocolate jar is now transformed by the appearance of the tiger cat, leaping on the table and pissing "into the pot, right down its delicate spout," without so much as "disturbing a hair / of the flowers' breathless attention." Here again, polar opposites—motion and stasis, delicacy and crudity—are reconciled; the absurd contrast between tiger piss and the delicate teapot spout is especially effective.

These polarities now yield to the metamorphosis of the instant. "A whisper of steam goes up from that porcelain / urethra. 'Saint-Saëns!' it seems to be whispering." So tiger-cat piss becomes steam becomes the sound of the composer's name and, by implication, his music. And this *vertige* delights the poet; he declares playfully: "Ah be with me always, spirit of noisy / contemplation in the studio, the Garden / of Zoos, the eternally fixed afternoons!" Here sound is pitted against silence, flux against eternity. Finally, the "brute beast" rests, "caressing his fangs," subdued by the "exact peril" (his mistress, Jane), which "only a moment before dropped aspirin / in this sunset of roses and now throws a chair / in the air to aggravate the truly menacing." The poem's ending is like a whirlpool: the tongue of the tiger-cat, the aspirin, sunsets, roses, chair thrown into the air—all these disparate images come together to create a dizzying, "truly menacing" vortex.

It is interesting to compare "Chez Jane" to Stevens's "Earthy Anecdote" or his "Anecdote of a Jar."[54] In the former, Stevens uses the "bucks . . . clattering / Over Oklahoma" and the firecat as symbols of two opposing sets of values: the bucks represent chaos, mindlessness, brute strength, the masculine principle, while the firecat stands for order, imaginative transformation, vitality, the feminine. At the end, the firecat, having won the day, "closed his bright eyes / And slept."

Again, in "Anecdote of a Jar," the round jar which the poet places in Tennessee transforms the "slovenly wilderness" which "sprawled around, no longer wild"; it functions as an ordering principle.

But in a Surrealist poem like "Chez Jane," the dialectic of opposites has no "meaning" beyond itself. The "white chocolate jar" and tiger cat do not stand for any particular set of values; rather, the poet is interested in capturing the moment of metamorphosis itself, the moment when tiger piss turns into the sound of "Saint-Saëns." Unlike Stevens's jar, O'Hara's is sometimes agent, sometimes acted upon. Everything is potentially something else, and the game is to record these changes.

In "Chez Jane," O'Hara was therefore doing something rather new in American poetry which was, despite the influx of French Surrealism during the war years, still essentially the poetry of Symbolism. Some readers may find O'Hara's poem excessively cold and intellectual; the poet himself is not yet present *in* the poem as mediator of polarities. But, taken on its own terms, "Chez Jane" has a kind of perfection and finish not yet found in the more prolix *Oranges,* written three years earlier. It is also quite free of the coyness—what we might call the "Dada giggle"—of such poems as "Night Thoughts in Greenwich Village" or "Tarquin," written at Ann Arbor.

A more personal vision of Surrealism is found in the long experimental poem "Easter" (1952), which O'Hara did not choose to publish during his lifetime. Critics have generally been unreceptive to this poem, calling it "messy," "strident," "bombastic," and "formless."[55] But when we read "Easter" in the context of its probable models, the long catalogue poems of Tzara and Péret, its form, so oddly reminiscent of a Walt Disney film like *Fantasia,* becomes more comprehensible. Here is a passage from Tzara's "Drugstore Conscience" (*Droguerie-conscience*) in Michael Benedikt's translation:

> the lamp of a lily will give birth to so great a prince
> that fountainheads will flourish in factories
> and the leech transform itself into a sickness-tree
> I'm searching for the roots of things my immovable lord. . . .
>
> wet parrot
> lignite cactus swell yourself up between a black cow's horns . . .
>
> (*Poetry of Surrealism,* p. 89)

"Easter" contains many passages that similarly juxtapose natural and mechanistic items in a dream landscape wholly devoid of logic:

> an army of young married couples' vanilla hemorrhages
> a spine-tingling detonation nested in leaves
> alfalfa blowing against sisters in a hanky of shade
> and the tea ship crushes an army of hair
> in rampant jaws those streets whose officer deploys a day of
> hairs strutting the rosy municipal ruts. . . .
>
> birdie, birdie
> on the uptown train. . . .
>
> (*CP*, 98)

An even closer model for "Easter" is found in Péret: "Nebulous" (*Nebuleuse*), also translated by Michael Benedikt, begins:

> When the night of butter just emerged from the churn
> inundates the moles of railway stations announced by the
>   trumpets of eyes
> and enlarges like a subway platform coming closer and closer
> only to obliterate your image
> which revolves in my brains like a heliotrope in the grip
>   of a bad case of seasickness
> then collar buttons leap into the air like lambkins formerly
>   perched upon a powder keg. . . .
>
> (*Poetry of Surrealism*, p. 237)

This passage is echoed by the following lines in "Easter":

> When the world strips down and rouges up
> like a mattress's teeth brushed by love's bristling sun
> a marvelous heart tiresomely got up in brisk bold stares
> when those trappings fart at the feet of the stars
> a self-coral serpent wrapped round an arm with no jujubes . . .
>
> (*CP*, 97)

O'Hara has now mastered Péret's style. In both cases, "when . . . " clauses and similes ("like a heliotrope," "like a mattress's teeth") are purposely designed as verbal traps, making us look for a logic that doesn't exist. Causality and analogy are consistently subverted; disparate images juxtaposed so as to create an antilandscape that no longer "refers" to a recognizable world.

Another important source for "Easter" is the poetry of Rimbaud, particularly the long, obscene, purposely outrageous "Ce qu'on dit au poète," in which Rimbaud inverts all values, treating the conventionally beautiful as if it were ugly and vice-versa. Lilies become enema syringes; the "sea of Sorrento" is filled "With the dung of a thousand swans"; "bright butterflies . . . Leave droppings all over The Pansy"; and at one point the poet asks:

> In brief: is any flower, weed
> Or lily, alive or dead
> Worth a sea gull turd?
> Worth a candle flame?[56]

O'Hara similarly debunks the "beautiful" and elevates the obscene to poetic status: "the glassy towns are fucked by yaks"; there are "floods of crocodile piss" and "shadows of prairie pricks dancing"; the poem refers to "a hardon a sequoia a toilet tissue," to "your deflowered eyeballs," "the pubic foliage of precarious hazard," "the ship sawed up by the biting asses of stars," the "orchids of the testicles," the "Boom of pregnant hillsides / awash with urine," and so on.

An interesting commentary on these images, and on the poem in general, is provided by Kenneth Koch:

> Another of his works which burst on us all like a bomb then [1952] was "Easter," a wonderful, energetic, and rather obscene poem of four or five pages, which consisted mainly of a procession of various bodily parts and other objects across a vast landscape. It was like Lorca and Whitman in some ways, but very original. I remember two things about it which were new: one was the phrase "the roses of Pennsylvania" and the other was the line in the middle of the poem which began "It is Easter!" (Easter, though it was the title, had not been mentioned before in the poem and apparently had nothing to do with it.) What I saw in these lines was 1) inspired irrelevance which turns out to be relevant (once Frank had said "It is Easter!" the whole poem was obviously about death and resurrection); 2) the use of movie techniques in poetry (in this case coming down hard on the title in the middle of the work); 3) the detachment of beautiful words from traditional contexts and putting them in curious new American ones ("roses of Pennsylvania").[57]

This is a very acute reading. The claim for Lorca and Whitman may be somewhat exaggerated because "Easter" is still predominantly a third-person impersonal poem, lacking the bardic intensity of these two poets. But Koch quite rightly notes that O'Hara's technique is to detach beautiful words from traditional contexts, that the poem centers around a procession of bodily parts across a vast landscape, and that at the word "Easter," the tone and mood of the poem undergo a definite shift, death giving way to resurrection, separation to union. Thus images like "the ship sawed up by the biting asses of stars" and "sins of sex and kisses of birds at the end of the penis" give way, after "the balm of Easter floods, my tongue's host / a rivulet of purple blood" to positive references: "the ship shoves off into the heady ocean of love," or "The day passes into the powdery light of your embrace." Indeed, the poem ends on a note of joy:

> the Sun sings in the stones of the savage
> when the world booms its seven cunts
> like a river plunged upon and perishing
> Sun, to the feast!
> to be pelted by the shit of the stars at last in flood
> like a breath.   (*CP*, 100)

Despite the references here to "cunts" and "shit," the poet is presenting a vision of new beauty. Sexual ecstasy is the keynote: the Sun activates the stones; the "seven cunts" open up the floodgates and rivers shoot out, meeting "the shit of the stars" in a marvelous "feast"—a "flood / like a breath." This is in sharp contrast to the opening of "Easter," in which "The perforated mountains of my saliva leave cities awash." The dry mouth of the poet is finally infused with new "breath"; the "perforated mountains" turn into the sunlit "seven cunts."

"Easter" does, then, display a sense of form. Its consistent use of high-low polarities, its anaphoric "When the world . . . " clauses—clauses that are regularly left suspended but that nicely tie lines together—and the elaboration of its central Easter theme (here, of course, a secular, even a blasphemous Easter) make this a very exciting, innovative poem.

Yet the cataloguing technique of "Easter"—the endless piling up of polarized images in exclamatory phrases—is not without its dangers. Six months or so after he completed "Easter," O'Hara tried to carry its form one step further and the result is his most Byzantine and difficult poem, *Second Avenue,* written in the spring of 1953 and first published in book form by Totem Press in 1960.

Kenneth Koch was enthusiastic about *Second Avenue.* He describes it as "a poem in eleven parts," whose "chief persona is a sort of Whitmanian I, though other voices appear and disappear as they do for example in the *Cantos* and *Paterson.* . . . Mr. O'Hara is the best writer about New York alive . . . he succeeds in conveying the city's atmosphere not by writing directly about it but by writing about his emotions, all of them somehow filtered through its paint supply stores and its inspiring April smog." The language, Koch adds, resembles that of Williams in being "convincing and natural." "To speak histori-cally," he concludes, "I think *Second Avenue* is evidence that the avant-garde style of French poetry from Baudelaire to Reverdy has now infiltrated American consciousness to such an extent that it is possible for an American poet to write lyrically in it with perfect ease."[58]

This would be a good description of O'Hara's later poems, but I wonder if it accurately describes *Second Avenue.* John Ashbery speaks of "the obfuscation that makes reading 'Second Avenue' such a diffi-cult pleasure" (*CP,* ix), and O'Hara himself seems to be somewhat defensive about this particular poem. In "Notes on *Second Avenue,*" apparently sent to the editor of a literary magazine in 1953,[59] he insists that the "philosophical reduction of reality to a dealable-with system . . . distorts life," that the "meaning" of the poem can't be paraphrased, but then, evidently recognizing the obstacles in the reader's path, he does an about-face and proceeds to "explain" certain passages.

"There are," O'Hara points out, "several scenes in the poem with characters," for instance, "a flier in his plane over the ocean" (*CP,* 143); "a little Western story" (*CP,* 144); "a newspaper clipping report of Bunny Lang's trip in the Caribbean" (*CP,* 144); "a true description of not being able to continue this poem and meeting Kenneth Koch for a sandwich while waiting for the poem to start again" (*CP,* 146); "a talk with a sculptor (Larry Rivers, who also sculpts) about a piece in progress" (*CP,* 147); "a description of a poetry critic and teacher: (tirade?)" (*CP,* 148); "a description of Grace Hartigan painting" (*CP,* 149); and finally, "a little description of a de Kooning WOMAN which I'd seen recently at his studio" (*CP,* 147).

O'Hara admits that the poem may "seem very jumbled, while actually everything in it either happened to me or I felt happening (saw, imagined) on Second Avenue." The "verbal elements," he concludes, "are not too interesting to discuss although they are intended consciously to keep the surface of the poem high and dry, not wet, reflective and self-conscious. Perhaps the obscurity comes in here, in the relation between surface and meaning, but I like it that way since the one is the other (you have to use words) and I hope the poem to *be* the subject, not just about it" (*CP*, 495–97).

This last statement affords some interesting clues as to the strengths and weaknesses of *Second Avenue*. It is perhaps too painterly a poem, O'Hara's most ambitious attempt to do with *words* ("you have to use words") what the Abstract Expressionists were doing with paint. Surely it is not coincidental that Grace Hartigan considers *Second Avenue* "Frank's greatest poem, one of the great epic poems of our time." She loves the poem's endless transformations: "It has everything art should have. It has imagery, emotional content, leaps of imagination, displacements of time and place going back and forth, flashings of modern life and inner feelings. Name it, name anything, and it's got it."[60]

O'Hara does indeed include "everything," and yet the question remains whether a poem, especially such a long poem, can "*be* the subject, not just about it," whether verbal structure can be so insistently nonmimetic. For the mode of *Second Avenue* seems to be one of intentional displacement and disorientation. Take the opening passage, whose bardic intensity and aureate diction recall Hart Crane:

> Quips and players, seeming to vend astringency off-hours,
> celebrate diced excesses and sardonics, mixing pleasures,
> as if proximity were staring at the margin of a plea . . .
> $\qquad\qquad\qquad\qquad$ (*CP*, 139; spaced dots, O'Hara's)

No sooner does O'Hara provide us with this lyric model than he undercuts it:

> This thoroughness whose traditions have become so reflective,
> your distinction is merely a quill at the bottom of the sea. . . .

Lines 4 and 5 prick the balloon, as if to say, "Oh, so you thought I was going to be *poetic*, did you? But why be poetic when our 'traditions have become so reflective? And what, after all, is the poet's pen but 'a quill at the bottom of the sea'?"

Grace Hartigan has pointed out to me that the use of pronouns in these lines is especially artful. The poem moves from "*This* thoroughness" (what thoroughness?) to "*your* violet dinginess" and "*your* distinction," to "*One* distinguishes," and finally to "*I* must bitterly . . ." These constantly shifting pronouns and referents create a fantasy landscape in which one cannot distinguish subject from object, interior from exterior, past from present or future, time from space. The reader is, so to speak, lost in the funhouse.

For Grace Hartigan, the inclusion of such varied references to person, place, and time within the space of ten lines is an amazing feat, making *Second Avenue* a ground-breaking poem, a kind of lyric *Who's Who*. I myself am less convinced that the principle of disorientation can keep a poem going for some six hundred lines without boring the reader a little. For one thing, O'Hara's range of styles in *Second Avenue* is perhaps too variable. There are, for example, a number of documentary-realistic passages, like the opening of Part 9, where the poet is discussing art and literature with Larry Rivers in the latter's studio:

> Now in November, by Josephine Johnson. The Heroes,
> by John Ashbery. Topper's Roumanian Broilings. The Swimmer.
> Your feet are more beautiful than your father's, I think.
> does that upset you? admire, I admire youth above age, yes,
> in the infancy of the race when we were very upset we wrote,
> "O toe!" and it took months to "get" those feet. Render. Rent.
> Now more features of our days have become popular, the nose
> broken, the head bald, the body beautiful. Marilyn Monroe.

(*CP*, 147)

As this "conversation" continues, the poet remembers all sorts of unrelated incidents:

> As I walked into the Dairy B & H Lunch, I couldn't remember
> your other eye, I puked.

Or this memory of his father's admonition:

> My father said, "Do what you want but don't get hurt,
> I'm warning you. Leave the men alone, they'll only tease you.

> When your aunt comes I want you to get down off that horse
> And speak like a gentleman, or I'll take it away from you.
> Don't grit your teeth at me."   (*CP*, 148)

And this memory is, in turn, followed by the satiric portrait of the literary critic as "chicken . . . pecking and dribbling," and "grinning Simian fart, poseur among idiots / and dilettantes and pederasts."

These passages, introducing a new note of harsh realism, immediacy, and "Personism," look ahead to the later poems, but they don't quite seem to belong in the same poem that contains the following description of a de Kooning portrait of a woman:

> You remained for me a green Buick of sighs, o Gladstone!
> and your wife Trina, how like a yellow pillow on a sill
> in the many-windowed dusk where the air is compartmented!
> her red lips of Hollywood, soft as a Titian and as tender,
> her grey face which refrains from thrusting aside the mane
> of your languorous black smells, the hand crushed by her chin,
> and that slumberland of dark cutaneous lines which reels
> under the burden of her many-darkly-hued corpulence of linen
> and satin bushes, is like a lone rose with the sky behind it.
>   (*CP*, 147)

Here the coy and rather labored metaphors look back to O'Hara's earlier style.

One is, in short, hard put to find any line of development in *Second Avenue;* individual sections appear in no particular sequence; scenes and images are juxtaposed without a view of their place in the larger scheme. Perhaps O'Hara wanted it that way, wanted to stun us by his insistent dislocations, as in "I hold all of night in my one eye. You," or "are you myself, / indifferent as a drunkard sponging off a car window?" (p. 142), but such *vertige* ultimately cannot sustain the poem, and I would agree with Helen Vendler that, at least in this case, there is too little design, although the poem's meanderings are less those of a diary than those of a catalogue of insufficiently related items.[61]

Yet in many ways *Second Avenue* represents a real stylistic advance. It is, for instance, one of the first poems to invoke O'Hara's friends by name.[62] I have already referred to John Ashbery, Grace Hartigan, and

Bunny Lang; here is a portrait of Joe LeSueur:

> I met Joe, his hair pale as the eyes of the fields of maize
> in August, at the gallery, he said you're the first Creon
> of 1953, congrats. Your costume, he said, was hand
> over fist. If you worked harder you could remake
> old Barrymore movies, you're that statuesque, he said. (*CP*, 143)

And Kenneth Koch:

> Kenneth in an abandoned storeway on Sunday cutting ever more
> insinuating lobotomies of a yet-to-be-more yielding world
> of ears, of a soprano rallying at night in a cadenza. . . .   (*CP*, 146)

And there are many lines and passages throughout *Second Avenue* that have the immediacy, excitement, and sense of *presence* that characterizes the later poetry. Here, for example, is the opening of the eleventh and final section:

> My hands are Massimo Plaster, called "White Pin in the Arm of the Sea"
> and I'm blazoned and scorch like a fleet of windbells down the /
>   Pulaski Skyway
> tabletops of Vienna carrying their bundles of cellophane to the laundry,
> ear to the tongue. . . .
> I emulate the black which is a cry but is not voluptuary like a warning,
> which has lines, cuts, drips, aspirates, trembles with horror. . . .
>   (*CP*, 150)

Here the poet's sense of personal energy, fluidity, vitality is rendered in terms of the everyday things in his life—the Massimo plaster, carefully designated by its precise name, "White Pin in the Arm of the Sea," the "fleet of windbells down the Pulaski Skyway," the black paint, cutting, dripping, aspirating.

By late 1953, then, all the necessary ingredients were present: the passages of casual, colloquial diction capturing actual speech or actual events, the unique O'Hara syntax with its ambiguous verbal positioning, its odd line breaks and consistent enjambement—all working together to give the reader a sense of tautness and breakneck speed; the versions of painting rendered "poetically"; the vignettes of artists, friends, enemies, people in the street; the images of the city; the art world, the private world. But after *Second Avenue,* O'Hara learns to relate individual elements more intricately, to forge them into a coherent whole. And he now begins to put what we might call "straight Surrealism" behind him. In the poems of 1954–61, O'Hara's great period, we can no longer identify the echoes of Péret or Tzara or Desnos as readily; Surrealism has now been assimilated into an American idiom.

Nevertheless, when one looks at the *oeuvre* of these early years— years of testing—one is astonished by the poet's range, his daring, his willingness to experiment—and his frequent successes. If we replaced *A City Winter* with a more representative collection of early poems—a collection that would include "Autobiographia Literaria," "A Pleasant Thought from Whitehead," "The Critic," "An Image of Leda," "A Postcard from John Ashbery," "Les Etiquettes Jaunes," "Poem (I've got to tell you")," "Memorial Day 1950," "Easter," *Second Avenue,* and "Chez Jane"—O'Hara's central place in the literary scene of the early fifties would already be assured.

3
POET
AMONG
PAINTERS

—Sometimes I think I'm "in love" with painting.
(*CP,* 329)

IN 1965, FRANCINE DU PLESSIX, who was editing a special issue on the relationship of poetry to painting for *Art in America,* asked twenty-two painters to choose a contemporary poem they especially liked and "make for it a work in black and white in the medium of their choice." "To avoid duplications," she explains, "I set a 'first come, first served' system of choice. Three New York painters who asked to illustrate Frank O'Hara, for instance, had to take a second choice because Jasper Johns had been the first to reply to our project, and had asked to interpret the work of this particular poet." [1]

O'Hara's popularity among the leading artists of his day is by now legendary. As René d'Harnoncourt, then director of the Museum of Modern Art, explained it in his preface to *In Memory of My Feelings* (the deluxe memorial volume published in 1967, in which thirty O'Hara poems are illustrated by artists with whom the poet had been closely associated): "Frank was so sure of his own reactions toward works of art that he did not need to be aggressive. He had absolute integrity without self-righteousness. . . . many of us, because of Frank's presence, learned to see better." [2] The thirty illustrations in the book naturally vary in quality, style, and appropriateness to the poem in question, but, taken as a whole, they provide an eloquent testimony to O'Hara's extraordinary rapport with painters as diverse as Larry Rivers, Robert Motherwell, Jasper Johns, Grace Hartigan, Barnett Newman, Robert Rauschenberg, Alfred Leslie, Norman Bluhm, Joe Brainard, Helen Frankenthaler, and Willem de Kooning. From the early fifties, when he sold Christmas cards at the front desk of the museum, to the year of his death when, as curator, he had begun work on a major retrospective of Jackson Pollock and had at last secured de Kooning's agreement to organize a large retrospective of his paintings, O'Hara worked closely with many of these artists, organizing their exhibitions, visiting their studios, interviewing them, and writing about their work. The collaborations ("poem-paintings" and related mixed-media performances) that grew out of these associations are often important art works in their own right although literary people have tended to dismiss them. I shall discuss these collaborations later in the chapter.

It is often argued that the visual arts took up too much of O'Hara's time and prevented him from devoting himself to his real vocation—poetry. John Ashbery, for example, remarks: "I sometimes wish he had not been so fruitfully involved with the Museum and with the art world. Due to the economics of art, Frank, unlike most of the artists who illustrated his book, could not support himself from his work although he was an internationally acclaimed poet. This meant that he could never devote more than a fraction of his time to his poetry."[3]

Practically speaking, this is quite true: dashing off poems during one's lunch hour or at a crowded party as O'Hara regularly did would not seem to be the best way of polishing one's craft. But like Williams, whom he resembles in so many ways, O'Hara used—and indeed needed—his other role as a source of inspiration. Joe LeSueur recalls that O'Hara's only leave of absence from the Museum (January–June 1956), when he accepted a grant from the Poets' Theatre in Cambridge, Mass., turned out to be "sheer hell for him":

. . . he hated being away from New York and all of his friends and returning to the scene of his college years, and while he was up there he wrote no play and only a few poems. When he could manage it he stormed back to New York, drank more than I ever saw him drink, and talked about how provincial Cambridge was. . . . Frank clearly wasn't cut out for grants, which he never applied for, or for places like Yaddo, where he never went; they created what I think he viewed as artificial writing situations. But the museum set-up worked for him, it seems to me. Not that he liked the routine and paper work, which in fact frequently drove him to the point of despair; it was simply that he must have needed the reality and discipline of the workaday world. . . . And finally, he believed in what he was doing. It wasn't just a job to him, it was a vital part of his life's work.[4]

The Museum thus served O'Hara as a *point de repère,* a fixed and stable center whose nine-to-five routine could offset his otherwise freewheeling and disorganized mode of living. But then, even Frank's fabled all-night drinking and talking sessions, whether at the Cedar Bar or at parties on Long Island, served an important function. As LeSueur remarks:

> . . . he seemed to be inspired and exhilarated by all of his painter friends, from Bill de Kooning, whom he idolized, to certain painters who appeared in the sixties, such as Alan d'Arcangelo. He devoted so much time to looking and thinking about their work you'd have thought he had a vested interest in their development as artists. But I don't entirely go along with the idea, suggested by several of Frank's friends, that his generosity took him away from his own work. That wasn't exactly what happened. He offered them encouragement, inspired them with his insights and his passion; they impinged upon and entered his poetry, which wouldn't have been the same and probably not as good without them.
> ("Four Apartments," p. 292)

The poetry certainly wouldn't have been the same. In the first place, painters and painting provided O'Hara with one of his central subjects. Consider the role that Grace Hartigan, whose life was closely bound up with Frank's from the early fifties to 1960,[5] plays in the poems. By her account, painter and poet would often use the same image as starting point. Thus, when Grace Hartigan painted *Oranges,* the series that corresponds to O'Hara's twelve pastorals by that name written some years earlier, she used the poet's words in the most ingenious ways, sometimes crowding a whole poem onto a corner of the canvas, sometimes spreading just a few words of text across the surface so as to create patterns of great tension and excitement. Words are played off against semiabstract, suggestive shapes of dazzling bright

color, as in *What Fire Murmurs Its Sedition,* in which the entire text of
the third prose poem, partly in script and partly in large and small
block print, is scattered across and around the reclining nude figure of
the poet (Fig. 1). Interestingly, poet and painter treat the word "oranges" in similar ways: O'Hara never mentions it except in the title;
Hartigan uses the color occasionally, but it is by no means prominent
in her series.

Here, then, we have a case of poetry inspiring painting. The con-
verse is equally true. Grace (the name has, of course, endless possibilities) appears in poem after poem, beginning with the early love sonnet,
"Poem for a Painter," in which the speaker exclaims: "Grace, / you
are the flowergirl on the candled plain / with fingers smelled of tur-
pentine" (*CP,* 80). In her painting, O'Hara evidently found a visual
confirmation of his own aesthetic; consider the remarks he makes in
the 1954 essay "Nature and the New Painting":

> She began as an abstract painter. . . . her early work shows the influence
> of Hans Hofmann's teachings and Jackson Pollock's free, iconoclastic
> spirit. She is said to have awakened one morning to the decision that she
> could paint abstractly no longer. . . . She put behind her the exclusively
> esthetic concerns of her abstractions, her new canvases erupting with
> images and influences hitherto repressed: fantastic nudes and costumed
> figures, loaded still lifes like rock quarries, overt references to the monu-
> mental bathers of Cezanne and Matisse. . . . Essentially a painter of *het-*
> *erogeneous pictures* which bring together *wildly discordant images*
> through insight into their functional relationship . . . her method is seen
> in bold relief next an abstract painter like Philip Guston, for instance,
> whose varied periods and explorations culminate in the pure, unified and
> perfect silence of his present work. (*SS,* 44–45, my italics)

What O'Hara calls Hartigan's "progress of inclusion" is beautifully
conveyed in the following passage from *Second Avenue,* which is, the
poet tells us, "a description of Grace Hartigan painting."[6]

>   Grace destroys
> the whirling faces in their dissonant gaiety where it's anxious,
> lifted nasally to the heavens which is a carrousel grinning
> and spasmodically obliterated with loaves of greasy white paint
> and this becomes like love to her, is what I desire
> and what you, to be able to throw something away without yawning

"Oh Leaves of Grass! o Sylvette! oh Basket Weavers' Conference!"
and thus make good our promise to destroy something but not us.

(CP, 149)

Notice how O'Hara's heterogeneous images and syntactic dislocations "imitate" the process of painting itself. The pronoun "it" ("It's
anxious") has no antecedent, the relative clause "which is . . . " no
specific referent, and yet we are told that "this" (the "dissonant gai-
ety"? the "heavens" seen as a "carrousel"? the "loaves of greasy white
paint"? or all these things taken together?) becomes "like love to her"
and is also "what I [the poet] desire." The shorthand phrase "and what
you" in line 6 again shifts perspective: "you" is now Grace herself; her
painting is all she desires it to be—a structure of "wildly discordant
images" that manages to avoid all bombast ("Oh Leaves of Grass! o
Sylvette! oh Basket Weavers' Conference!"), that can *deconstruct*
("throw away without yawning") pure abstraction in favor of hetero-
geneity ("Images . . . hitherto repressed," "chaotic brushwork and
whirling impasto," *SS,* 45), that is charged with personal *passion* ("and
thus make good our promise to destroy something but not us").

In such bittersweet love poems as "Christmas Card for Grace Hartigan" (*CP,* 212) and "For Grace after a Party" (p. 214), O'Hara lets one
image "bleed" into another even as Hartigan does in her painting.
"Put out your hand," he says in the latter, "Isn't there / an ashtray
suddenly, there? beside / the bed?" Or again, in the famous "In Memory of My Feelings" (1956), dedicated to Grace Hartigan, the aphoris-
tic phrase, "Grace / to be born and live as variously as possible" (*CP,*
256), is embedded in a long meditation on the nature of identity, the
ability to assume roles, to have "sordid identifications." The painter
herself has pointed out to me that this reference to "Grace" relates
back to the preceding lines:

> One of me is standing in the waves, an ocean bather.
> or I am naked with a plate of devils at my hip.

Here O'Hara alludes to two Hartigan nudes.[7] He seems to identify
even with the figures in Grace's paintings, entering, so to speak, the
world of her canvas.

Perhaps the best example of the personal role Grace Hartigan plays
in the poems is found in " 'L'Amour Avait Passé Par Là' " (1950). Here

the poet appears as a Pierrot figure, lamenting the loss of his love, and his shift in mood from a gently self-mocking sorrow to consolation is rendered chiefly in art images. The poem begins:

> Yes
> like the still center of a book on Joan Miró
> blue red green and white . . .
> and the huge mirror behind me blinking, paint-flecked
> they have painted the ceiling of my heart
> and put in a new light fixture
> and Arte Contemporáneo by Juan Eduardo Cirlot
> and the Petit Guide to the Musée National Russe. . . .

The poet is about to turn into a blank page in an art book. But then he recalls that he must "get to the Cedar to meet Grace," and he declares with a wonderful flaunting of logic:

> I must tighten my moccasins
> and forget the minute bibliographies of disappointment
> anguish and power
> for unrelaxed honesty. . . .

And the "unrelaxed honesty" of his tête-à-tête with Grace may lead to new thresholds:

a candle held to the window has two flames
and perhaps a horde of followers in the rain of youth
as under the arch you find a heart of lipstick or a condom
left by the parade
of a generalized intuition
it is the great period of Italian art when everyone imitates Picasso
afraid to mean anything
as the second flame in its happy reflecting ignores the candle and the wind

(CP, 333)

Here the "second flame" with its "happy reflecting" is associated with Grace and counters the bleak "light fixture" earlier suspended from the poet's heart.

A second strategy found in O'Hara's poems about art is to use an allusion to artists or works of art as a touchstone for grounding and authenticating a particular mood. This occurs in "Having a Coke with You" (1960), where the object of the poet's love (Vincent Warren) is comically compared and found superior to Rembrandt's *Polish Rider,* Duchamp's *Nude Descending a Staircase,* and the equestrian figures of Marino Marini, who (in what I find a penetrating insight) fails somehow to "pick the rider as carefully as the horse" (*CP,* 360). In "A Warm Day for December" (*CP,* 375), the poet makes the round of the 57th Street galleries and notes that he is "Isolated by my new haircut / and look more Brancusi than usual." Or take "Radio," written in 1955:

> Why do you play such dreary music
> on Saturday afternoon, when tired
> mortally tired I long for a little
> reminder of immortal energy?
>   All
> week long while I trudge fatiguingly
> from desk to desk in the museum
> you spill your miracles of Grieg
> and Honegger on shut-ins.
>   Am I not
> shut in too, and after a week
> of work don't I deserve Prokofieff?
>
> Well, I have my beautiful de Kooning
> to aspire to. I think it has an orange
> bed in it, more than the ear can hold.   (*CP,* 234)

The charm of this poem depends upon the comic inversion of the last three lines, the seemingly absurd logic that the poet doesn't need music because his "beautiful de Kooning" gives him "more than the ear can hold." But of course O'Hara is perfectly serious: being "shut in" at the museum, far from making him "shut out" from the pleasures of music, has taught him to "listen" to paintings. All the arts—visual, aural, verbal—are interdependent. Perfect one, the poem suggests, and you will come closer to the others. What is especially interesting is that O'Hara's reference to the de Kooning, far from being an offhand remark, is based on actual fact. Indeed, one of O'Hara's peculiar strengths is the loving attention he bestows on the documentary detail that provides authenticity. Kenneth Koch makes this point in a letter to Frank, dated 22 March 1956:

RADIO is perfect. I was in the Cedar Tavern last night and Bill de Kooning was there, so I asked him if he'd seen your poem about his picture. He said, Yeah . . . but how can I be sure it's about my picture, is it just about a picture? I quoted him "I have my beautiful de Kooning / to aspire to. I think it has an orange / bed in it . . . " He said "It's a couch. But then it really is my picture, that's wonderful." Then he told me how he had always been interested in mattresses because they were pulled together at certain points and puffed out at others, "like the earth." (*CP*, 536)

Another group of poems inspired by art can be classified as meditations on particular paintings with the intent of "translating" the tone of the painting into a verbal medium. These are poems that, unlike the passages from *Second Avenue* and "In Memory of My Feelings" discussed above, treat the painting as an independent object, without reference to the artist. "Poem (The eyelid has its storms . . .)," for example, tries to capture what O'Hara calls, in his monograph on Jackson Pollock, "the tragedy of a linear violence" (*AC*, 33). It begins:

> The eyelid has its storms. There is the opaque fish-
> scale green of it after swimming in the sea and then sud-
> denly wrenching violence, strangled lashes, and a barbed
> wire of sand falls to the shore.   (*CP*, 223)

As a commentary on one of Pollock's "all-over" paintings, this is an effective poem, but I wonder if it can be said to lead a life of its own. I have similar reservations about "Blue Territory," a poem "about" Helen Frankenthaler's painting by that name.[8] Again, if one knows this abstract painting, whose curvilinear shapes, vibrant colors, and shimmering surfaces carry minimal suggestions of an ocean landscape, O'Hara's rendition is interesting:

> Big bags of sand   until they came,
>   the flattering end
> of the world
>   the gulls were swooping and gulping and filling
> the bags
>   as helpful creatures everywhere were helping
> to end
>   the world
>   so we could be alone together at last, one by one
>   Who needs an ark? . . .   (*CP*, 270)

But if we take this impressionistic "tone poem" on its own terms, its "picture" fails to come into focus.

A more interesting "translation" of painting into poetry is "Joseph Cornell," written in 1955. Cornell was a master of the Surrealist assemblage; his intriguing shadow boxes combine exotic words and images with ordinary materials—thimbles, eggshells, mirrors, and maps—to create strange fables of the unconscious. "Taglioni's Jewel Casket" (1940), which is owned by the Museum of Modern Art, is a good example. A box made of wood, velvet, glass, and plastic, it contains four rows of glass cubes. On the inside of the cover, which is made of blue velvet, we find the following "message" on white paper: "On a moonlight night in the winter of 1835 the carriage of Maria Taglioni was halted by a Russian highwayman, and that enchanting creature commanded to dance for this audience of one upon a panther's skin spread over the snow beneath the stars." Such a box, as William Rubin points out,[9] becomes a kind of "spatial theatre," combining three-dimensional space and scenic illusion. The stilted narrative about Madame Taglioni is wittily juxtaposed to the prosaic plain box with its arithmetically precise rows of glass blocks.

In his poem, O'Hara gives us the equivalent of Cornell's boxes:

> Into a sweeping meticulously-detailed disaster the violet light pours. It's not a sky, it's a room. And in the open field a glass of absinthe is fluttering its song of India. Prairie winds circle mosques.
>
> You are always a little too young to understand. He is bored with his sense of the past the artist. Out of the prescient rock in his heart he has spread a land without flowers of near distances.

(*CP*, 237)

Here the verbal experience closely approximates the visual. In the first "box," the poet gives his version of a Cornell "message," an exotic and stylized description reminiscent of the passage about Maria Taglioni. The second box abruptly shifts to the response of the viewer, the "You" (all of us) who is "always a little too / young to understand" that the artist must, like Cornell, create new forms because "He is / bored with his sense of the / past." The third sentence aphoristically conveys the very spirit of Cornell's art: "the land without / flowers of near distances" (even the line break here emphasizes the deprivation), the bare "thing itself," as Wallace Stevens would say, made "Out of the / prescient rock in his heart."

Even here, of course, we need to know something about Cornell's work in order to understand O'Hara's poem. But in certain cases, when O'Hara worked very closely with a particular painter, the poem absorbed the spirit of the painting thoroughly enough to become independent. This is true, I think, of "On Seeing Larry Rivers' *Washington Crossing The Delaware* at the Museum of Modern Art" (*CP*, 233). Rivers explains what he was trying to do in this particular painting in an interview with O'Hara for *Horizon* (1959):

> ... what could be dopier than a painting dedicated to a national cliché— Washington Crossing the Delaware. The last painting that dealt with George and the rebels is hanging in the Met and was painted by a coarse German nineteenth-century academician who really loved Napoleon more than anyone and thought crossing a river on a late December afternoon was just another excuse for a general to assume a heroic, slightly tragic pose.... What I saw in the crossing was quite different. I saw the moment as nerve-wracking and uncomfortable. I couldn't picture anyone getting into a chilly river around Christmas time with anything resembling hand-on-chest heroics. (*AC*, 112)

"What was the reaction when George was shown?" O'Hara asks. "About the same reaction," Rivers replies, "as when the Dadaists introduced a toilet seat as a piece of sculpture in a Dada show in Zurich. Except that the public wasn't upset—the *painters* were. One painter, Gandy Brodie, who was quite forceful, called me a phony. In the bar where I can usually be found, a lot of painters laughed" (*AC*, 113).

O'Hara himself, however, understood the Rivers painting perfectly. His poem, written in 1955, treats Washington's Crossing of the Delaware with similar irreverence and amused contempt:

> Now that our hero has come back to us
> in his white pants and we know his nose

>   trembling like a flag under fire,
>   we see the calm cold river is supporting
>   our forces, the beautiful history.   (*CP*, 233)

The next four stanzas continue to stress the absurdity of what O'Hara, like Rivers, presumably regards as a nonevent, the "crossing by water in winter to a shore / other than that the bridge reaches for." Here the silly rhyme underscores the bathos of what is meant by our "beautiful history" (note that the crossing takes place in a "misty glare"); and the poem ends with a satiric address to George, culminating in the pun on "general":

>   Don't shoot until, the white of freedom glinting
>   on your gun barrel, you see the general fear.   (*CP*, 234)

Although O'Hara's poem is especially witty if read in conjunction with Rivers's painting, it can be read quite independently as a pastiche on a Major Event in American History, an ironic vision of the "Dear father of our country," with "his nose / trembling like a flag under fire."

O'Hara's poetic response to the painting of Larry Rivers, like his lyric celebrations of Grace Hartigan, suggests that he was really more at home with painting that retains at least some figuration than with pure abstraction. Pollock, Kline, and Motherwell may well have been O'Hara's Gods, but, practically speaking, it was difficult to carry over into poetry the total abstraction of, say, Frankenthaler's "Blue Territory." Words, after all, have meanings, and thematic implications thus have a way of coming in by the back door. When, in the next chapter, we consider O'Hara's major poems, we shall see that he did, of course, make use of such major concepts of Abstract Expressionism as "push and pull," "all-over painting" (composition as continuum with no beginning or end), and Harold Rosenberg's famous observation that in Action Painting the canvas becomes an arena upon which to *act* rather than a space in which to reproduce. But as a poet, O'Hara displays a certain ambivalence to the great Abstract Expressionists, an ambivalence that creates interesting tensions in his art criticism to which I now turn.

"SITTING IN A CORNER OF THE GALLERY"

—I dress in oil cloth and read music
by Guillaume Apollinaire's clay candelabra.   (*CP*, 18)

O'Hara's criticism reveals striking parallels with that of his life-long hero, Guillaume Apollinaire.[10] In his introduction to the French poet's collected art criticism, LeRoy Breunig writes: "Apollinaire possessed a gift that most professional critics will envy, and that was his flair. He knew how to recognize greatness. His innate taste and his faith in the 'nobility' of art permitted him to choose from among the mass of unknown painters swarming in the salons and the galleries of the period those who were destined to survive."[11] A good example of Apollinaire's unorthodox approach to art criticism may be found in his review of the *Salon d'Automne* of 1911, the first Salon in which the Cubists were included. "In a tiny room, Room 8," Apollinaire begins, "are the works of a few painters known by the name of cubists. Cubism is not, as is generally thought, the art of painting everything in the form of cubes." After giving some background about Picasso's earliest Cubist paintings and the relationship between Cubists and Fauves, Apollinaire comments acutely:

> However, the public, accustomed as it is to the brilliant but practically formless daubs of the impressionists, refused to recognize at first glance the greatness of the formal conceptions of our cubists. People were shocked to see contrasts between dark forms and lighted segments, because they were used to seeing only painting without shadows. In the monumental appearance of compositions that go beyond the frivolities of contemporary art, the public has refused to see what is really there: a noble and restrained art ready to undertake the vast subjects for which impressionism had left painters totally unprepared. Cubism is a necessary reaction that will give rise to great works, whether people like it or not. (p. 183)

With hindsight, we know what a prophetic statement this was in 1911, even though Apollinaire provides us neither with a theory of Cubist painting nor with practical analyses of individual works. In O'Hara's art criticism, we find the very same qualities: an absence of theoretical discourse and, except in rare cases, close technical analysis, counterbalanced by an astonishing ability to recognize greatness, to distinguish between the first-rate and the second-best. Like Apollinaire, O'Hara had the innate gift of entering a gallery in which a large group show was installed and immediately spotting *the* important painting or paintings.

This peculiar genius is nowhere more evident than in the three "Art Chronicles" O'Hara wrote while art editor for *Kulchur* in 1962 and 1963. In the third "Chronicle," O'Hara reviews the Museum of Modern Art retrospective of Mark Tobey and concludes: "Tobey has done fine things in his own way . . . but they will never be major, any more than Redon will ever challenge Renoir. . . . Not while Willem de Kooning and Barnett Newman are about."[12] This is a judgment time has certainly borne out. Today we hear little about Tobey while de Kooning, still at the height of his powers, is increasingly recognized as perhaps the greatest painter of the period. In the same "Chronicle," O'Hara distinguishes between Pop artists like Andy Warhol or Robert Indiana, who "tend to make their art *out of* vulgar (in the sense of everyday) objects, images, and emblems," and Claes Oldenburg, who "makes the very objects and symbols themselves, with the help of papier-mâché, cloth, wood, glue, paint and whatever other mysterious materials are inside and on them, *into* art" (*SS,* 141). This distinction between what we might call commercial Pop Art and the brilliant illusionism of Oldenburg's "seven-foot pistachio icecream cone" or his "monstrous wedge of chocolate and vanilla layer cake" seems increasingly valuable as we look back at Pop Art from the vantage point of the later seventies.

The "Art Chronicles" are chiefly concerned with the great abstract painters, but because O'Hara always cared more for individuals than for movements, he was one of the first critics to recognize the genius of Alex Katz, whose realistic "flat sculptures" were painted, so to speak, against the grain. Katz's "large free-standing figures," O'Hara notes, "are modern in ethos, emphasizing almost inadvertently the spatial absence which surrounds them. . . . They have an air of watchfulness, without ever being silhouettes" (*SS,* 136). This account of Katz's work in the Summer 1962 "Art Chronicle" is amplified in one of O'Hara's best critical essays, "Alex Katz," written for *Art and Literature* shortly before his death. Here he defines Katz's pictorial world as "a 'void' of smoothly painted color . . . where the fairly realistic figure existed (but did not rest) in a space which had no floor, no walls, no source of light, no viewpoint. . . . Katz's people simply existed somewhere. They stayed in the picture as solutions of a formal problem, neither existential nor lost. . . . They were completely mysterious pictorially, because there seemed to be no apparent intent of effect. They knew they were there" (*AC*, 145–46). Certainly, Katz's "flat" sculptural portrait of O'Hara himself (see *AC*, 146) testifies to that sense of peculiar *presence*, of being *there* that the poet speaks of.

Perhaps O'Hara is at his most trenchant in the "Art Chronicles" when he discusses the reception of *Art* in these exciting years. In 1962, for example, the Guggenheim mounted a show called *Abstract Expressionists and Imagists,* which was evidently a mixed bag, reflecting, in O'Hara's view, "a living situation," whose "free-wheeling accuracy" "keeps you fresh for looking" (*SS,* 128). But the art audience, longing for certainties, was evidently indignant. "Unfortunately," says O'Hara, "many people wanted to see a justification, packaged in a new Sherry's container, with a card saying, 'Because of this show you are entitled to keep on admiring abstract expressionism.' Hence the criticism the Guggenheim has gotten about the quality of the show, some of it near hysteria: "A WEAK HOFMANN! HOW COULD THEY!" None of the reviewers seems to have thought, "How could he!" (*SS,* 128).

Such witty deflation is typical of O'Hara. And his conclusion acts as the perfect squelch: "A lot of people would like to see art dead and sure, but you don't see them up at the Cloisters reading Latin." Here, and in his hilarious, if admittedly bitchy attack on two leading art reviewers of his day, John Canaday and Emily Genauer,[13] O'Hara recalls the Apollinaire of "Watch Out for the Paint!," the droll essay in which the poet tells the anecdote about the bourgeois lady who came to Mallarmé when the latter was a lycée teacher and begged him to excuse her son from after-school detention because she wanted to take him to the Manet exhibit. "All Paris," said the lady, "is going to it to laugh at his paintings. I will never forgive myself if my child is deprived of this unique amusement, which, furthermore, will help to educate his taste." Whereupon Mallarmé doubled the punishment. "How prudently," Apollinaire concludes, "one must refrain from pronouncing hasty judgments. It is so easy to be wrong; and there is not always a Mallarmé around to double the punishment called for by sacrilegious laughter." [14]

Like Apollinaire, O'Hara was always fighting "sacrilegious laughter," exposing narrow-minded reviewers and obtuse critics. And it is especially useful to read his art criticism against the background of Apollinaire's because it helps us to understand what O'Hara was *not,* what demands we cannot make on his reviews, essays, and museum catalogues. When *Art Chronicles* was published in 1974, a number of reviewers complained that O'Hara was too "subjective" and "impressionistic" a critic, and that he merely adopted the going view of such theorists as Harold Rosenberg on Abstract Expressionism, providing no original insights into the movement. [15]

There is some truth to these strictures. O'Hara is at his weakest when he tries to generalize about such abstractions as Art, Beauty, Reality, or Nature. The early essay, "Nature and the New Painting" (1954) is particularly interesting in this connection because it illustrates both the poet's strengths and his weaknesses as a critic. Much of this essay contains specific description of the work of Grace Hartigan (quoted earlier in this chapter), Robert di Niro, and Larry Rivers, and what O'Hara says of their art is consistently useful. Yet it is never clear what he means by "nature." He says, for example, "In past times there was nature and there was human nature; because of the ferocity of modern life, man and nature have become one. . . . In the abstractions of Willem de Kooning and in his female figures, we perceive structures of classical severity: the implacable identifications of man with nature. This is not symbolized. It is painted" (*SS,* 42). The implication is that in Abstract Expressionist art, "nature" is absorbed into painting so fully that the canvas presents a perfect union of the two. Yet a page or so later, O'Hara explains that Grace Hartigan rejected abstraction in order to "return to nature"—that is, to figurative images—a change in style that "introduced a passion which was only implied in the early work" (p. 45). But if this is the case, what happens to the perfect fusion of art and nature in the abstractions of de Kooning?

Similarly questionable generalizations are found in the pioneering and frequently brilliant monograph on Jackson Pollock. Contrasting Cubism and Surrealism ("Surrealism destroyed where Cubism only undermined. . . ."; "Cubism was an innovation, Surrealism an evolution"), O'Hara declares: "Surrealism enjoined the duty, along with the liberation, of saying what you mean and meaning what you say, above and beyond any fondness for saying or meaning" (*AC*, 18). This sounds profound but what is O'Hara actually saying? He seems to imply that Surrealism is somehow more literal than other schools of art, and yet the Surrealists themselves thought of their work as precisely the opposite: the embodiment of dreams, hallucination, unconscious thought—the art of free association and hidden erotic meanings.

O'Hara's importance as an art critic does not, then, emerge from his formal essays or set pieces: the introductions he wrote for the catalogues of the exhibitions he organized at the Museum, *New Spanish Painting and Sculpture* (1960); *Franz Kline* (1960); *Motherwell* (1962); *Nakian* (1964); or *David Smith* (1966). These essays are full of brilliant aperçus about individual works, but too often we find sentences like the following: "If the motto of American art in recent years can be said to be 'Make it new,' for the Spanish it is 'Make it over.'"[16] Or: "Underlying, and indeed burgeoning within, every great work of the Abstract Expressionists . . . exists the traumatic consciousness of emergency and crisis experienced as personal event" (*AC*, 67). Or: "Stylization was the order of the day, whether the archaistic stylization of a Manship, a kind of mock-heroic idealization of the proletariat, or a belated Art Nouveau stylization of human and animal forms . . ." (*AC*, 82).

But if we look at O'Hara's occasional criticism—his reviews in *Art News* and *Kulchur,* his interviews and memoirs—a very different critical intelligence emerges. The early reviews (1953–54) are curiously literary; the young Harvard graduate is not yet wearing his learning lightly. Thus he says of the figures in Kenneth Callahan's painting: "Their anatomy is that of El Greco, but their habitat comes from Romantic poetry, not painting, and they appear through the pearly mists of Shelley—which on canvas is sometimes just grey."[17] Kees Van Dongen's women have bosoms that "rise and fall as in a revelatory chapter of Proust."[18] Helen Frankenthaler's "heavily-painted pictures" have "the compact sordidness of one of those 'unspeakable' chapters in Henry James."[19] Yet at the same time, reviewing Adolph Gottlieb's April 1954 show at the Kootz Gallery, O'Hara comments acutely on "the multiplicity of grids and events in space both between and behind these grids" and notes that "often the thick surface strokes are not so much signs of specific meaning as signals of that speed which results from force as well as felicity."[20]

In 1955, O'Hara joined the Museum of Modern Art as a special assistant in the International Program, and for the next few years, the organization of traveling exhibitions kept him so busy that he produced relatively little art criticism. But these were the years of intense exposure to the world of contemporary painting and sculpture, and by the late fifties, when O'Hara was at the height of his poetic powers, he was also writing much more casually and spontaneously, and yet more seriously, about art. Between 1958 and 1960 alone, O'Hara published the following: the book on Jackson Pollock for the Braziller "Great American Artist" series, the important interviews with Franz Kline and Larry Rivers, a witty and penetrating essay on the latter's *Next to Last Confederate Soldier,* and a number of interesting short pieces on Pollock, Cavallon, Norman Bluhm, or, again, on such topics as American versus non-American Art.

When *Jackson Pollock* appeared in 1959, Hilton Kramer called it an example of "the 'poetical' school of criticism," and a number of art critics objected to the poet's purple prose and intensely personal response to the painter.[21] Yet the book turned out to be immensely popular, and despite the lapses cited earlier, it was and continues to be an important assessment of Pollock's work. The general principles put forward about Action Painting may be no more than a restatement of Harold Rosenberg's (e.g., the conception of "wall" as opposed to "easel"; the painting as field of force which the poet enters; the rejection of metaphor and symbol in favor of the thing itself—paint as paint, wire mesh as wire mesh). Nevertheless, O'Hara's Paterian comments on particular paintings are often very valuable in that they force the reader to take another look at the canvas, to *see* it as if for the first time.

Pollock's *White Light,* for example, "has a blazing, acrid, and dangerous glamor of a legendary kind, not unlike those volcanoes which are said to lure the native to the lip of the crater, and by the beauty of their writhings and the strength of their fumes cause him to fall in" (*AC,* 29). *Number 1, 1948,* on the other hand, derives its strength from a very different strategy: it replaces the brooding languor of *White Light* with "an ecstatic, irritable, demanding force, an incredible speed and nervous legibility in its draftsmanship; and the seemingly blood-stained hands of the painter, proceeding across the top just beyond the main area of drawing, are like a postscript to a terrible experience" (*AC*, 31).

It is interesting to turn from the formal, distant, somewhat man-nered style of the Pollock monograph—a style dictated, at least in part, by the conventions governing the writing of an "art book"—to the very different essays on Larry Rivers. O'Hara seems to have been happiest as a critic when he could write about a painter who was also a close personal friend, and his pieces on Rivers constitute a kind of prose counterpart to his "I do this, I do that" poems like "A Step Away From Them" or "Joe's Jacket."

The interview "Larry Rivers: Why I Paint as I Do" is, like all of O'Hara's interviews, notable for the poet's self-effacement.[22] His questions are brief and pointed; he obviously knows the work thor-oughly but is not anxious to parade his knowledge. On the other hand, the Rivers presented in this interview consistently sounds like O'Hara himself, so that, in a second, more devious way, the poet is present after all. Interestingly, the interview thus embodies the doctrine of "Personism"; the words are squarely between two people; poet and painter become one.

The dialogue is prefaced by a graphic picture of Rivers's studio:

> In the daytime, the light pours in from three skylights, but at night it is a vast, dim place, lit by seven naked light bulbs hanging high up near the ceiling. At night the studio looks very much like the set for Samuel Beck-ett's *Endgame;* it's hard to believe you can find out anything about the outside world without using a ladder; the windows are way up.
>
> (*AC*, 106)

After describing the members of the Rivers household, including "a friendly, frantic shepherd dog named Amy," and mentioning the paintings currently on the studio walls, O'Hara adds:

> Another wall has the huge *Journey* of 1956, a painting which looks small in the space of the studio; lurking under a nearby potted plant is a plaster

commercial figure of Psyche or Aphrodite which Rivers rescued from a night club; she is holding an orange light bulb in her uplifted hand and Rivers uses her as a night light. (p. 107)

This note of comic eclecticism sets the scene for the dialogue that follows.

Rivers's aesthetic turns out to be remarkably close to O'Hara's despite their very different backgrounds. Rivers came from a poor Jewish family and grew up "in the streets of . . . the Bronx" (p. 109). He started out as a jazz musician, worked for a time as delivery boy for an art-supply house, and only then turned to the study of painting, working with Hans Hofmann and attending N.Y.U. at night, while his former mother-in-law, the Mrs. Bertha Burger who acted as one of his main models, kept house for him and his two sons and helped to support him.[23] His world was thus quite unlike the provincial Catholic milieu of Baltimore and Grafton, Mass., in which Frank was raised, or the Harvard of John Ashbery and Kenneth Koch, or even the sophisticated world of the Museum of Modern Art.

Nevertheless, Rivers's view of art is immediately familiar to anyone who has read O'Hara. He rejects the primacy of subject matter in painting, insisting that the *how* supercedes the *what*. Like O'Hara, he stresses the importance of "the immediate situation" (p. 108), of energy, of the role of "accident" in art (p. 117), and of the need to evade "the discomforts of *boredom*." "One of my theories," he says, sounding just like O'Hara, "about the art of the last hundred years is that more alterations to the image of painting have been brought about by the boredom and dissatisfaction of the artist and his perversity than anything else" (p. 113). Like O'Hara, he has a predilection for campy humor, as in the George Washington painting which fuses, in Sam Hunter's words, "history, nostalgic sentiment, the world of commonplace objects and emblems," assimilating "popular folklore to the high style of advanced art."[24]

A painting, says Rivers, is best defined as "a smorgasbord of the recognizable":

I may see something—a ribbon, say, and I'll use it to enliven a three-inch area of the canvas. Eventually it may turn into a milk container, a snake, or a rectangle. . . . I may even have private associations with that piece of ribbon, but I don't want to *interpret* that association. . . . I feel free to use the appearance of a thing—that piece of ribbon—without assigning any specific meaning to it as an object. (*AC,* 118)

And when Frank asks him to apply these principles to the recently painted *Second Avenue with THE,* Rivers explains:

What you see is the view from a studio on Second Avenue—a top-floor studio—looking across at the buildings opposite. The canvas shows a selected few of the multitude of objects I could see from where I stood. The rectangles are reflections from glass windows across the street. The dark vertical lines are the studio floor boards. I looked down, saw them, and painted them. The horizontal lines are the window sills. The semi-circles on the right are the rims of a drum. The line of little white squares are the white keys of a piano I had there in the studio. And the rocket-woman figure, she was in the studio too, a statue which was in my field of vision. That little shape up there by the letters THE—just to the left—that's a woman leaning out of a window opposite. I should have had the letters ALPINE up there too. That was the title—a chic one, don't you think—some builder had given one of those buildings. (*AC,* 118)

"What about those letters THE?" Frank asks. "Those letters were pasted on the studio window by some movie director who photographed them for THE END of his picture. The END part of it had disappeared" (*AC,* 118).

I cite this passage at length because it makes clear the close affinities between Rivers's painting and O'Hara's poem *Second Avenue,* written a few years earlier in Rivers's studio.[25] Just as Rivers takes recognizable objects (the studio floor boards and window sill, the woman, and the lettering on the window) and displaces them, creating a new tension between illusionistic detail and abstract configurations, so O'Hara takes his images from Second Avenue street scenes, cutting, distorting, and reassembling them so that his finished composition retains no more than "traces" of that which is being represented:

Candidly. The past, the sensations of the past. Now!
in cuneiform, of umbrella satrap square-carts with hotdogs
and onions of red syrup blended, of sand bejewelling the prepuce
in tank suits, of Majestic Camera Stores and Schuster's,
of Kenneth in an abandoned storeway on Sunday cutting even more

insinuating lobotomies of a yet-to-be-more-yielding world
of ears, of a soprano rallying at night in a cadenza, Bill, of
"Fornications, la! garumph! tereu! lala la! vertigo! Weevy! Hah!",
of a limp hand larger than the knee which seems to say "Addio"
and is capable of resigning from the disaster it summoned ashore.
Acres of glass don't make the sign clearer of the landscape
less blue than prehistorically, yet less distant, eager, dead!

(CP, 146–47)

The isolation of the adverb "Candidly," creating ambiguity of reference, the shift from "The past" to "now!", the images of storefronts and pushcarts "dissolving" into thoughts of Kenneth Koch, memories of a concert, and the ridiculous allusions to *The Waste Land* in line 8, the final contradictory image of a blue landscape "less distant, eager, dead!"—all these features find their way into the poem as if by random penetration of the artist's consciousness, just as Rivers describes the entry of similar elements into his painting.

O'Hara is thus the ideal interpreter of Rivers's work for, like Grace Hartigan, Rivers is a painter who rejects pure abstraction on the one hand and "straight" representational painting—what Rivers calls "cornball realism" (*AC,* 119)—on the other. Both artists explore the expressive potential of commonplace objects; the white piano keys and window sills of Rivers's *Second Avenue with THE* correspond to images like the "old Roman coin," the "bolt-head," or "the construction workers with silver hats on" in O'Hara's "Personal Poem" (*CP,* 235).

In the 1965 memoir "Larry Rivers," O'Hara recapitulates the qualities that link poet and painter. Rivers's arrival on the New York painting scene is comically compared to the appearance of "a demented telephone. Nobody knew whether they wanted it in the library, the kitchen or the toilet, but it was electric" (*CP,* 512). Like O'Hara himself, Rivers was "restless, impulsive and compulsive"; he could not abide an aesthetic that separated the visual arts from his other two loves, jazz and poetry. "His work," says O'Hara, "is very much a diary of his experience.... Where much of the art of our time has been involved with direct conceptual or ethical considerations, Rivers has chosen to mirror his preoccupations and enthusiasms in an unprogrammatic way" (p. 514). What O'Hara means here, I think, is that at a certain moment in our history, when Abstract Expressionism was in danger of moving toward standardization and mere repetition, Rivers, following de Kooning, who had always retained certain figurative elements (outlines of his own fingers, written letters, the silhouette of a woman's face, and other illusionistic gestures), deflected the course of New York painting. His art is thus particularly close to the lyric mode of O'Hara. And accordingly, the collaboration of two such cognate sensibilities was bound to produce interesting results.

POEM-PAINTINGS

Collaboration between poets and painters is largely a twentieth-century phenomenon. Genuine collaboration—as opposed to *illustration* which is something quite different, being, by definition, *ex post facto*—is rare at any time because it is so hard to strike a balance between two such seemingly inimical arts. A so-called *poem-painting,* whether done by a single artist or as a collaboration, tends to be either a painting with a few words of text used as part of the visual scheme, or, conversely, an illustrated poem in which visual images are subordinated to verbal meaning. Under the right circumstances, however, the poem-painting, done as a collaboration, has enormous potential. Like opera, ballet, the masque, or the animated film, it can provide the special pleasure created by the interaction of seemingly unrelated media.

As in the case of his art criticism, O'Hara's concept of the poem-painting can be traced back to Apollinaire, who wrote poems "after" paintings (pasting "Les Fenêtres" on the back of Delaunay's work of the same name so as to create a kind of double image), and whose *Calligrammes* contain fascinating experiments with verbal-visual composition. In "Il Plêut," for example, the words float down the page from left to right like rain drops; in "La Cravate et La Montre," the arrangement of words imitates the two objects named in the title; and in "Visée" ("Aim"), the variations in position of the lines correspond to the shifting attitudes of the poet.[26]

But these are not, strictly speaking, poem-paintings. A closer model for O'Hara's collaborations is found in Dada and Surrealist art, although the *peinture-poésie* of Picabia, Schwitters, Magritte, or Ernst is almost never the result of collaboration. A painting like Picabia's famous *M'Amenez-Y* (1919–20) is a good example of Dada experimentation with verbal-visual patterning.[27] Its banal mechanical shapes (two half-circles, a cylinder, a screw) are juxtaposed to the title which is based on one of Marcel Duchamp's verbal "readymades": "M'amenez-y" ("bring me there") is a substitution for the correct "Amenez-y-moi"; it is also a play on the word "amnésie." Across the top of the canvas, Picabia has comically announced that this is a portrait painted in castor oil ("l'huile de ricin"), and within the circles, we find the words "peinture crocodile" and "ratelier [dentures] d'artiste"—an amusing word play. The artist's signature is prominently placed in the bottom right-hand corner, the pointless reference to "Pont-L'Evêque" (a small town in Normandy where cheese is made) as the place where *M'Amenez-Y* was painted, in the bottom left. Picabia's words do not, of course, make a poem, but his composition does depend upon a particular conjunction of verbal and visual images.

Kurt Schwitters's collages of the same period are poem-paintings of a rather different type. In his essay *Merz* (1920), Schwitters declares: "It was my desire not to be a specialist in one branch of art but an artist. My aim is the Merz [a play on *merde*] composite art work. . . . First I combined individual categories of art. I pasted words and sentences into poems in such a way as to produce a rhythmic design. Reversing the process, I pasted up pictures and drawings so that sentences could be read in them."[28] These two processes may be illustrated by *Collage* (1920) and *Sonata* (1923), both of which are reproduced in Motherwell's *The Dada Painters and Poets,* a book O'Hara knew and loved.[29] *Sonata* is primarily verbal; short nonsense words are arranged in columns in various phonetic configurations, and the small rectangular collage in the bottom right-hand corner plays a subordinate role. This is an early example of Concrete Poetry. *Collage,* on the other hand, cuts up newspapers and posters and then reassembles them, so that bits of headlines, words, phrases, and parts of phrases are scattered across the surface, right side up and upside down. These two collages are interesting experiments, but the relationship between word and visual image seems largely arbitrary.

René Magritte's *peinture poésie* looks ahead to Pop Art. A painting like *The Wind and the Song* (1928-29) contains what seems to be a realistic replica of a large pipe against a blank background. Across the bottom of the canvas is the legend "Ceci n'est pas une pipe."[30] But, as William Rubin argues, the painting is not as simplistic as it first appears, for "merely reproducing any three-dimensional object on a delimited flat surface—that is, picturing it—automatically engenders a set of aesthetic rapports that have no necessary relation to the meaning of the object qua object" (p. 94). The image of the pipe is not, in other words, equivalent to a real pipe. The didactic legend "Ceci n'est pas une pipe" further complicates the scheme, for the word "pipe" releases different signals than either the painted image of the pipe or a real pipe. A resonance, albeit a limited one, is thus set up between verbal and visual images.

The most interesting Surrealist poem-paintings are, however, those of Max Ernst, in whose work word and image are not merely juxtaposed as in the collages of Magritte or Picabia, but fused so as to form what Lucy Lippard has called "a genuinely 'intermediary' statement."[31] In an essay called "Beyond Painting," written in the mid-thirties, Ernst defines *collage* as an "alchemical composition of two or more heterogenous elements resulting from their unexpected reconciliation ... toward systematic confusion and 'disorder of the senses' (Rimbaud), or to chance, or to a will to chance."[32] Ernst's own favorite "collage word" (e.g., the key word governing the form the collage will take) is *phallustrade,* which he defined as "an alchemical product composed of the following elements: an *autostrada,* a balustrade, and certain amounts of phallus." Thus, the Dada collage, *The Hat Makes the Man* (Fig. 2), is, as Lippard says, "a *phallustrade* in every sense, the visual pun [being] extended by the verbal puns in the accompanying inscription: '*Bedecktsamiger stapelmensch nacktsamiger wasserformer* ('*edelformer*') *kleidsame nervatur auch UMPRESS NERVEN!* (*C'est le chapeau qui fait l'homme, le style c'est le tailleur*).'"[33]

It is impossible to translate this into literal English because every word is a pun or double-entendre: "*Bedecktsamiger*" means "covered" plus "seeded" ("covered with seed"?); "*edelformer*" combines the meaning of "edel" (lofty, noble, precious, aristocratic) with erotic connotations because "edle Teile" are private parts, and so "edelformer" may connote "one who has elegant private parts" or merely a person who observes the forms or who creates elegance. The collage itself is a page from a hat catalogue, transformed by means of watercolor, pencil, scissors, and glue into a series of sculpted vignettes with mechanistic, organic, cartoonlike, even narrative characteristics. In this witty and intricate *phallustrade,* "Words and forms begin to bounce on and off each other in a trans-disciplinary, cross-referential action that continues to provide surprises long after the initial decoding." (Lippard, p. 13).

Ernst carried this form of "literary art" (note that it is not at all an illustration in the conventional sense) even further in *La Femme 100 têtes,* a "collage novel" in which the artist took a series of perfectly ordinary nineteenth-century wood engravings found in magazines and cut them up so as to discover a new figurative "reality" brought about by the chance encounter of previously unrelated images. Each resulting picture was given a poetic caption. Neither the picture nor the caption carries the "plot" alone; rather, in Lippard's words, they offer "a double viewpoint that forms a stereophonic unity. The reader must literally read between the lines provided by the verbal-visual interaction and project himself into that intermediary space." The collage-novel has, moreover, important analogues to film: "The pictorial dislocation of action and sequence juxtaposed against the ambiguous captions, apparently out of sync, suggest a silent movie with subtitles in a foreign language. The mixing is done, impressionistically, in the mind" (Lippard, p. 13).

Ernst's use of the "collage-novel" and the *phallustrade* thus looks ahead to the poem-paintings of our own time. But it is important to remember that he was primarily a visual artist, that even his so-called collaborations with Paul Eluard on *Répétitions* (1921) and *Les Malheurs des Immortels* (1922) are not true collaborations, for in these books, Ernst takes an Eluard poem already written and then proceeds to illustrate it. The next step was for poet and painter to work simultaneously on the same spatial area, playing off words against visual images so as to create new forms. This is what happens in *Stones,* the series of lithographs made by O'Hara and Rivers between 1957 and 1960.

In a very amusing essay called "Life Among the Stones" (1963),[34] Rivers describes the genesis of these lithographs. "It started," he recalls, "with this Siberian lady Tanya who came to my house in the summer of 1957. Her life at the time called for an activity. She found it and dedicated herself with gentle fury to the production of lithographs. . . . She wanted me to work on lithograph stones with a poet. She had the devotion, the press, and she would print" (p. 91).

"The Siberian lady Tanya," as Rivers jokingly calls her here, was Tatyana Grossman, whose print workshop in West Islip, Long Island, is now world famous. "Both technically and aesthetically," writes Calvin Tompkins in his study of contemporary printmaking, "the prints published by Tatyana Grossman's Universal Limited Art Editions [they include more than a hundred lithographs by Jasper Johns, and Robert Rauschenberg's intriguing *Shades,* a series of lithographs on Plexiglas] are·generally acknowledged to be equal or superior to anything being done in Europe or anywhere else." [35]

Tatyana Grossman's choice of Frank O'Hara as Rivers's collaborator was the result of a series of fortunate coincidences. She recalls:

> I went to see . . . Barney Rosset of the Grove Press to ask if he could perhaps suggest a poet for such a book [i.e., of lithograph stones], and he suggested Frank O'Hara. Well, I read some of O'Hara's poems, but I didn't really understand them very well, they were so abstract. But then a few days later . . . I drove out to Larry Rivers' studio in Southampton. . . . I talked to Larry about this idea of a book that would be a real fusion of poetry and art, a real collaboration, not just drawings to illustrate poems, and Larry listened, and then he called out, "Hey, Frank!" And down the stairs came a young man in blue jeans. It was Frank O'Hara. [36]

Rivers was delighted that "This Siberian lady didn't just find some painter and some poet who would work together. She asked two men who really knew each other's work and life backwards." [37] Despite their "super-serious, monstrously developed egos," Rivers and O'Hara saw what had to be done: "Frank O'Hara wasn't going to write a poem that I would set a groovy little image to. Nor were we going to assume the world was waiting for his poetry and my drawing which is what the past 'collaborations' now seem to have been" (p. 93).

Working on the lithograph stone proved to be a new challenge for O'Hara and Rivers, who saw themselves as carrying on the tradition of "Picasso, Matisse, Miro, Apollinaire, Eluard, and Aragon" (p. 92).

Rivers describes the difficulties posed by the medium as follows:

> The lithograph stone surface is very smooth. The marks going on it can be made with a rather difficult to handle almost rubbery crayon or with a dark liquid called Touche. . . . Whatever you do comes out the opposite to the way you put it down. In order for the writing to be read it must be done backwards. It is almost impossible to erase, one of my more important crutches. Technically it was really a cumbersome task. One needed the patience of another age, but our ignorance and enthusiasm allowed us to jump into it without thinking about the details and difficulties.
>
> (p. 93)

The first of the twelve *Stones* was called *US* (Fig. 3). Rivers's detailed account of its genesis will help us to understand the actual process of collaboration:

> Each time we got together we decided to choose some very definite subject and since there was nothing we had more access to than ourselves the first stone was going to be called "us." Oh yes, the title always came first. It was the only way we could get started. U and S were written on the top center of the stone backwards. I don't know if he wrote it. I remember decorating the letters to resemble some kind of flag and made it seem like the letters for our country. Then I put something down to do with his broken nose and bumpy forehead and stopped. From a round hand-mirror I eked out a few scratches to represent my face. The combination of the decorated U and S, his face and mine [see top left], made Frank write ". . . they call us the farters of our country. . . ." I did something, whatever I could, which related in some way to the title of the stone and he either commented on what I had done or took it somewhere else. . . . Sometimes I would designate an area that I was sure I was going to leave empty. He might write there or if I did put something down I would direct him to write whatever he wished but ask that it start at a specific place and end up a square or rectangular thin or fat shape of words over or around my images. (pp. 93–94)

Here Rivers stresses the *improvisational* character of the collaboration, its status as an event or happening rather than as a predetermined, planned "work of art." This is not to say, however, that anything goes; the account makes quite clear that, at each step of the way, the two artists depended upon one another's response. It is therefore misleading to call *Stones,* as does one reviewer, "no more than props to support an avant-garde party game of two addressed to those who can recognize names, allusions, and events and the spirit of exclusiveness they exalt."[38] For although *US* is not one of the best lithographs in the series (the surface is perhaps too cluttered, and O'Hara has not yet mastered the technique of lettering, writing backwards being extremely cumbersome unless one uses a mirror), it has a definite structure.

The predominant visual motif is Frank's face in profile with its broken nose. It appears in the upper left-hand corner, next to the sketch of Rivers himself seen frontally; then again in reverse (an enlarged mirror image) in the upper right, this time shaded in and superimposed on other shapes; again in the lower left, where the head is turned upside down and attached to a contorted torso, the whole pose reminiscent of Picasso's *Guernica* figures; and finally, in the lower right-hand corner, we find, embedded in a sort of valentine, the poet's face, cheek-to-cheek with Rivers's face, again seen frontally. These faces are placed against a background of doodles, some resembling hands, legs, phalluses, and animal shapes; others reminiscent of Chinese ideograms.

O'Hara's verbal images are intimately related to this landscape of stance and gesture. The pun on the word US is not just a local joke ("They call US the Farters of our Country") but the theme of the whole poem-painting, which portrays heroism and anti-heroism in various guises. Thus at the very center, O'Hara places a letter from James Dean (the Hollywood hero as victim) to Jane (the painter Jane Freilicher); the foolishly empty letter: "It's swell out here. How are you?" is viewed upside down and almost bumps into the sign: "A HERO of the '50's is arriving in Hollywood." The artists themselves are seen as comically out of step with the times:

> poetry was declining
> > Painting advancing
> > we were complaining
> it was '50

The immediate postwar years, as every literary historian has noted, were lean ones for American poetry. The tone of the period is conveyed by O'Hara's references to the petty bickering ("Poetry belongs to Me, LARRY, and *Painting* to you") and innuendo: "THAT'S what G said to P, and . . ." (evidently Gertrude Stein to Picasso),[39] a line leading straight into the bubble, "Look where it got them." The young artists are, moreover, a bit precious: "Parties were 'given' / we 'went'" is ironically placed right under what I have called the *Guernica* figure. At bottom center, O'Hara places the lines:

> A very soft rain
> we were sitting on the stairs

The absolute simplicity of these words in which poet and painter become two ordinary human beings, sharing a moment of love, forms an effective contrast to the bravado of the opening lines. So, too, the "valentine scene" in the lower right, next to the lines just cited, is juxtaposed to the two rather formal, sharply etched portraits of O'Hara and Rivers in the upper left.

The composition of *US* is thus both complex and ingenious, words and pictures fusing so as to create interesting spatial tensions. An even more effective poem-painting is number 3, entitled *Rimbaud & Verlaine* (Fig. 4). The lettering is now much surer than in *US*, O'Hara having mastered the art of "mirror-writing." Rivers's account of the composition of this particular lithograph is especially valuable:

There was a photo of Rimbaud and his depressed friend Verlaine in the studio. I began to make a drawing looking at it. We then remembered a ballet night at the City Center. During an intermission we were making our way down the wide staircase from the cheap seats to the mezzanine when our mutual friend and my dealer John Myers thinking he was being funny screamed out for general use "there they are all covered with blood and semen." This is a reference to something said about Rimbaud and Verlaine that Verlaine's wife hounded him with for his whole life. After recalling this Frank decided to use it and in a delicate two-line series he began writing. . . . His first two lines had to do with the poetry of Rimbaud and Verlaine. He brought the lines up to my drawing and stopped. . . . He then went on about the staircase and something about the ballet. I waited till he was through and in the spaces left (I directed the space between the lines and the general distribution) I tried a staircase . . . no good. Here I found out how hard it was to get rid of anything—in order to erase you must scrape with a razor. Finally I began making bullets that were also penises with legs. Simple Simon's response to what Frank had written about the corps de ballet. If there is "art" somewhere in this lithograph its presence remains a mystery. (p. 94)

There is, of course, plenty of "art" here. The sketch of Rimbaud and Verlaine, a contrast of lights and darks, is brilliantly rendered: a light-haired, handsome Rimbaud with strange visionary eyes is contrasted to the small, somewhat petty, dark Oriental figure of Verlaine. Rimbaud clearly dominates the scene as he did in the real affair. O'Hara's lines, "The end of all existences / is a pint of blood on a / windowsill," an allusion to the terrible Brussels drama in which Verlaine shot Rimbaud, provide a nice ironic commentary on Rivers's static, understated portrait of the two poets. The blood motif then returns in the reference to Myers's snide remark made at the ballet, a remark that relates O'Hara and Rivers to Rimbaud and Verlaine. The image of the bullets (penises with legs) is especially effective: these shapes are related not only to the "beats / of the corps de ballet," and the movements of poet and painter descending the City Center staircase, but also the relationship of Rimbaud and Verlaine, culminating in the shooting. There are other ingenious visual details: note the chairlike shape at the left, suggesting a balcony seat, and the silhouette of a person sitting in the audience near it. The black spots scattered across the surface, moreover, resemble drops of blood. Relatively little of the available space is used in this lithograph so that whiteness predominates, in keeping with O'Hara's reference to "white air" in the last line. *Rimbaud & Verlaine* is a poem-painting in the full sense of the word.

Love (Fig. 5), one of the finest plates in the series, relates word to picture in a rather different way. "We decided," Rivers recalls, "to do a LOVE stone. I distributed male and female over the surface with a few genitalia for the sex of it. He wrote in between and on the drawing and never even mentioned man or woman or bodies or sex" (p. 97).

This is quite accurate. In the spaces between Rivers's silhouettes of athletic males and phallic shapes, O'Hara places the words of a poem whose tone wholly undercuts the visual impression:

LOVE
To be lost
the stars go out a broken chair
is red in the dark a faint lust
stirs like a plant in the creased rain

Here O'Hara typically cuts at odd junctures so that "a faint lust" belongs to "in the dark" rather than to its complement: "stirs like a plant. . . ." The tone is wistful, sad, resigned. This stanza, in turn, modulates into two passages written in parody-nineties diction: "where the gloom / swells into odour / like earth in the moon," and "lightless the arrow wears its sigh of depth and its sorrows of snow." The strange tension between the verbal ("pretty" images, rhymes, sonorous vowel sounds) and the visual (broad-shouldered supermen, giant genitalia, a top hat) creates a delicately ambiguous vision of *Love.* The reader-viewer is confronted by contradictory signals that arrest the attention.

Not all the *Stones* are as interesting as the three I have discussed. *Springtemps,* their second plate, consists of a self-contained O'Hara poem to Joseph Rivers on the left, and blurred, semiabstract images of flowers, butterflies, and human bodies on the right; neither the picture nor the poem seems to gain much from this juxtaposition. Again, *Music,* the sixth plate (Fig. 6), is strictly speaking an illustrated poem rather than a poem-painting. The lower half of this lithograph reproduces O'Hara's poem "Students" (*CP,* 290); above the text, Rivers places what he calls his "own version of Batman. Violinman." The painter himself remarks shrewdly that this *Stone* "is a little more old-fashioned: our unintegrated style." In this case, Frank had already written the poem and asked Larry to respond. "A good poem," says Rivers, "but for the kind of mind I have, useless" (p. 96).

The point here is not so much whether Rivers liked the poem as that it was a finished product, a condition which leaves the painter with no role but that of illustrator. True artistic collaboration must, however, involve simultaneity. One of the loveliest *Stones* is *Melancholy Breakfast* (Fig. 7), which contains semiabstract images of such breakfast items as eggs, toasters, gas burners, griddles, and a table. These images are distorted as if seen through the blur of half-sleep or a hangover. Everything in the scene is disconnected: in O'Hara's words, "the silent egg thinks / and the toaster's electrical ear waits." And the bottom line sums it up: "The elements of disbelief are very strong in the morning." Here poet and painter seem to be on the very same wavelength.

To turn from *Stones* to *Poem-Paintings,* the collaborations made by O'Hara and Norman Bluhm in 1960,[40] is to move into a much more lyrical, delicate, evanescent, but equally interesting pictorial world. Bill Berkson describes the genesis of *Poem-Paintings* as follows:

> One dreary Sunday midday in October 1960, the painter Norman Bluhm and Frank O'Hara, poet and self-confessed *balayeur des artistes,* met at Bluhm's studio in the old Tiffany Building on Park Avenue South, and, as the inclement weather wasn't helping either's mood or conversation, they decided to get on with a collaboration project they had talked about weeks before. A few hours later, they had made these twenty-six poem-paintings.[41]

And John Perreault, reviewing *Poem-Paintings* for *Art News,* suggests that the two artists put together the series "all in one short frenzy of creativity that must have been like two collaborating Zen monks in a zany dance of the seasons."[42]

It didn't quite happen in this romantic way. Norman Bluhm told me in an interview that it took many Sundays (not just a few hours!) to complete *Poem-Paintings.* Here is his account:

> Frank and I enjoyed music. We used to meet Sunday mornings at my studio, listen to music and talk and look at the paintings, and then go to my house and listen to records. One time, listening to opera (Toti del Monte, the famous 300-pound soprano, singing *Madame Butterfly*), I said to Frank: "I have all this paper, let's put it on the wall." And we decided we'd like listening to the music and playing around with words and paint. But it wasn't a serious art project. We just wanted to do something while the music was going on. For instance, if we were listening to a Prokofiev symphony, you could feel the boots in my painting.[43]

Music, Bluhm insists, was the driving force behind the collaboration. An Italian on his mother's side, Bluhm had, as a child, longed to be an opera singer; Frank, of course, had longed to be a concert pianist. For both artists, music was terribly important, and both believed that all the arts are interrelated, that the modern compartmentalization of the arts is hopelessly limiting.

The work on *Poem-Paintings,* Bluhm recalls, "was a terrific event, a Happening—a way of amusing ourselves. They were done as an event by two people who had this special feeling for each other and for art, music, and literature." As for technique, "the words are more important than gesture. Basically, we tried to keep the art as just a gesture [hence the decision to use only black and white paint], not an illustration of the poem. The idea was to make the gesture relate, in an abstract way, to the idea of the poem. Only rarely did we do a thing à la Dali where you pick up the drip and throw it into the word."

Sometimes Bluhm would do a drawing and O'Hara would invent an appropriate set of words; sometimes the procedure was reversed. But each poem-painting, Bluhm told me, "grew out of some hilarious relationship with people we knew, out of a particular situation. The tone was comic or satiric—a kind of operatic buffo. We thought of our collaboration as a theatrical event, an amusement. We did it for fun, forgetting our miseries, our love affairs—our more serious problems."

Take, for example, *Homage to Kenneth Koch* (Fig. 8). This picture displays a large abstract shape, etched in black, with a thick white drip running through it, and on the right side, in O'Hara's beautiful writing, the following poem:

> I was standing
> outside your window
> how lucky I was
> you had just washed it
>
> and later I thought of you
> in the car barn,
> my head was inside the hood
> and I felt very hot
>
> are you inside the hood too?

This charmingly absurd poem in which lovers hope for a rendezvous inside the boiling hood of a car was inspired, according to Bluhm, by the following incident: "One time, we (Kenneth Koch and I) picked up two girls at a cocktail party. He ended up with the better-looking one but she did have big feet. I told Frank about it and drew the shape of a foot (the big black abstract form)." Frank responded by writing an appropriately foolish love poem.

Or again, *Welcome to Kitty Hawk* (Fig. 9) evidently grew out of a conversation about airplanes. "My father," Bluhm recalls, "was a flyer, and I told Frank a story about a mechanic who built his own airplane and as it reached 200 feet, the engine split off and the plane crashed." This is not exactly a happy story, but Bluhm's black shape (he calls it a "bad airplane") looks like a chicken hawk and so O'Hara's caption is very amusing.

Few of the *Poem-Paintings* contain real poems. Number 3 boasts the single word *Bust;* number 6, the letters B-A-N-G in the four corners, surrounding a shape that looks like a comical furry phallus. Many are no more than in-jokes: number 19 refers to Chicago because it was Bluhm's birthplace; number 13 contains the phrase "sale morbidité," which is, as Bill Berkson says, "a *Gabin-erie* picked up during his [Bluhm's] decade in Paris." Number 5, which contains no visual images, is a more or less direct transcript of O'Hara's conversation: the words "I'm so tired of all the parties, it's like January and the hangovers on the beach" are scrawled across the surface of the picture.

Individually, these poem-paintings may be quite negligible—a stroke or two of paint, a few curved lines and drips, and a phrase like "reaping and sowing / sowing and reaping . . . Skylark," as in number 1. But John Perreault is surely right when he compares these collaborations to "footprints of a wild ballet."[44] Like Chinese ink drawings, they have a lyric charm quite different from the more complex and subtle *Stones.* For one thing, O'Hara has a chance to display his beautiful handwriting which looks like calligraphy. The technique of making lithographs made this impossible in *Stones,* where the poet uses block print. The combination of O'Hara's rounded letters and Bluhm's curling horseshoe shapes, his thick white paint flecks, and suggestive, fleeting gestures, make *Poem-Paintings* real works of art even if their verbal messages hardly qualify as "poems." Take *Hand* (Fig. 10), which presents the shape of a clenched fist, outlined in thick black paint, with a splash of white across its center. The word HAND appears in the upper left; within each of the five "fingers," there is delicate small writing:

> You eat all the time
> you even know how to use
> chopsticks
> so why don't you write me
> a letter
> forget it

The final "forget it" is placed inside the thumb; so, as we come to the last finger, we also come to the end of O'Hara's little Dada poem with its naive address to someone's hand. In itself, the poem is trivial, but the placement of words and phrases within the thick black outlines of finger-shapes, and the further contrast of black and white create a lovely spatial configuration. Indeed, the twenty-six collaborations should be seen as an integral whole, a total event, rather than as separate paintings. Their inventiveness, wit, and charm become increasingly apparent as we study the relation of gesture to gesture, footmark to handprint, lyric phrase to four-letter word, proverb to sexy innuendo, white drop to black letter, and so on.

The "collaborations" of the sixties with such artists as Joe Brainard and Jasper Johns are no longer, strictly speaking, poem-paintings. The untitled ink-and-paper collage below (Fig. 11), for example, is one of a series of twenty-odd Pop cartoons O'Hara made with Joe Brainard between 1963 and 1966.[45] It combines tacky blue-and-white flowered wallpaper with bits of a dollar bill bearing George Washington's picture, a ticket for the Paris metro, a piece of memo pad, the letters of "9th Street," and, at dead center, a page from *Nancy* comics with the bubble caption: "Would you like a coke?" These juxtapositions are entertaining but fairly obvious; one misses the intricate verbal-visual counterpoint of *Stones* or the fragile lyricism of the O'Hara–Bluhm *Poem-Paintings*. In these cartoons, we are back in the world of Picabia and Schwitters; the "Nancy Collage" is an amusing assemblage, but it attempts—and achieves—less than O'Hara's earlier collaborations.

Jasper Johns's well-known *Skin with O'Hara Poem* (1963–65) takes us out of the realm of poem-paintings altogether (Fig. 12). The lithograph contains two large imprints of hands on either side. In the center are two blurred black shapes suggesting facial outlines; black smudges move across the surface connecting the hands to these facial shapes. Above the right hand, Johns has reproduced the text of "The Clouds Go Soft" (*CP,* 474), typed to scale. The bottom lines of the poem are slightly covered by black smudges. The poem thus becomes part of a game of lost-and-found; now we see it (although at first the viewer barely notices its existence), now we don't. It is an exciting composition, combining realistic figuration and Dada game-playing, but *Skin with O'Hara Poem* is *by* Jasper Johns; it is not a collaboration. The poem, an already completed work, is used as part of a spatial structure.[46]

We may conclude that the poem-painting, in the sense of a genuine collaboration, presents unusual challenges but also difficulties to the artist. Peter Schjeldahl calls it an "exotic hybrid of the two loneliest and traditionally 'highest' arts";[47] and Bill Berkson notes: "Collaboration between serious artists (even in the best of spirits . . .) involves always a brisk atmosphere of competition. Strategy may amount to a step-by-step oneupmanship: by painting a wide black line down the middle of the sheet, artist A lets artist B know that he knows what B's muse is up to and 'pardon my dust.'"[48]

This chapter has concentrated on O'Hara as a "poet among painters," and I have, accordingly, neglected his perhaps equally important collaborations with composers, choreographers, and film-makers. Certainly films like Alfred Leslie's *The Last Clean Shirt,* for which O'Hara wrote subtitles to create a double-scenario, or the text he provided for Ned Rorem's *Four Dialogues* would repay study. But painting had a special place in O'Hara's poetic universe, and so I have stressed its place in O'Hara's artistic development. The poet himself made the crucial distinctions in a letter written to Gregory Corso in 1958:

> Several people you know are around lately, Kerouac whom I've only seen once or twice but liked a lot, Howard Hart and [Philip] Lamantia who are reading with a French hornist as the Jazz Poetry Trio. . . .
> I don't really get their jazz stimulus but it is probably what I get from painting . . . that is, you can't be inside all the time it gets too boring and you can't afford to be bored with poetry so you take a secondary enthusiasm as the symbol of the first—for instance, I've noticed that what Kerouac and "they" feel as the content of jazz in relation to their own work (aspirations), I feel about painting with the corresponding difference in aspiration, that is where one takes Bird for inspiration I would take Bill de Kooning: partly because I feel that jazz is beautiful enough or too, but not fierce enough, and where jazz is fleeting (in time) and therefore poignant, de K is final and therefore tragic. . . . Then also, I don't have to see what I admire while I'm writing and would rather not hear it, which seems unavoidable in the jazz milieu since even if they don't whistle while they work they read with it. Maybe I should try to give a reading somewhere in front of a Pollock or a de K. . . . I guess my point is that painting doesn't intrude on poetry.[49]

To give a poetry reading in front of a de Kooning—this is the kind of aspiration we expect from O'Hara. But note that he doesn't want painting to "intrude on poetry," that it remains his "secondary enthusiasm." When asked by Lucie-Smith whether he had ever wanted to be a painter, O'Hara replied that he had not, although he admitted to "fooling around" with painting whenever he happened to be waiting around a studio for someone. "I might do some little thing, you know. But I never really did it seriously because . . . it seems to me that painting and sculpture take so much concentration over such a period of time that I'm not sure I can do it. Whereas one *can* write relatively fast" (*SS,* 21).

This amounts to no more than saying that his own particular genius was not for painting; surely the statement that painting is more difficult and time-consuming than writing poetry is tongue-in-cheek, for many abstractionists and Pop Artists of O'Hara's day hardly excercised the "concentration" over long periods of time that he talks of here. And in any case, the question, "Why are you not a painter?" must have struck O'Hara as wonderfully absurd. His pseudo-answer to this pointless question became the subject of one of his greatest poems:

WHY I AM NOT A PAINTER

I am not a painter, I am a poet.
Why? I think I would rather be
a painter, but I am not. Well,

for instance, Mike Goldberg
is starting a painting. I drop in.
"Sit down and have a drink" he
says. I drink; we drink. I look
up. "You have SARDINES in it."
"Yes, it needed something there."
"Oh." I go and the days go by
and I drop in again. The painting
is going on, and I go, and the days
go by. I drop in. The painting is
finished. "Where's SARDINES?"
All that's left is just
letters, "It was too much," Mike says.

But me? One day I am thinking of
a color: orange. I write a line
about orange. Pretty soon it is

a whole page of words, not lines.
Then another page. There should be
so much more, not of orange, of
words, of how terrible orange is
and life. Days go by. It is even in
prose, I am a real poet. My poem
is finished and I haven't mentioned
orange yet. It's twelve poems, I call
it ORANGES. And one day in a gallery
I see Mike's painting, called SARDINES.   (*CP*, 261–62)

Readers often assume that O'Hara is stressing differences: the painter like Mike Goldberg is constantly "taking out," and finally nothing remains of SARDINES but the letters, whereas the poet keeps "putting in" and "putting in." But on a second reading, it becomes clear that the poem is a profound jest. If someone asks a stupid question, O'Hara implies, he deserves a stupid answer. For in fact, Frank's art turns out to be just like Mike's. If Mike's painting finally contains no sardines, so Frank's "Oranges" never mentions the word "orange." In both cases, the original word or image merely triggers a chain of associations that ultimately leads straight to its demise. O'Hara is a poet not a painter for no better reason than that is what he *is*. But of course the poem is also saying that poetry and painting are part of the same spectrum, that in the final analysis SARDINES and ORANGES are one. This is why the rhetorical device governing the poem is repetition ("I drink; we drink"; "I go and the days go by"; "I drop in; I drop in again"). Art does not tolerate divisions; it must be viewed as process, not product.

1. Grace Hartigan. What Fire Murmurs Its Sedition. *1952. Oil on paper, 48 x 38½". No. 3 of* Oranges. *Collection Mr. and Mrs. Leonard Kasle. Reproduced with permission of the artist.*

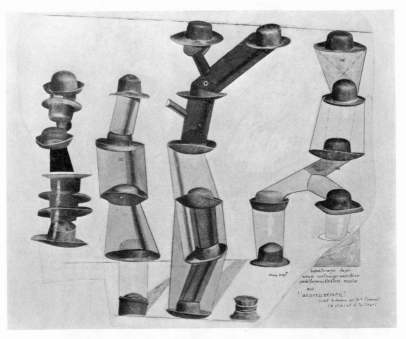

2. *Max Ernst.* The Hat Makes the Man. *1920. Collage with
pencil, ink and watercolor, 14 x 18″. Museum of Modern Art,
New York.*

4. *Larry Rivers and Frank O'Hara.*
Rimbaud & Verlaine. *Plate 3 of*
Stones, *1957–60. Lithograph,
19 x 23¼″. Museum of Modern Art,
New York (Gift of Mr. and Mrs. E.
Powis Jones).*

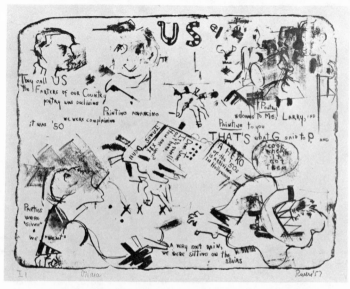

3. *Larry Rivers and Frank O'Hara.* US, *Plate 1 of* Stones, *1957–60. Lithograph, 19 x 23¼″. Museum of Modern Art, New York (Gift of Mr. and Mrs. E. Powis Jones).*

5. *Larry Rivers and Frank O'Hara.* Love. *Plate 4 of Stones, 1957–60. Lithograph, 19 x 23¼". Museum of Modern Art, New York (Gift of Mr. and Mrs. E. Powis Jones).*

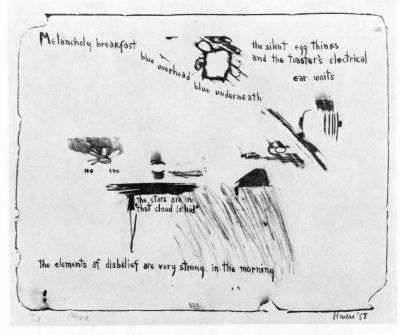

7. *Larry Rivers and Frank O'Hara.* Melancholy Breakfast.
Plate 8 of Stones, *1957–60. Museum of Modern Art, New York
(Gift of Mr. and Mrs. E. Powis Jones).*

6. *Larry Rivers and Frank O'Hara.*
Music. *Plate 6 of* Stones, *1957–60.
Lithograph, 19 x 23¼″. Museum of
Modern Art, New York (Gift of Mr. and
Mrs. E. Powis Jones).*

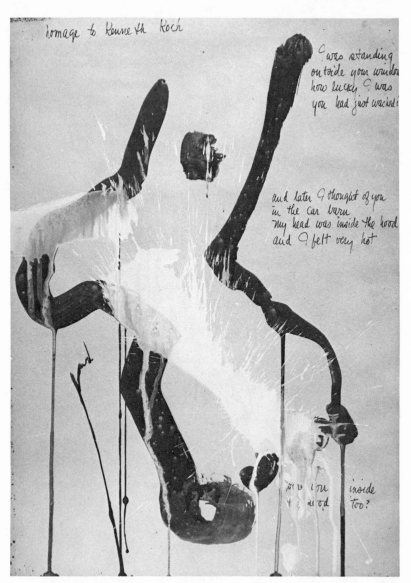

8. *Norman Bluhm and Frank O'Hara.* Homage to Kenneth Koch. *1960. Gouache and ink, 19¼ x 14". New York University Art Collection.*

9. *Norman Bluhm and Frank O'Hara.* Welcome to Kitty Hawk.
*1960. Gouache and ink, 19¼ x 14". New York University Art
Collection.*

10. Norman Bluhm and Frank O'Hara. Hand. *1960. Gouache
and ink, 19¼ x 14". New York University Art Collection.*

11. *Joe Brainard and Frank O'Hara.* Untitled. *1964. Collage with ink on paper, 10 x 8". Collection Frank O'Hara Estate.*

12. *Jasper Johns.* Skin with O'Hara Poem. *1963–65. Lithograph, printed in black, 22 x 34". Museum of Modern Art, New York (Gift of the Celeste and Armand Bartos Foundation).*

4

IN FAVOR
OF ONE'S TIME
(1954-61)

—and it was given to me
 as the soul is given the hands
 to hold the ribbons of life!
 as miles streak by beneath the moon's sharp hooves
 and I have mastered the speed and strength which is the armor of the world.

("There I Could Never Be A Boy," CP, 216)

IN 1954, FRANK O'HARA was twenty-eight. Within the seven "green and turbulent" years that followed, he produced his finest poems and collaborations as well as his best art criticism. It was, both personally and artistically, the golden period of his life. During the summer of 1955, for example, he wrote to Fairfield Porter that he had written a new batch of poems, "so summery I don't know how they'll make the difficult transition to fall. Perhaps just shrivel up, turn brown and blow away. That would make me feel very grand. After all, if we can't make leaves, neither can god poems."[1]

By the late fifties, O'Hara was at the center of a circle of artists that included not only the painters discussed in the last chapter, but the poets John Ashbery (then living in Paris but in close communication),

James Schuyler, Barbara Guest, Kenneth Koch, Edwin Denby, Allen Ginsberg, John Wieners, and LeRoi Jones; the composers Ned Rorem, Ben Weber, and Virgil Thompson; the dancers Merce Cunningham, Paul Taylor, Vincent Warren, and Merle Marsicano. I do not mean to imply that all these artists belonged to one circle. There were, of course, many related circles, and diversity was O'Hara's special gift: the composers he knew, for example, ranged from the conservative Samuel Barber to the avant-garde Morton Feldman and Lucia Dlugoszewski. Or again, moving out into a wider circle, he was friendly with Leonard Bernstein and Tennessee Williams.

The poet's closest personal friendships—with Joe LeSueur, with whom he shared four apartments between 1955 and 1965, with Vincent Warren, the object of his most tender love poems, and with Grace Hartigan and Patsy Southgate—took place during this period.[2] And although he was now assistant curator at the Museum of Modern Art, organizing important exhibitions, his duties were not yet so extensive that there wasn't plenty of time for movies, concerts, operas, ballet, late evenings at the Cedar, parties all over town, and weekends at Southampton. In a letter to John Ashbery, characteristically dashed off in spare moments over a four-day period (1–4 February 1961), O'Hara lists a dizzying series of gallery openings and plays attended, new Balanchine ballets, and even his and Vincent's "assiduous TVing"; the following paragraph gives a good idea of his daily life:

> Hello, it is now February 4th, Friday thank heaven, and I think I am going to paint my bedroom this weekend. I veer between orange and blue, though Mario says the latter is the brightest color and would be very nerve-wracking. (That might be quite appropriate.) The opera [Aaron Copland's *The Second Hurricane*] was a lot of fun and afterwards we went to Donald Droll's for supper where were Elaine de Kooning, Edwin, John Button, Edward Bagaline (who is very nice and is supposed to have a great collection—as I said above; we couldn't accept his invitation to see it as it was 2:00 when he issued it), and Beatrice Monti, who is Joan and Jean-Paul's dealer in Milano. She was very interesting and the quiche lorraine was divine.[3]

"It's lucky," Joe LeSueur has commented wryly, "that he didn't become famous because it would have intruded upon his working hours and the way he lived."[4]

O'Hara certainly didn't work at becoming a famous poet. All his friends agree that he was reluctant to submit poems for publication or to assemble them in a volume. The selection for *Meditations in an Emergency* (1957) was largely the work of James Schuyler and Kenneth Koch; later when O'Hara was supposedly putting together *Lunch Poems* for City Lights Books at the request of Lawrence Ferlinghetti, he kept procrastinating so that Ferlinghetti had to send him constant reminders like "How about LUNCH? I'm hungry," to which O'Hara would respond "Cooking" or something similar.[5] Thus the "lunch poem" project, initiated at least as early as 1959, did not come to fruition until 1964, and when O'Hara supplied a biographical note for the dust jacket, he adopted the playful stance of "Personism":

> Often this poet, strolling through the noisy splintered glare of a Manhattan noon, has paused at a sample Olivetti to type up thirty or forty lines of ruminations, or pondering more deeply has withdrawn to a darkened ware- or fire-house, to limn his computed misunderstandings of the eternal questions of life, co-existence and depth, while never forgetting to eat Lunch his favorite meal.[6]

Many of the important poems of this period—for example, "A True Account of Talking to the Sun at Fire Island" (1958)—remained unpublished during O'Hara's lifetime. And those that did get into print often did so by chance. Diane di Prima, whose *Floating Bear* published such major O'Hara poems as "Mary Desti's Ass" and "For the Chinese New Year and Bill Berkson,"[7] has given an amusing account of how she acquired the poet's manuscripts:

> I would go over to Frank O'Hara's house pretty often. He used to keep a typewriter on the table in the kitchen, and he would type away, make poems all the time, when company was there and when it wasn't, when he was eating, all kinds of times. There would be an unfinished poem in his typewriter and he would do a few lines on it now and again, and he kept losing all these poems. They would wind up all over the house. . . . The poems would get into everything and I would come over and go through, like, his dresser drawers. There would be poems in with the towels, and I'd say, "Oh, hey, I like this one," and he'd say, "OK, take it." Very often it would be the only copy. My guess is that huge collected Frank O'Hara has only about one-third of his actual work.[8]

O'Hara's attitude toward his poetry thus struck most people as casual, if not downright careless. "As far as I could tell," Joe LeSueur recalls, "writing poetry was something Frank did in his spare time. He didn't make a big deal about it, he just sat down and wrote when the spirit moved him." He didn't need much time "because he usually got what he was after in one draft, and could type very fast, hunt-and-peck fashion. And from the very beginning it seemed to me that he never tried to get a poem going, never forced himself to write; he either had an idea or he didn't, and that was all there was to it" ("Four Apartments," pp. 288–89).

Because speed and spontaneity were of the essence, the typewriter was the essential instrument. LeSueur recalls only two non-typewriter works: "his poem about James Dean, 'written in the sand at Water Island and remembered' and his 'Lana Turner has collapsed' poem, which he wrote on the Staten Island Ferry on the way out to a reading at Wagner College" (p. 290). And indeed, during Frank's six months' leave of absence from the Museum in the winter of 1956 when he accepted a grant from the Poets' Theatre in Cambridge, he wrote to Mike Goldberg: "There were a couple of weeks of foul depression, gnashing teeth, pacing and boredom, when I felt that I would never, NEVER . . . be able to play the typewriter again. But the presence of this Steinway you all gave me [a Royal portable donated by his friends after Frank lost his own typewriter in Penn Station] has finally asserted itself, and I now stagger from bed, stride to the desk, and begin my scales each morning, or almost each."[9]

"Playing the typewriter" rather than writing in longhand inevitably leads the poet to emphasize visual prosody. For example, O'Hara used long lines frequently, evidently because he liked their appearance on the page—their ability to convey sensuality and strength.[10] When spoken, however, these lines tend to break down into groups of twos or threes, as in the following example:

Now the violets are all gone, // the rhinoceroses, // the cymbals
(*CP*, 346)

What is heard does not, then, reflect what is seen. O'Hara was not, for that matter, a particularly good reader of his own poetry. Like Williams, he wrote primarily for the eye rather than the ear; like Williams, he placed special emphasis on speed and spontaneity, only rarely revising more than a phrase or two of a poem. But this is not to say that he didn't take his poetry very seriously. As Joe LeSueur remarks with great insight: "I didn't realize right away that if you took poetry so much for granted as you did breathing it might mean you felt it was essential to your life" (p. 288).

Poetry and life—O'Hara refused, at least consciously, to make a distinction between the two. He regarded both as part of the same vital process, living every moment as if it were his last, forcing himself to go without sleep so as not to miss anything. "There's nothing so spiritual about being happy," O'Hara says in a poem of 1956 (CP, 244), "but you can't miss a day of it, because it doesn't last." We are now in a better position to understand why O'Hara was so reluctant to judge or to rank his own poetry. Given his intense relationships with people, he naturally tended to prefer whatever poem he had just written because it could remind him of a particular person or incident. All his best poems grow out of personal relationships. I have already talked of the "Grace Hartigan" poems; other important figures in the lyrics of the later fifties are Mike Goldberg, Kenneth Koch, Joan Mitchell, and of course Joe LeSueur and Vincent Warren. It is interesting that the poems written for Joe LeSueur—"Joe's Jacket," "Waking Early Sunday," "Adieu to Norman, Bonjour to Jean-Paul"—are written in the realistic, documentary "I do this, I do that" mode which LeSueur himself admires most,[11] whereas the love poems to Vincent Warren, whom O'Hara met in 1959, tend to be less factual, more emotional, direct, Romantic. And the lyrics addressed to Bill Berkson or directly concerned with him have a very different quality again—they are more elusive, detached, abstract.

To understand O'Hara's method of composition in this period, we might begin by looking at a specific poem whose genesis has been amusingly described by LeSueur in "Four Apartments":

> Sometimes . . . the details in a poem will remind me of a day I would otherwise have forgotten. Mother's Day, 1958, for example. Frank was struck by the title of a *Times* book review, "The Arrow That Flieth by Day," and said he'd like to appropriate it for a poem. I agreed that the phrase had a nice ring and asked him for the second time what I should

do about Mother's Day, which I'd forgotten all about. "Oh, send your mother a telegram," he said. But I couldn't hit upon a combination of words that didn't revolt me and Western Union's prepared messages sounded too maudlin even for my mother. "You think of a message for my mother and I'll think of one for yours," I suggested. We then proceeded to try to top each other with apposite messages that would have made Philip Wylie applaud. Then it was time to go hear a performance of Aaron Copland's *Piano Fantasy* by Noel Lee. "It's raining, I don't want to go," Frank said. So he stayed home and wrote "Ode on the Arrow That Flieth by Day," which refers to the Fantasy, Western Union, the rain, and Mother's Day. (rpt. *CP*, 541).

The Ode does indeed "refer" to these seemingly unrelated items but in a very oblique way. The key to O'Hara's transformation of the materials LeSueur describes is the poem's title, taken from Psalm 91:5: "Thou shalt not be afraid of the terror by night; nor the arrow that flieth by day." How *not* to be afraid—this is the theme of the poem. To capture the mood of deepening anxiety, O'Hara eliminates all narrative, giving us instead snatches of his conversation, both spoken and unspoken. The opening note is one of deceptively light-hearted banter:

> To humble yourself before a radio on a Sunday
> it's amusing, like dying after a party
> "click" / and you're dead from fall-out, hang-over
>   or something hyphenated   (*CP*, 300)

One might note that the awareness of death is introduced right away, however comically, but it is then deflected by the wonderfully absurd distillation of pseudo-Mother's Day Greetings invented by Frank and Joe on this occasion:

(hello, Western Union? send a Mother's Day message to Russia: SORRY NOT TO BE WITH YOU ON YOUR DAY LOVE AND KISSES TELL THE CZAR /

LA GRANDE JATTE WASN'T DAMAGED IN THE MUSEUM OF MODERN ART FIRE / S / FRANK)

David Shapiro has suggested that this kind of parenthetical injection, the mimetic representation of sending a telegram, corresponds to the introduction of noise in the "musique concrète" of Satie, one of

O'Hara's favorite composers.[12] It creates a discontinuity of texture, forcing the reader to shift gears, as it were, and commanding our attention. Such attention is important, for, despite the playful fantasy of the telegram, its "message" has serious implications in that the very thought that this *is* Mother's Day introduces a note of irritation and malaise.

> the unrecapturable nostalgia for nostalgia
> for a life I might have hated, thus mourned
>
> but do we really need anything more to be sorry about
> wouldn't it be extra, as all pain is extra

The poet tries to comfort himself with this last thought but he knows only too well that he will never "WIN A DREAM TRIP . . . somehow." And indeed, in the next passage he must confront "the arrow that flieth by day" directly:

> for God's sake, fly the other way
> leave me standing alone crumbling in the new sky of the Wide World
> without passage, without breath
>
> a spatial representative of emptiness
>
> if Joan says I'm wounded, then I'm wounded

The cause of his "wound" cannot be named. Neither tortured at the stake like Joan of Arc nor reviled by hostile critics like André Gide, he cannot put the blame on "moral issues or the intercontinental ballistics missile / or the Seer of Prague" [Kafka]. Indeed, the poet's anxiety has no cause. And this is precisely why it is so devastating:

> (you're right to go to Aaron's PIANO FANTASY, but I'm not up to it this
> time, too important a piece not to punish me
>   and it's raining)

It is a nice irony that the poet's original joke comes true: he does, after all, die from "something hyphenated"; he is gunned down by a nameless source, turning him, at least momentarily, into the "death of a nation / henceforth to be called small."

What the "Ode" does, then—and this is entirely absent from Le-

Sueur's narrative of the incident—is to reenact the mental process whereby amusement and horseplay gradually give way to anxiety and ultimately to withdrawal. But O'Hara's comic self-depreciation precludes sentimentality. The implication is that under other circumstances (if only it weren't Mother's Day and weren't raining to boot!) he could and does resist "the arrow that flieth by day." "All pain," as he puts it, "is extra." Something amusing, distracting, challenging is sure to turn up. Maybe the air will once again "salute" him as he stands "leaning on the prow."

The poem's mode reflects O'Hara's gradual shift from the Tzara-Péret model of his earlier years to the more open, flexible forms of Apollinaire and Reverdy, the laconic informality of the later Auden, the brutal and personal intensity of Mayakovsky. Williams continues to be a central influence, but Pound now becomes equally important. I shall return to the question of influence later in this chapter. But first I want to look at the poetic signature, the particular style that identifies a given lyric as a "Frank O'Hara poem," the sort of poem that has been so widely imitated, if never quite reproduced, during the past decade.

"WHATEVER ENERGY I BURN FOR ART"

"Music," the opening poem of *Lunch Poems,* written in 1954, contains most of the stylistic devices I wish to discuss.

> If I rest for a moment near The Equestrian
> pausing for a liver sausage sandwich in the Mayflower Shoppe,
> that angel seems to be leading the horse into Bergdorf's
> and I am naked as a table cloth, my nerves humming.
> Close to the fear of war and the stars which have disappeared.
> I have in my hands only 35¢, it's so meaningless to eat!
> and gusts of water spray over the basins of leaves
> like the hammers of a glass pianoforte. If I seem to you
> to have lavender lips under the leaves of the world,
> I must tighten my belt.
> It's like a locomotive on the march, the season
> of distress and clarity
> and my door is open to the evenings of midwinter's
> lightly falling snow over the newspapers.
> Clasp me in your handkerchief like a tear, trumpet
> of early afternoon! in the foggy autumn.

As they're putting up the Christmas trees on Park Avenue
I shall see my daydreams walking by with dogs in blankets,
put to some use before all those coloured lights come on!
    But no more fountains and no more rain,
    and the stores stay open terribly late.   (*CP*, 210)

This is at once an "easier" and a "more difficult" poem than such earlier lyrics as "Chez Jane," "Easter," or "Memorial Day 1950." As in the case of "Ode (to Joseph LeSueur), "one's first impression is that "Music" is no more than a record of daily trivia; it recounts an uneventful lunch hour spent in the former Mayflower Donut Shoppe on Fifth and 59th, detailing Frank's random thoughts about the Plaza fountain across the way, the equestrian statue nearby, Bergdorf Goodman's down the street, the thirty-five cents in his pocket, the liver sausage sandwich he has ordered, and the impending Christmas season with its giant trees on Park Avenue, colored lights, and long shopping hours.

But the real strategy of the poem is to remove objects from what Viktor Shklovsky has called "the automatism of perception,"[13] by adapting the techniques of film and action painting to a verbal medium. For one thing, the poem is framed as a series of cuts and dissolves, whether spatial, temporal, or referential. Thus in line 3, the highly concrete setting—the Mayflower Shoppe on the Plaza—dissolves into a comic fantasy scene, created by the optical illusion of staring into the Plaza fountain on a rainy day: "that angel seems to be leading the horse into Bergdorf's." Or again, the poem suddenly cuts from Fifth Avenue to Park, where the giant Christmas trees are being put up, and one's "daydreams," whoever they are, emerge with their "dogs in blankets."

Temporal dissolves work the same way. The "real" time of the poem is "early afternoon! in the foggy autumn" (line 16), a rainy day in that in-between time of the year after the leaves have fallen and before the Christmas lights come on, a time of half-light and shadow in "this season / of distress and clarity." Yet in line 13, the poet says "and my door is open to the evenings of midwinter's / lightly falling snow over the newspapers," and the end of the poem presents the Christmas season itself: "But no more fountains and no more rain, / and the stores stay open terribly late."

Time shifts are not, of course, anything new in poetry, but it is one of O'Hara's trademarks to maintain the present tense (or conditional present as in "If I rest . . .") regardless, and to supply no adverbial pointers (e.g., "when," "after," "before," "during") that signal a shift. The concept of person is similarly fluid. The "I"—a very familiar, intimate, *open* "I"—is omnipresent but whom is he addressing? If the first "you" (line 8) is a close friend or lover, the second, to whom the poet says rapturously, "Clasp me in your handkerchief like a tear, trumpet / of early afternoon!" is clearly a larger "you"—perhaps the Manhattan traffic, the rising moon, the sky, or indeed the whole universe as if to say, "You out there!" While the poet's self thus remains a constant center, anything or anyone that comes within its field of vision can be addressed or called by name. The repetition of definite articles and demonstratives reinforces this sense of intimate conversation and invites the reader's participation: "*The* Equestrian" (note the ellipsis of the noun here), "*the* Mayflower Shoppe," "*that* angel," "*the* Christmas trees on Park Avenue"—all these references suggest that the reader is familiar with the scene, indeed that he is part of it.

The syntax of "Music" may be described as a system of nonsequiturs. "If I rest for a moment . . ." the poet begins, but no "then" clause ever follows, and the conditional clause dissolves into the parenthesis of line 3. The second "If I seem to you" clause in line 8 is completed by "I must tighten my belt," a clause that follows grammatically but makes no sense. Appositives and parallel nouns similarly turn out to be pseudo-appositives and pseudo-parallels: "It's like a locomotive on the march, the season / of distress and clarity"; or "the fear of war and the stars which have disappeared." In what sense is a "season" a "locomotive on the march"? And why "distress *and* clarity," or "the fear of war *and* the stars"? The use of "and" to introduce coordinate clauses is similarly illogical: "That angel seems to be leading the horse into Bergdorf's / *and* I am naked as a table cloth," or "it's so meaningless to eat! / *and* gusts of water spray . . ." and so on.

The syntactic dislocations of "Music" are by no means as radical as those found in such earlier poems as "Second Avenue," with its all but impenetrable verbal surface, its total ambiguity of reference. But the repeated nonsequiturs act to undercut the documentary realism of the poem's scene and introduce the opposing note: an element of fantasy, of imaginative transformation. Not "I rest," but "*If* I rest"; not "I have lavender lips," but "*If* I *seem* to you to have lavender lips." Or again, "I *must* tighten my belt," and "It's *like* a locomotive on the march." Nothing really *happens* to the poet; it is all potential, conditional, projected into a possible future ("I *shall see* my daydreams"). And individual images and metaphors are often comically or grotesquely far-fetched, reinforcing the fantasy note: "and I am naked as a table cloth"; "Clasp me in your handkerchief like a tear / trumpet of early afternoon!"; "If I seem to you to have lavender lips"; "I shall see my daydreams walking by with dogs in blankets."

How do all these elements work together? Again, the title gives us a clue, for the poem is like a melodic graph of the poet's perceptions. The varied sound images—some documentary and realistic, some fanciful and surreal—fuse to create a pattern that brings to mind modern dance (another favorite O'Hara art form) rather than a "poem" in the traditional sense of the word. "Music" begins on a note of suspended animation: the poet rests "for a moment near The Equestrian / pausing" for his sandwich. But immediately his imagination begins to transform the external scene: "that angel seems to be leading the horse into Bergdorf's," and "gusts of water spray over the basin of leaves / like hammers of a glass pianoforte." The tempo now accelerates as the poet's self increasingly *opens* to experience. It merges with the land-scape of the coffee shop, becoming as "naked as a table cloth," and his door is "open to the evenings of . . . snow over the newspapers." A sense of anticipation, of excitement, of brinkmanship pervades the poem: nerves hum, the speaker is "Close to the fear of war and the stars which have disappeared," he finds it "so meaningless to eat!" The leaves in the Plaza fountain become, in a truly filmlike dissolve, "the leaves of the world," and underneath them, the poet's lips, with a hint of impending doom, turn lavender. The initial "pause" gives way, precisely at the midpoint of the poem, to the urgency of the "locomo-tive on the march," the mood of yearning and ecstasy coming to a head with the imperative "Clasp me . . . !" But the vision of the pre-Christ-mas season with its "dogs in blankets" doesn't last. The moment gives way to stasis: "no more fountains and no more rain."

"Music" thus captures the sense of magic, urgency, and confusion of the modern cityscape in its "season of distress and clarity." It presents an impression of total fluidity, conveyed by the repeated use of present participles: "pausing," "leading," "humming," "falling," "putting," "walking." And the deliberate indeterminacy of the long verse lines is offset and heightened by repetitive internal sound patterning: "*rest*" / "Eque*str*ian"; "*p*a*us*ing" / "*saus*age"; "*se*ems to b*e* l*ea*ding," "*l*avender *l*ips under the *l*eaves of the wor*l*d," "C*l*asp me in your h*a*ndkerchief," and so on. The effect of all these devices is to create an aura of intense animation.

Like an action painting, "Music" presents the poet's act of coming to awareness rather than the results of that act. Accordingly, it traces the shift from calm to the crescendo of anticipation and excitement associated with "gusts of water" spraying over the leaves and the rapturous imperative, "Clasp me . . . !" After this crescendo, the mood gradually darkens as time, which has haunted the poet from the beginning, freezes. He can, after all, rest only "for a moment," "pausing" to take in a scene so animated ("my nerves humming") that there is hardly time to eat lunch. And in the course of the poem, lunchtime imperceptibly modulates into the foggy "early afternoon" and finally into darkness, when the fountains and rain are no longer visible and "the stores stay open terribly late." By the time the colored lights come on, the poet's "daydreams" will have vanished.

To recapitulate, let us consider "Music" in the broader context of O'Hara's poetry.

1. Imagery

"Music" fuses realism and surrealism, the literal and the fanciful. In so doing, it marks a clear-cut rejection of the Symbolist mode that had dominated American poetry for the first half of the century. Unlike Prufrock's "sawdust restaurants with oyster shells," with their symbolic connotations of aridity, sterility, and decay, O'Hara's Mayflower Shoppe points to nothing beyond itself; it has no underlying significance that demands interpretation. The name "Mayflower," for example, does not, in this context, call to mind our Founding Fathers or the innocence of an Early America; the coffee shop is simply *there,* an authentic presence we can all locate and recognize. Or again, whereas

Prufrock's fear of eating a peach reflects his fear of ripeness and fertility, O'Hara's "liver sausage sandwich" has no particular symbolic properties; it could, for that matter, be a salami or cheese sandwich just as easily.

Like the landscapes of Williams, of Reverdy, or of Apollinaire, O'Hara's is thus what Charles Altieri has called a "landscape without depth,"[14] a presence stripped of its "ontological vestments." Aerial perspective, three-dimensionality give way to a world of surfaces. In poem after poem of this period, what looks like a flat literalism predominates:

> It is 12:20 in New York a Friday
> three days after Bastille day, yes
> it is 1959 and I go get a shoeshine
> because I will get off the 4:19 in Easthampton
> at 7:15 and then go straight to dinner
> and I don't know the people who will feed me   (*CP*, 325)

> It's my lunch hour, so I go
> for a walk among the hum-colored
> cabs. First, down the sidewalk
> where laborers feed their dirty
> glistening torsos sandwiches
> and Coca-Cola. . . .   (*CP*, 257)

> I cough a lot (sinus?) so I
> get up and have some tea with cognac
> it is dawn
>   the light flows evenly along the lawn
> in chilly Southampton and I smoke
> and hours and hours go by I read
> Van Vechten's SPIDER BOY then a short
> story by Patsy Southgate and a poem
> by myself. . . .   (*CP*, 341)

The matter-of-fact realism of these passages has been widely imitated: "It is 12:20 in New York a Friday" (the first line of "The Day Lady Died") has become a kind of formula for New York poets. But whereas any number of minor poets can offer us such a *catalogue raisonné*,[15] O'Hara's empiricism is deceptive for it modulates easily and surprisingly into fantasy and artifice. The lessons of Dada and

Surrealism have, after all, been learned; even the most casual personal poems retain the witty modulations and sudden polarization of images found in the poetry of Tzara, Péret, and Breton, or, for that matter, in the poetry of Apollinaire, which is one of the dominant influences on O'Hara's poetry of this period. Take the following passage from "Rhapsody":

> I am getting into a cab at 9th Street and 1st Avenue
> and the Negro driver tells me about a $120 apartment
> "where you can't walk across the floor after 10 at night
> not even to pee, cause it keeps them awake downstairs"
> no I don't like that "well I didn't take it"   (*CP*, 326)

This bit of "supper-club conversation for the mill of the gods" strikes the poet as "perfect in the hot humid morning on my way to work," and he realizes that

> it isn't enough to smile when you run the gauntlet
> you've got to spit like Niagara Falls on everybody or
> Victoria Falls or at least the beautiful urban fountains of Madrid
> as the Niger joins the Gulf of Guinea near the Menemsha Bar. . . .

By the time we come to this last line, the *real* New York scene has dissolved, the Menemsha Bar becoming part of an exotic tropical landscape, an imaginary "jungle of impossible eagerness."

"Naphtha" (*CP*, 337–38) displays a similar development:

> Ah Jean Dubuffet
> when you think of him
> doing his military service in the Eiffel Tower
> as a meteorologist
> in 1922
> you know how wonderful the 20th Century
> can be
> and the gaited Iroquois on the girders
> fierce and unflinching-footed
> nude as they should be
> slightly empty
> like a Sonia Delaunay
> there is a parable of speed

somewhere behind the Indians' eyes
they invented the century with their horses
and their fragile backs
which are dark

Lines 1–7 are perfectly straightforward, but the "and" at the beginning of line 8 is a false connective, for who are these "gaited Iroquois"
who appear "on the girders"? Construction workers who are not afraid
of heights? Statues? The Indian as primitive life source? Or what? And
then the whole tableau turns into a Sonia Delaunay painting which is
"slightly empty." Emptiness, and the concomitant need to maintain
one's "fragile," precarious balance is the keynote here, and so we can
forget all about the Eiffel Tower and shift to the intimate conversation
of the third verse paragraph:

how are you feeling in ancient September
I am feeling like a truck on a wet highway. . . .
apart from love (don't say it)
I am ashamed of my century
for being so entertaining
but I have to smile

Such surprising conjunctions of literal reference and comic fantasy are
typical of O'Hara; he shifts from *real* to *surreal* and back again with
astonishing speed. And this is why his poetry is ultimately so difficult
to imitate. It is easy enough to begin a poem with "It is 12:23 in New
York, a rainy Monday," or "I am walking up Broadway and I meet
Ernie," but without O'Hara's Dada or fantasy context, such empiricism (the literalism of simple Pop Art) becomes monotonous.

2. Proper Names

O'Hara's poetry is, as everyone has remarked, one of constant name-
dropping. Interestingly, proper names are not used very frequently in
the early work. "Easter," with its "razzle-dazzle maggots," "glassy
towns," and "yaks," is a poem of wholly imaginary landscapes, but
"Music" refers to "The Equestrian," "the Mayflower Shoppe," "Bergdorf's," "Park Avenue"—authentic New York settings. By the late

fifties, O'Hara had established an elaborate network of cross-references to close personal friends, artists, film stars, city streets, bars, exotic places, titles of books, movies, operas, and ballets—in short, the name of anyone or anything that happens to come across the poet's path. The following are typical:

> Richard Barthelmess as the "tol'able" boy barefoot and in pants,
> Jeanette MacDonald of the flaming hair and lips and long, long neck,
> Sue Carroll as she sits for eternity on the damaged fender of a car
> and smiles, Ginger Rogers, with her pageboy bob like a sausage
> on her shuffling shoulders, peach-melba-voiced Fred Astaire of the feet,
> Eric von Stroheim, the seducer of mountain-climbers' gasping spouses. . . .
>
> (*CP,* 232)

> Where is Mike Goldberg? I don't know
> he may be in the Village, far below
> or lounging on Tenth Street with the gang. . . .   (*CP,* 301)

> Shirley Goldfarb continues to be Shirley Goldfarb
> and Jane Hazan continues to be Jane Freilicher (I think!)
> and Irving Sandler continues to be the balayeur des artistes
> and so do I (sometimes I think I'm "in love" with painting)
> and surely the Piscine Deligny continues to have water in it
> and the Flore continues to have tables and newspapers   and people under them
> and surely we shall not continue to be unhappy
> we shall be happy
> but we shall continue to be ourselves everything continues to be possible
> René Char, Pierre Reverdy, Samuel Beckett it is possible isn't it
> I love Reverdy for saying yes, though I don't believe it   (*CP,* 329)

One's first response to these endless allusions is that they are part of a tiresome in-joke. Why should we know who Shirley Goldfarb is, or whether Jane Hazan has retained her married name (Freilicher) or where Mike Goldberg is "lounging"? And don't these very private allusions make excessive demands on readers, especially future readers who will need extensive annotation in order to understand a given O'Hara poem?

Perhaps we can answer these questions by looking at some possible sources for this naming technique. Paul Carroll suggests that O'Hara may have been influenced by the Dada poems of Pierre Albert-Birot,[16] translations of which appear in Motherwell's *Dada Painters and Poets* (1951), one of the central source books for the New York poets. "At the Paul Guillaume Gallery," for example, begins:

> The 13th day of November this year of 1917
> We were at Paul Guillaume the negrophile's place
> 108 Faubourg St. Honoré at 8 o'clock
> A short time after we were there
> Along came Apollinaire
> He sat down on a leather chair
> And spoke first of a new art that one day he had implied
> To be a sort of "technepheism"
> To use a very simple term. . . .

Another Albert-Birot poem, "Openings," begins:

> The 1st of March 1919 I was
> at Rosenberg's where Herbin the painter
> Was showing his pictures
> Rue de la Beaume
> It's a street
> Where one sees nothing but stone
> And you ask yourself as you go in
> Are there people there
> You push the little half open door
> And you find some
> Here's Cendrars Hello
> And Soupeault   (you arrive)
> How are you   (I depart)
> Fine Hello Severini
> Good day my friend
> Good day Max Jacob. . . .[17]

How important is it to recognize the names and addresses in these poems? The references to Severini, Apollinaire, and Jacob surely count for something because their conversations, gestures, and manners conjure up the artistic milieu of the time and give the poem an air of authenticity: this *really* happened at a *real* show! The day (1 March 1918) and place (Rosenberg's) are immortalized. But we cannot press much further, for the proper names in these Dada poems do not resonate with meaning. A similar process occurs in Pound's more personal Cantos. In Canto 80, we read:

> which is what I suppose he, Fordie, wanted me to be able to picture
> when he took me to Miss Braddon's
>   (I mean the setting) at Richmond
> But that New York I have found at Périgeux
>   *si com' ad Arli*
> in wake of the sarascen
>   As the "Surrender of Breda" (Velásquez)
> was preceded in fresco at Avignon[18]

O'Hara is squarely in the Pound as well as in the Dada tradition. In the passage cited from "To the Film Industry in Crisis," we do miss a lot of the fun if we aren't familiar with Ginger Rogers–Fred Astaire movies or have never seen an Eric von Stroheim film, and the allusions to Reverdy, Char, and Beckett in "Adieu to Norman" serve to ground the poet's experience even as the reference to "Fordie" (Ford Madox Ford) and Velásquez's *Surrender of Breda* authenticate Pound's artistic world. But in most cases (as in "Where is Mike Goldberg?"), the referential quality of the names is purposely undercut. As Charles Altieri remarks:

> His [O'Hara's] texture of proper names gives each person and detail an identity, but in no way do the names help the reader understand anything about what has been named. To know a lunch counter is called Juliet's Corner or a person O'Hara expects to meet is named Norman is rather a reminder for the reader that the specific details of another's life can appear only as momentary fragments, insisting through their particularity on his alienation from any inner reality they might possess.[19]

This seems to me precisely the point. To give another instance: when one says, "It is 12:20 in New York," one is recognizing that numbers no longer have any mystical significance. In this respect, O'Hara goes one step further than Pound, who still uses historical, literary, and mythological figures as touchstones. In O'Hara's poetry, such touchstones have largely disappeared; only the arts continue to be endowed with a certain value. His poetic world is thus one of immanence rather than transcendence; persons and places, books and films are named because they are central to O'Hara's particular consciousness, but they have no "inner reality." Compare O'Hara's treatment of, say, Jane Freilicher to Yeats's mythologizing portraits of Lionel Johnson or Lady Gregory, and the difference will become clear.

3. Syntactic Ambiguity

One of the central features of O'Hara's style is what Eric Sellin has called, with reference to Reverdy's poetry, "syntactic ambiguity." As we have seen in the case of "Music," O'Hara's poetic structure is a system of nonsequiturs, making use of false connectives and demonstratives, pronouns with shifting referents, dangling conditional clauses, incomplete declarative sentences, confusing temporal and spatial relationships, and so on. Sellin quite rightly calls such ambiguity "irreducible" (as distinguished from the semantic ambiguities discussed by William Empson and his followers), because its effect is "to render two or several contextual meanings simultaneously possible for a given passage."[20] Or, as Ernst Gombrich puts it in a brilliant short discussion of Cubism, "If illusion is due to the interaction of clues and the absence of contradictory evidence, the only way to fight its transforming influence is to make the clues contradict each other and to prevent a coherent image of reality from destroying the pattern in the plane." A Cubist painting resists all our attempts to apply "the test of consistency." "Try as we may to see the guitar or the jug suggested to us as a three-dimensional object and thereby to transform it, we will always come across a contradiction somewhere which compels us to start afresh." By intentionally scrambling his representational clues, the Cubist painter thus forces us "to accept the flat surface with all its tensions."[21] The ambiguity cannot, in other words, be resolved.

This is precisely what happens in O'Hara's poetry which carries on what Sellin calls "the cubist-surrealist esthetic [of] simultaneity" (p. 112). Indeed, if the Surrealists taught O'Hara how to mix semantic spheres, moving from literal to hallucinatory, it is the Cubist or proto-Cubist poets who provide the model for his syntax. Take the following example from Apollinaire's "Zone":

Today you walk through Paris the women are blood-stained
It was and I would prefer not to remember it was during beauty's decline

Surrounded by fervent flames Notre Dame looked at me in Chartres
The blood of your Sacred Heart flooded me in the Montmartre
I am ill from hearing happy words
The love from which I suffer is a shameful sickness
And the image which possesses you makes you survive /
                                        in sleeplessness and anguish
It is always near you this passing image[22]

In this nine-line passage, the present dissolves into the past and
vice-versa without explanation. More important, the "you" of line 1
and "I" of line 2 both refer to the poet, a pattern repeated in lines 6–7.
To further complicate things, the familiar you ("tu") of the opening
lines gives way, in line 4, to the formal "your Sacred Heart" ("votre
Sacré-Coeur"), referring to Christ. Clausal relationships are also obscure: in the first line we have simple juxtaposition of two declarative
sentences without punctuation ("Today you walk through Paris," and
"the women are blood-stained"). These present-tense observations are
now followed by the gnomic "It was" ("Cétait") and a confusing conjunction: "*and* I would prefer not to remember it."

Reverdy's poetry, which O'Hara especially loved,[23] furnishes similar examples. "Trace de Pas" has, as Sellin notes, an interesting example of a "bridge phrase" or, as I prefer to call it, a "floating modifier."

> Five branches have lit up
> The trees hold back their tongues
> By the window
> A head still stuck out
> A new star was going to appear
> Above
> The airplane competed
> With the stars for quickness . . .[24]

Here lines 5–7 are syntactically ambiguous. Does "above" ("Là-haut")
belong with the line that precedes it ("A new star was going to appear
above") or the one that follows ("Above, the airplane competed with
the stars")? The syntax forces us to consider both possibilities.

O'Hara's poetry abounds in such "Cubist" syntax. A few examples
must suffice here.

From First to Second Person:

> yet *I* always loved Baltimore
> the porches which hurt *your* ass
> no, they were the steps
> well, *you* have a wet ass anyway
> if they'd only stop scrubbing   (*CP,* 402)

From First to Third Person:

> I stop for a cheeseburger at JULIET'S
> CORNER. . . .
> and *one* has eaten and *one* walks
> past the magazines with nudes
> and the posters for BULLFIGHT and
> the Manhattan Storage Warehouse
> which they'll soon tear down. *I*
> used to think they had the Armory
> Show there.   (*CP,* 258)

Second-Person Shifts:

> How funny *you* are today New York
> like Ginger Rogers in *Swingtime*
> and St. Bridget's steeple leaning a little to the left
>
> here I have just jumped out of a bed full of V-days
> (I got tired of D-days) and blue *you* there still
> accepts me foolish and free
> all I want is a room up there
> and *you* in it.   (*CP,* 370)

AMBIGUOUS REFERENCE

> *There* I could never be a boy,
> though I rode like a god when the horse reared
> At a cry from mother I fell to my knees!
> *there* I fell, clumsy and sick and good. . . .   (*CP,* 216)

PSEUDO-CONNECTIVES

>   this country
> has everything but *politesse,* a Puerto Rican cab driver says
> *and* five different girls I see
>   look like Piedie Gimbel
> with her blonde hair tossing too   (*CP,* 340)

so the weight
　　　　　of the rain drifting amiably is like a sentimental breeze
and seems to have been invented by a collapsed Kim Novak balloon

yet Janice is helping Kenneth appeal to The Ford Foundation. . . .

(CP, 346)

　　　　　　　　　　　considering
　　　　my growingly more perpetual state *and* how
　　　　can one say that angel in the Frick's wings
　　　　are "attached" if it's a real angel?　　　　*(CP,* 393)

FLOATING MODIFIERS

　　　　the warm walking night
　　　　　　　　　wandering

amusement of darkness. . . .　　　　　　　　　*(CP,* 269)

　　　　First, down the sidewalk
　　　　where laborers feed their dirty
　　　　glistening torsos sandwiches
　　　　and Coca-Cola, *with yellow helmets
　　　　on.* They protect them from falling
　　　　bricks, I guess.　　　　　　　　　*(CP,* 257)

normally I don't think of sounds as colored unless I'm feeling *corrupt*
concrete Rimbaud obscurity of emotion which is simple and very definite
even lasting. . . .　　　　　　　　　　　　　*(CP,* 331)

　　　　Someone else's Leica sitting on the table
　　　　the black kitchen table *I am painting*
　　　　the floor yellow, Bill is painting it. . . .　　　　*(CP,* 393)

SPATIAL AND TEMPORAL DISSOLVES

　　　　now it is dark on 2d Street near the abbatoir
　　　　and a smell as of hair comes up the dovecotes
　　　　as the gentleman poles a pounce of pigeons
　　　　in the lower East Sideness rippling river
　　　　where have you gone, Ashes, and up and out
　　　　where the Sorbonne commissions frigidaires
　　　　from Butor and Buffet and Alechinsky storages
　　　　Beauty! said Vera Prentiss-Simpson to Pal Joe
　　　　and the hideaway was made secure against the hares　　*(CP,* 324)

I walk through the luminous humidity
passing the House of Seagram with its wet
and its loungers and the construction to
the left that closed the sidewalk if
I ever get to be a construction worker
I'd like to have a silver hat please   (*CP*, 335)

When these syntactic and prosodic devices are used in conjunction, we get a poetry of great speed, openness, flexibility, and defiance of expectations. Like the "all-over" painting, an O'Hara lyric often seems intentionally deprived of a beginning, middle, and end; it is an instantaneous performance. Syntactic energy is thus equivalent to the painter's "push and pull"—the spatial tensions that keep a surface alive and moving. The rapid cuts from one spatial or temporal zone to another, moreover, give the poetry its peculiar sense of immediacy: everything is absorbed into the NOW.

4. *The Engaged Self: Personism in Action*

"Personism . . . does not have anything to do with personality or intimacy, far from it." What does O'Hara mean by this enigmatic statement in the Manifesto? And what is the meaning of his frequent slurs on confessional poetry?[25] Let us try to sort out these distinctions.

In O'Hara's major poems, as is surely apparent to even the most casual reader, the first person is ubiquitous. In "Music," the pronoun "I" and its cognates appear ten times in the space of twenty-one lines. Yet, unlike the typical autobiographical poem with its circular structure (present–past–return to the present with renewed insight), "Music" does not explore the speaker's past so as to determine what has made him the person he is; it does not, for that matter, "confess" or "reveal" anything about his inner psychic life. The role of the "I" is to respond rather than to confess—to observe, to watch, to be attentive to things. The poet's ruminations are "Meditations in an Emergency" not "*on* an Emergency"—an important distinction for it suggests that the self, no longer able to detach itself from the objects it perceives, dissolves and becomes part of the external landscape. As in Pasternak's

Safe Conduct, one of O'Hara's favorite books,[26] the "I" fragments into the surfaces it contemplates. Hence the poet can only tell us what he *does* (what books he buys, what he eats, where he is walking, what he is saying and to whom); how he *responds* to external stimuli, whether traffic jams, headlines, nasty remarks made by friends, or a visit to an art gallery; and what he *recalls* (fragments from the past in the form of sharply visualized scenes float up into his conscious mind). But he makes no attempt to reflect upon the larger human condition, to derive meaning from a series of past incidents, or to make judgments upon his former self, as Robert Lowell does in the *Life Studies* poems. Indeed, the past is often so immediate that it becomes the present, as we shall see when we consider some of O'Hara's great memory poems. In this connection, it is interesting to note that O'Hara substitutes titles like "In Memory of My Feelings" for Yeats's "In Memory of Major Robert Gregory" or Lowell's "My Last Afternoon with Uncle Devereux Winslow." It is a matter of reifying a feeling rather than remembering another person or a particular event; in so doing, that feeling becomes part of the poet's present.

Here the shift in pronouns, discussed in the preceding section, is relevant. When O'Hara switches from "I" to "one" in "A Step Away From Them," he enlarges the poem's horizons, making the seemingly personal situation (going for a walk during lunch hour) fictive, theatrical. Rimbaud's "Je est un autre" ("I is somebody else") provides a key to O'Hara's Personism. The poet's "I" is distanced by various devices: self-deprecatory humor, long-angle shots, fantasy—"If I seem to you / to have lavender lips under the leaves of the world. . . ." Again, the confusing second-person references extend the range of the poem, drawing the reader into the situation. "Clasp me in your handkerchief like a tear!" the poet exclaims, and immediately we are drawn into the magic circle. We are *there.*

Kenneth Koch has called the *Collected Poems* "a collection of created moments that illuminate a whole life," and many readers have agreed that the volume is in essence one long poem, that once they began to read O'Hara, they could not put the book down.[27] This suggests to me that "Personism" works in a special way. In the course of the *Collected Poems,* we come to know the speaker very much as we know a friend; we see him in all his moods—exuberant, sensual, ecstatic, playful, interested, attentive, remote, bored, depressed, despairing, alternately loving and bitchy. The more one reads the poems, the more one longs to know how "Frank" will react to a particular event, whether it is a headline, a lovers' quarrel, or a traffic jam. The "aesthetic of attention" invites our response so that ultimately the poet's experience becomes ours.

Perhaps the closest model I can find for O'Hara's lyric voice is that of Mayakovksy, whose poetry O'Hara had been reading avidly since the early fifties.[28] Here is a section from the famous "I Love" of 1922 in the George Reavy translation:

> Adults have much to do.
> Their pockets are stuffed with rubles.
> Love?
> Certainly!
> For about a hundred rubles.
> But I,
> homeless,
> thrust
> my hands
> into my torn pockets
> and slouch about, goggle-eyed.
> Night.
> You put on your best dress.
> You relax with wives and widows.
> Moscow,
> with the ring of its endless Sadovayas
> choked me in its embraces.
> The hearts
> of amorous women
> go tic-toc.
> On a bed of love the partners feel ecstatic.
> Stretched out like Passion Square
> I caught the wild heartbeat of capital cities.[29]

Despite Mayakovsky's straightforward syntax and short lines, his tone looks ahead to O'Hara's. Thus he shifts from flat statement ("Adults have much to do") to an unexpected question and answer ("Love? / Certainly!"), from first person ("But I, / homeless") to second ("You put on your best dress. / You relax with wives and widows"), from present tense (lines 1-14) to past (lines 15-17) and back to the present. The last three lines juxtapose third-person observation (it is not clear whether the poet is himself one of the partners "On a bed of love") to personal recollection, as "Stretched out like Passion Square / I caught the wild heartbeat of capital cities."

The mood of the poem is buoyant, exclamatory, highly emotional. Gradually, Mayakovsky draws the reader into his personal circle so that we too catch "the wild heartbeat of capital cities." And yet "I Love" skirts sentimentality because the poet knows how foolish he is; in the second stanza, we read, "I know where lodges the heart in others. / In the breast—as everyone knows! / But with me / anatomy has gone mad: / nothing but heart / roaring everywhere" (p. 161).

Such rapid transitions from lyricism to buffoonery characterize many of O'Hara's best poems, for example: "Adieu to Norman, Bon Jour to Joan and Jean-Paul," "Poem (Khrushchev is coming on the right day!)," "Mary Desti's Ass," and especially "A True Account of Talking to the Sun at Fire Island," which is O'Hara's adaptation of Mayakovsky's "An Extraordinary Adventure which befell Vladimir Mayakovsky in a Summer Cottage."[30]

To recapitulate: O'Hara's poetry is characterized by a remarkable confluence of styles. Aside from the influence of painting, discussed in the last chapter, and the close bonds between O'Hara's lyric and the arts of film and music, the poems reflect an unusual combination of literary influences. Dada and Surrealism continue to stand behind O'Hara's distinctive imagery—an imagery inclining toward artifice and the landscape of dream. The colloquialism and celebration of ordinary experience recall Williams and, to a lesser extent, the later Auden; but the use of proper names and documentary "evidence" seems to derive from Pound rather than Williams. I have also noted that O'Hara's syntactic structures were influenced by Apollinaire and Reverdy, while his peculiar brand of Personism can be traced back to Mayakovsky, Pasternak, and Rimbaud.[31]

The *Collected Poems* is, in short, a very learned (detractors would say, an eclectic) book. O'Hara's reputation as casual improvisator, unschooled doodler, could hardly miss the mark more completely. Indeed, he used to call aspiring poets who wanted to "tell it like it is," to throw convention to the winds, the "Campfire Boys."[32] His own sense of poetic form was very different. As he once wrote to Bill Berkson with reference to musical composition, "you don't know whether it's a piece or not unless some convention is at least referred to." "There is," he adds, "about as much freedom in the composition of music as there is in a prison recreation yard."[33] Surely "freedom" in poetry has similar limitations.

RESHAPING THE GENRES

One of the special pleasures of reading O'Hara's poetry is to see how the poet reanimates traditional genres. Ode, elegy, pastoral, autobiographical poem, occasional verse, love song, litany—all these turn up in O'Hara's poetry, although his tendency is to parody the model or at least to subvert its "normal" conventions. Let us look at some of the poet's most interesting generic transformations.

1. The "Surreal-Autobiographical" Poem

This group, which includes such poems as "There I Could Never Be a Boy," "In Memory of My Feelings," "Ode to Michael Goldberg ('s Birth and Other Births)," "Crow Hill," and "A Short History of Bill Berkson" has its source in the Romantic tradition. "There I Could Never Be a Boy," for example, with its allusions to Keats's "Endymion" and its echoes of Dylan Thomas's "Fern Hill," is a kind of Wordsworthian portrait of the poet as imaginative child, whose heightened sensibility can create its own worlds ("I rode like a god when the horse reared"; "in the billowing air I was fleet and green / riding blackly through the ethereal night / toward men's words which I gracefully understood"), but who suffers from the terrible repression of adults: "At a cry from mother I fell to my knees!" and "All things are tragic / when a mother watches!" (*CP*, 216–17). This last note is Rimbaldian, recalling "Les poètes de sept ans," and gives a slightly ironic edge to the poet's Romantic vision.

"Ode to Michael Goldberg" similarly presents Wordsworthian moments of vision, but its structure offers a more complex network of variations and oppositions. The mood is alternately somber and light-hearted; events are viewed seriously only to be parodied a moment later. Thus the mowing scene, during which the boy has his first glimpse of sex:

> Yellow morning
> > silent, wet
> > > blackness under the trees over stone walls
> hay smelling faintly of semen. . . . (CP, 291)

is juxtaposed to short, staccato quatrains, comically recalling Frank's first experiences at the movies:

> Karen Morley got shot
> in the back by an arrow
> I think she was an heiress
> it came through her bathroom door. . . .

This scene now modulates into a momentary return to a realistic present: "I'd like to stay / in this field forever / and think of nothing / but these sounds, / these smells and the tickling grasses / "up your ass, Sport," and then dissolves, in turn, into the touching account of the poet's first intimations of his future vocation:

> Up on the mountainous hill
> behind the confusing house
> where I lived, I went each
> day after school and some nights
> with my various dogs. . . .
>
> the wind sounded exactly like
> Stravinsky
> > I first recognized art
> as wildness, and it seemed right,
> > I mean rite, to me
>
> climbing the water tower I'd
> look out for hours in wind
> and the world seemed rounder
> and fiercer and I was happier
> because I wasn't scared of falling off
>
> nor off the horses, the horses!
> to hell with the horses, bay and black (CP, 292)

Here the wind is very much a Romantic image, and lines 12–13 recall Wallace Stevens's "The World is Larger in Summer." Yet the punning (a slightly coy device) on "right" (*Rites of Spring*) parodies the Romantic theme as does the final "to hell with the horses." And the next passage moves away from Romantic heightened consciousness to a Rimbaldian scatological vision of adolescent masturbation:

> what one must do is done in a red twilight
>   on colossally old and dirty furniture with knobs,
>   and on Sunday afternoons you meet in a high place
>   watching the Sunday drivers and the symphonic sadness
>   stopped, a man in a convertible put his hand up a girl's skirt
> and again the twitching odor of hay, like a minor irritation
> that gives you a hardon, and again the roundness of horse noises
>
> (*CP*, 292)

The poem continues to shift ground in this way, passages that detail concrete particulars being foregrounded against a backdrop of more abstract ruminations. The overall structure is reminiscent of *Me II*, Larry Rivers's "painted autobiography," which is, according to Sam Hunter, "composed of small, scattered vignettes of family life from babyhood to full maturity. First family snapshots and then special aspects of illustrated journalism offered Rivers a sense of continuity with the movement of life, while putting the necessary distance between him and events."[34] So too O'Hara absorbs the family snapshot into the larger movement of life so as to create a dynamic composition.

"Ode to Michael Goldberg" is a charming poem, but I myself prefer the enigmatic, elliptical "In Memory of My Feelings" (1956)—in my opinion not only O'Hara's best autobiographical poem, but one of the great poems of our time. Its central theme, the fragmentation and reintegration of the inner self—a self that threatens continually to dissipate under the assault of outer forces—is a familiar Romantic topos, but O'Hara turns the autobiographical convention inside out, fusing fantasy and realism in a painterly collage-poem, whose form is at one with its meaning. Grace Hartigan, to whom "In Memory" is dedicated, suggests that O'Hara's aim in this poem is to define "inner containment"—"how to be *open* but not violated, how *not to panic.*"[35] The structure of the poem embodies this theme; it is an extremely

"open" lyric sequence that nevertheless never gives way to formlessness, never "panics."

O'Hara's actual biography plays a part in the poem, but it is subordinated to a series of hallucinatory visions and memories. The implication all along is that what matters is not what happened but how one
felt or feels about it; the poet writes, after all, in memory of his "feelings." And evanescent as these feelings are, O'Hara unifies his kaleidoscopic visions by repeating certain key images: the hunt (a hunt for
what or for whom?), nautical references (from the gondola of the
opening to the "German prisoners on the *Prinz Eugen*" of Part 4), and
a procession of circus animals, exotic locales (Borneo, Ramadan,
Venice's Grand Canal, the sands of Arabia, Persia, the mountains of
Greece), and Romantic characters (Manfred, the gondolier, Lord
Nelson, Shanghai Lil, a Hittite, an African prince, a "Chinaman
climbing a mountain," "an Indian / sleeping on a scalp.") In the
"midst" of all "these ruses" is the serpent, who stands here for the
poet's true self—the self that must triumph if he is to become an artist.

Part I begins:

> My quietness has a man in it, he is transparent
> and he carries me quietly, like a gondola, through the streets.
> He has several likenesses, like stars and years, like numerals.
>
> (*CP*, 252)

This enigmatic passage is best understood in terms of Rimbaud's concept of the "dédoublement du moi," the split between the ordinary,
empirical ego and the poet's created self. Rimbaud, for that matter,
stands squarely behind the poem, Part 4 echoing the catalogue of
assumed selves in Part IV of "Enfance."[36] Another probable source is
Apollinaire's "Cortège," in which the self is painfully assembled from
bits and pieces of the poet's past identities. At the outset, then, Frank
O'Hara the "poet" is still dominated by Frank O'Hara the man who
carries him "quietly, like a gondola, through the streets." He has not
yet articulated poetic speech; it is only a "quietness," containing "a
number of naked selves," longing to emerge but kept in check by "so
many pistols I have borrowed to protect myselves / from creatures
who too readily recognize my weapons / and have murder in their
heart!"

The "I" thus regards himself as victim but of whom or of what? The would-be murderers are especially frightening because they are wholly disguised: "in winter / they are warm as roses, in the desert / taste of chilled anisette." When the poet tries to escape his condition by assuming the role of Byron's Manfred, climbing to the mountain top "into the cool skies," he is attacked from all sides:

> An elephant takes up his trumpet
> money flutters from the windows of cries, silk stretching its mirror
> across shoulder blades. A gun is "fired."   (*CP*, 253)

And now, in a passage reminiscent of the "Circe" episode in *Ulysses,* the poet remembers moments of unspecified but terrible humiliation:

>   One of me rushes
> to window #13 and one of me raises his whip and one of me
> flutters up from the center of the track amidst the pink flamingoes
> and underneath their hooves as they round the last turn my lips
> are scarred and brown, brushed by tails, masked in dirt's lust,
> definition, open mouths gasping for the cries of the bettors for the lungs
> of earth.
>   So many of my transparencies could not resist the race!

After this nightmare scene, with its strong overtones of sexual fear, there is only emptiness, a self in fragments: "dried mushrooms, pink feathers, tickets, / a flaking moon drifting across the muddied teeth." The image of the serpent appears for the first time, and the "I" identifies with it, but this serpent does not yet have power. A victim of "the hunter," its eyes "redden at sight of those thorny fingernails," and "My transparent selves / flail about like vipers in a pail, writhing and hissing." Finally, the "acquiline serpent comes to resemble the Medusa." Part 1 ends on a note of death; the poet's old self must die if it is to be reborn.

In the poem's opening movement, memory thus appears in the guise of surrealistic fantasy, frightening in its very indeterminacy. The perspective of Part 2 is, by contrast, that of more straightforward autobiography, the connecting link between the two occurring in the opening lines: "The dead hunting / and the alive, ahunted."

> My father, my uncle,
> my grand-uncle and the several aunts. My
> grand-aunt dying for me, like a talisman, in the war,
> before I had even gone to Borneo. . . .   (*CP,* 253)

The irony, of course, is that these relatives did not die "for" the poet at all, but that their death was supposed to pain and trouble him whereas his recollection of the group merely resembles "the coolness of a mind / like a shuttered suite in the Grand Hotel / where mail arrives for my incognito." "Trying desperately to count them as they die" becomes a meaningless exercise: this is the way memory does not, indeed cannot operate.

But how to transcend "these numbers"? In Part 3, the speaker chooses one option: he assumes the role of hero. Like the "moi" of Rimbaud's *Saison en enfer,* he reappears as noble savage in the deserts of Arabia ("The most arid stretch is often the richest"), swallows "the stench of the camel's spit," and then reappears in a series of guises: French Revolutionary, Napoleonic platoon leader, and finally as "meek subaltern . . . violating an insane mistress." These various roles merge in a hallucinatory sequence, the mistress now following the poet "across the desert / like a goat, towards a mirage . . . and lying in an oasis one day, / playing catch with coconuts, they suddenly smell oil."

Absorption in history is one way of escaping the empirical self: "Beneath these lives / the ardent lover of history hides." But the moment doesn't last and in Part 4, we switch, once again, to the real Frank O'Hara visiting Chicago with Jane Freilicher ("the fountains! the Art Institute, the Y / for both sexes, absent Christianity"), a Frank who is enchanted by an early morning vision (before Jane is up) of a Norwegian freighter on the "copper lake," "on the deck a few dirty men . . . Beards growing, and the constant anxiety over looks." Remembering Grace Hartigan's portraits of himself,[37] he now merges his identity with that of the seamen. And out of this fusion, the poet achieves the breakthrough he has longed for all along:

> Grace
> to be born and live as variously as possible. The conception
> of the masque barely suggests the sordid identifications.
> I am a Hittite in love with a horse I don't know what blood's

in me I feel like an African prince I am a girl walking downstairs
in a red pleated dress with heels I am a champion taking a fall
I am a jockey with a sprained ass-hole I am the light mist
                              in which a face appears
and it is another face of blonde I am a baboon eating a banana
I am a dictator looking at his wife I am a doctor eating a child
and the child's mother smiling I am a Chinaman climbing a mountain
I am a child smelling his father's underwear I am an Indian
sleeping on a scalp
                    and my pony is stamping in the birches,
and I've just caught sight of the *Niña,* the *Pinta* and the *Santa Maria.*
                    What land is this, so free?   (*CP,* 256)

In the first version (1955) of this passage, O'Hara arranged these
images in four 4-line stanzas, each having the refrain "What land is
this, so free?" which appears only once in the final draft. The first
stanza, for instance, went like this:

> I don't know what blood's in me
> I feel like an African prince
> I am a girl walking downstairs
> in a red pleated dress with heels
>   what land is this, so free?

(See Notes to the *CP,* 538)

By running together two clauses in one line on the one hand, and
breaking a clause in half at a line-end, on the other, O'Hara stresses the
multiplicity of selves, the chaos and plenitude of life which cannot be
presented in the orderly little ballad stanzas of the original. In a moment of heightened consciousness, the poet is able to assume all roles:
he turns Indian, catching sight of the *Niña, Pinta,* and *Santa Maria,*
and watching the white men arrive (again an echo of Rimbaud's "Les
blancs débarquent" ["the white men are landing!"] in the *Saison*). And
these white men bring him, not a real horse (no more camels, goats, or
elephants!) but "the horse I fell in love with on the frieze"—in short, a
work of art.

In this moment of ecstasy, the fragmented self, victimized by nameless attackers, is reborn: "And now it is the serpent's turn. / I am not
quite you, but almost, the opposite of visionary." So begins Part 5. The

"visionary" is no longer needed, for what the poet has learned is that to be an artist is to come to terms with life itself: "When you turn your head / can you feel your heels, undulating? that's what it is / to be a serpent." Now "the heart . . . bubbles with red ghosts, since to move is to love." The poet can now reject the hero figure of Part 3: "The hero, trying to unhitch his parachute, / stumbles over me. It is our last embrace." Out of the body comes the "cancerous statue" which is the poet's real self, which "against my will / against my love" has "become art." And the poem concludes triumphantly:

> and I have lost what is always and everywhere
> present, the scene of my selves, the occasion of these ruses,
> which I myself and singly must now kill
> > and save the serpent in their midst.

> > > > *(CP, 257)*

Few poets of our time, I would posit, could manage the difficult structural and textural modulations of this poem, its swift and sudden transitions from long flowing line to short choppy one, from romantic melody to jazz syncopation, from fact to fantasy, past to present, self to other, nightmare landscape to the direct presentation of things. The French influence is as important as ever, but it is now thoroughly domesticated, absorbed into the fabric of colloquial American idiom: "My / 12 years since they all died, philosophically speaking" or "I'm looking for my Shanghai Lil." And on every rereading, some new marvelous detail strikes our attention. Notice how the "barrage balloon" of Part One's hunting scene reappears, quite unexpectedly, as the hero's parachute in Part 5. The poem ends on what Grace Hartigan has called a note of "inner containment"; the "serpent self" triumphs over "the occasion of these ruses."

2. Poems for Emergent Occasions: The "I do this, I do that" Poem

What are probably O'Hara's best known poems—"Adieu to Norman, Bon Jour to Joan and Jean-Paul," "A Step Away from Them," "Personal Poem," "Lana Turner has Collapsed!"—all belong to the genre of the occasional poem, although with rare exception, the occasion is not an important public one (or even a pivotal private event like a wedding or a *bon voyage* party), but an ordinary incident like a luncheon date or a weekend beach party.

Such occasional poetry gave O'Hara a chance to display his wonderful sense of humor. "Khrushchev is coming on the right day!", for example, explores the essential absurdity of our responses to the latest news. The poem is not really about Khrushchev at all; rather, it pokes fun at the American desire to make foreign dignitaries, especially from an alien country like Russia, feel "at home" in the United States. Even a dour leader like Khrushchev, a person who probably mistrusts all things American, the poem implies, will have to be pleased with New York on such a marvelous September day, a day on which "the cool graced light / is pushed off the enormous glass piers by hard wind / and everything is tossing, hurrying on up" (*CP,* 340). The irony, of course, is that Khrushchev himself couldn't care less; he has hardly come to America in order to savor the fall weather. But the poet's own mood is one of such buoyancy, such *joie de vivre,* that he wants even Khrushchev to enjoy his visit, and so, when the Puerto Rican cab driver complains to him that "this country / has everything but *politesse,*" the poet thinks, in a marvelously silly nonsequitur, that "Khrushchev was probably being carped at / in Washington, no *politesse.*" Ultimately, the poem implies, none of it matters; what matters is that it is one of those rare New York mornings when one actually loves walking to work because "the light seems to be eternal / and joy seems to be inexorable." And so the train that "bears Khrushchev on to Pennsylvania Station" becomes part of the "tossing," "blowing" life of the city, ultimately merging with the "hard wind."

Yet O'Hara's own attitude to his improvisatory occasional poems is curiously equivocal. In a letter to Fairfield Porter, he contrasts his own work to John Ashbery's with reference to the two sons (the "bad" one played by Frank's idol, James Dean) in the film *East of Eden:*

> I think one of the things about *East of Eden* is that I am very materialistic and John is very spiritual, in our work especially. As an example, the one boy gives the father $5000 he has earned by war-profiteering in beans for a birthday present, but the good boy gives him the announcement of his engagement which symbolizes the good life the father wants for both

sons. John's work is full of dreams and a kind of moral excellence and kind sentiments. Mine is full of objects for their own sake, spleen and ironically intimate observation which may be truthfulness (in the lyrical sense) but is more likely to be egotistical cynicism masquerading as honesty.[38]

This is unnecessarily harsh self-criticism, although the distinction O'Hara makes between his own mode and Ashbery's is not entirely beside the point. I shall return to this distinction in the next chapter. In any case, although some of O'Hara's lesser poems may suffer from what he calls "egotistical cynicism masquerading as honesty," his "ironically intimate observation" usually transforms life into art, preventing "objects" from being treated merely "for their own sake." Certainly this is the case in the witty Khrushchev poem.

My personal favorite among O'Hara's occasional poems is "Joe's Jacket," which was published in *Big Table* in 1960 but was not included in *Lunch Poems*. This poem was written during the summer of 1959 when Frank lived with Joe LeSueur at 441 East 9th Street. It was the summer he met and fell in love with Vincent Warren. This is the background of the poem which is "about" a weekend houseparty in Southampton and alludes obliquely to the complex set of relationships between Frank, Vincent, and Joe, as well as to Frank's long-standing literary friendship with Kenneth Koch and his wife Janice.

On the surface, "Joe's Jacket" is like a Scott Fitzgerald short story in miniature: the summer weekend parlor-car ride to Southampton, the drunken party, the morning after the night before, the return to the hot city, the Monday morning hangover. But these incidents are presented in a series of separate "shots," reminiscent less of Fitzgerald than of a film like Godard's *Weekend*. In this connection, the poem's metrics are especially ingenious. The whole "story" is told as if in one long breath. The poem's long (13-20-syllable) lines are almost wholly unpunctuated and almost all run-on; there is not a single full stop in the space of fifty-two lines. Once we have "entrained" with Frank, Jap, and Vincent, therefore, we cannot really stop until the whirlwind weekend is over. Yet this "action poem" simulates speed and acceleration by careful structural means; it is a good example of the "push and pull" technique O'Hara alludes to in his letter to Larry Rivers.

The poem opens on a note of pleasurable anticipation:

> Entraining to Southampton in the parlor car with Jap and Vincent, I
> see life as a penetrable landscape lit from above
> like it was in my Barbizonian kiddy days when automobiles
> were owned by the same people for years and the Alfa Romeo
> was only a rumor under the leaves beside the viaduct and I
> pretending to be adult felt the blue within me and the light up there
> no central figure me, I was some sort of cloud or a gust of wind
> at the station a crowd of drunken fishermen on a picnic Kenneth
> is hard to find but we find, through all the singing, Kenneth smiling
> it is off to Janice's bluefish and the incessant talk of affection
> expressed as excitability and spleen to be recent and strong
> and not unbearably right in attitude, full of confidences
> now I will say it, thank god, I knew you would   (*CP*, 329)

En route in the train with Jap (Jasper Johns) and Vincent, the poet feels euphoric and light-hearted; his is, at least for the moment, a stable and secure world. Like a painting of the Barbizon school, whose source of light comes from a definite point, his "landscape" seems "penetrable" as he recalls the orderly days of his childhood "when automobiles / were owned by the same people for years," and he "felt the blue" within himself. Blue is O'Hara's favorite color; a whole essay could be devoted to its appearances and uses in the *Collected Poems*. To feel "the blue within" oneself is to be free, happy, imaginative; to become, further, "some sort of cloud or gust of wind" is again a Romantic image of creative fulfillment. And even the dinner Janice has prepared is "bluefish."

It is interesting to note how different this whole passage is from the poems of O'Hara's mentors and contemporaries. The phrase "life as penetrable landscape" immediately recalls "Life changed to landscape" in Robert Lowell's "Beyond the Alps," but Frank's train ride is not a symbolic journey from the old world to the new; it is merely a trip on the Long Island Railroad. Again, "Joe's Jacket" marks a certain withdrawal from the Williams mode of O'Hara's earlier poems; for, whereas Williams would have captured the sense of the permanent moment in all its perceptual immediacy, O'Hara rapidly shifts from the present to the past and, later in the poem, to the future, absorbing both past and future into what happens *now*. And finally, despite its air of documentary realism, the opening scene of "Joe's Jacket" is some-how fantastic, with its dreamlike image of the Alfa Romeo, "only a rumor under the leaves beside the viaduct," and its condensed, amusingly devious account of the dinner conversation, where it is never clear who says what, the whole tone of the exchange being captured by the running together of verbal snatches: "now I will say it, thank god, I knew you would."

The "excitability and spleen" which begin to surface toward the end of this section come into the foreground in Part 2, which depicts "an enormous party mesmerizing comers in the disgathering light." Notice that the "light," previously coming from a known source, is now "disgathering." And Frank's memories of his "Barbizonian kiddy days" now give way to a drinking marathon:

> I drink to smother my sensitivity for a while so I won't stare away
> I drink to kill the fear of boredom, the mounting panic of it
> I drink to reduce my seriousness so a certain spurious charm
> can appear and win its flickering little victory over noise
> I drink to die a little and increase the contrast of this questionable moment
> and then I am going home, purged of everything except anxiety and selfdistrust
> now I will say it, thank god, I knew you would

When this last line is repeated, it no longer sounds good-humored or light-hearted. Something nasty and unexplained has happened, but we never learn what it is. A lovers' quarrel? An insult? A misunder-standing? A general feeling of malaise, of being unloved? In any case, it appropriately begins to rain.

Now this scene dissolves in its turn, giving way to the hour before dawn; the "enormous party" gives way to "an enormous window morning." The wind returns but the poet now views its force with total despair: "the beautiful desperation of a tree / fighting off strangula-tion." His bed has "an ugly calm"; the book he reaches for contains D. H. Lawrence's "The Ship of Death"; in the next line, ship and bed merge as the poet begins "slowly to drift and then to sink." Just as he reaches this low point, "the car horn mysteriously starts to honk, no one is there / and Kenneth comes out and stops it in the soft green lightless stare." This last phrase recalls Wallace Stevens's Green Night: it is the time of creativity and before we know it, Frank and Kenneth are working away on the latter's libretto, totally absorbed in their task. Frank's anxiety is temporarily dispelled: "I did not drift / away I did not die I am there with Haussmann and the rue de Rivoli / and the spirits of beauty, art and progress, pertinent and mobile / in their worldly way, and musical and strange the sun comes out."

The beauty of "Joe's Jacket" is that the poem refuses to end on this high Romantic note. Sunrise is all very well, but "Entraining" invariably means "returning," and so the fourth stanza begins:

> returning by car the forceful histories of myself and Vincent loom
> like the city hour after hour closer and closer to the future I am here

"I am here" counterpointed to the words "I am there," four lines above, is especially poignant. The poet realizes that he is not part of the exciting Paris art world; he is *here*. There is no escape. But returning to Joe (nothing is said of Vincent's departure or subsequent movements) has its comforts: "Joe is still up and we talk / only of the immediate present." At 4 A.M., the "sleeping city" is "bathed in an unobtrusive light which lends things / coherence and an absolute." This "unobtrusive light" replaces the earlier extremes; it is the light of common day, of neutrality, of things as they are in our normal, everyday lives. As such, it does lend things a kind of "coherence."

And so, in Part 5, the poet, now all alone after Joe has finally gone to bed, prepares "for the less than average" working day. The word "calm" is repeated three times within two lines, but this is not the pleasant tranquility of the parlor car; it is the calm of empty routine, dead ritual. Frank can only face the day by wearing Joe's seersucker jacket, a jacket he last wore on a European holiday:

> there it was on my Spanish plaza back
> and hid my shoulders from San Marco's pigeons was jostled on the /
> Kurfürstendamm
> and sat opposite Ashes in an enormous leather chair in the Continental
> (*CP*, 330)

Rome, Venice, Berlin, Paris with John Ashbery—Joe's jacket has seen him through all these places:

it is all enormity and life it has protected me and kept me here on
many occasions as a symbol does when the heart is full and risks no speech
a precaution I loathe as the pheasant loathes the season and is preserved
it will not be need, it will be just what it is and just what happens

Only now do we understand the title of the poem. "Joe's Jacket" is the talisman that protects Frank from daily misfortunes; as a synecdoche, it stands, of course, for Joe's love. But Frank also resents its protection ("a precaution I loathe"), and in a second, ironic sense, Joe's jacket is his straitjacket: "Entraining" with Vincent, he ultimately returns to Joe. The jacket is, then, an ordering principle which the poet alternately needs and resents.

"In Memory of My Feelings" explores the artist's need to protect his "naked selves" from external chaos. "Joe's Jacket" has a related theme: how to order one's life somehow, how to ward off anxiety in favor of some kind of coherence. But because this is a poem about the life of an artist, "order" is always to be distinguished from mere routine. The poet goes through the routine of "rising for the less than average day," and having his coffee, but he must fight routine just as he previously fought "anxiety and self-distrust." Happiness comes in those moments when life and art are one, when Frank and Kenneth work in harmony on the opera libretto while the rest of the household is asleep. Such moments of "soft green lightless[ness]" redeem life, but they are rare. Most of the time, one can only cope by accepting "just what it is and just what happens." And "what happens" is that Frank pursues Vincent, quarrels with Kenneth and his friends, and returns, worn out, to Joe. The tension between *just what is* and what one yearns for ("I am here"—"I am there") is beautifully dramatized in this most seemingly spontaneous but most carefully structured "I do this, I do that" poem.

3. Odes

In a reading given at Buffalo on 25 September 1964, O'Hara prefaced his rendition of "Ode on Lust" with the remark, "I wrote it because the ode is so formidable to write. I thought if I call it an ode it will work out."[39] This comment, facetious though it is, sheds some light on the group of long poems written in 1957–58 and published by the Tiber Press in 1960 under the title *Odes*. There are, of course, earlier as well as later odes scattered throughout the *Collected Poems* (and such long litanies as "To the Film Industry in Crisis" and "Ave Maria" also properly belong to this class); the term "ode," moreover, is used fairly loosely. "Ode to Michael Goldberg" is, as I have argued, an autobiographical poem on the Wordsworthian model; "Ode (to Joseph LeSueur) on the Arrow that Flieth by Day" resembles such occasional poems as "A Step Away from Them" and "Adieu to Norman." Nevertheless, most of the "odes" in the Tiber Press book do have certain common characteristics that merit discussion.

Such poems as "Ode to Joy," "Ode on Lust," and "Ode to Willem de Kooning" reveal a very different side of O'Hara from the one we have considered so far. Their tone is more oracular, impersonal, and exclamatory, their syntax insistently paratactic (the "and" clauses piling up to create an almost unbearable intensity), their prosody more formal and elaborate than is typical of O'Hara. "Ode to Joy" (*CP*, 281), for example, has traces of the Greater or Pindaric Ode. Not that its three stanzas resemble the Pindaric model (strophe—antistrophe—epode), but the subject is "elevated" (the triumph of love over time), the tone sublime, and the three "strophes" have an intricate and elaborate prosodic scheme. Each strophe has thirteen lines, longer lines alternating with somewhat shorter ones in a fixed pattern, with the final line invariably having only four or five syllables and two stresses. In each strophe, lines 2, 4, 7, 8, 12, and 13 are indented. The phrase "no more dying," which appears in the opening line, becomes the refrain, reappearing after the first strophe and again at the end of the ode. Thus, although O'Hara's strophes contain neither rhyme nor meter, and although enjambment is used so consistently that the integrity of the individual line is somewhat obscured, the overall pattern is considerably more formal than that of, say, "The Arrow that Flieth by Day." Certainly, its visual appearance on the page is very tidy, the three strophes looking exactly alike.

"Ode on Lust" (*CP*, 282) has a similarly structured visual pattern. Three boxlike stanzas whose lines have six to eight syllables are juxtaposed to two long, snakelike couplets, in which the lines range from seventeen to twenty-three syllables; the third "box" is followed by a kind of coda, made up of five such long lines. The effect is to create what looks like a composition for solo voice and chorus, the "long line" sections responding to the short, abrupt ones.

Thematically, these odes are curious for their avoidance of Personism; they are perhaps closer to such earlier long poems as "Second Avenue" and "Easter." "Ode to Joy" is a celebration of erotic love, of sexual bliss as a way of defying death. This theme is insistently Romantic but O'Hara's imagery is often surrealistic:

> and the streets will be filled with racing forms
> and the photographs of murderers and narcissists and movie stars
>   will swell from the walls and books alive in steaming rooms
>   to press against our burning flesh not once but interminably
> as water flows down hill into the full-lipped basin
> and the adder dives for the ultimate ostrich egg
> and the feather cushion preens beneath a reclining monolith
>   that's sweating with post-exertion visibility and sweetness
>   near the grave of love
>   No more dying

The "reclining monolith / that's sweating with post-exertion visibility and sweetness" is a sly sexual image reminiscent of a Miró painting; the poem contains many such comic-erotic images, thus undercutting its own high Romanticism:

> in the sky a feeling of intemperate fondness will excite the birds
>   to swoop and veer like flies crawling across absorbèd limbs
> that weep a pearly perspiration on the sheets of brief attention
> and the hairs dry out that summon anxious declaration of the organs
>   as they rise like buildings to the needs of temporary neighbors
>   pouring hunger through the heart to feed desire in intravenous ways

Yet despite this injection of parody, "Ode to Joy" is essentially quite serious about its theme: only the ecstasy of loving, the "lava flow[ing]" of sexual consummation has the power to make "Buildings . . . go up in the dizzy air," to "ride . . . heroes through the dark to found / great cities where all life is possible to maintain as long as time," to turn even "the grave of love" into "a lovely sight." "No more dying."

The finest of the 1957–58 odes is, I think, the "Ode on Causality" (*CP*, 302–03). This poem begins on an ironic note with the aphorism, "There is the sense of neurotic coherence," and we soon learn that there is no sense of any kind of coherence, the notion of causality being comically deflated in the last strophe: "what goes up must / come down, what dooms must do, standing still and walking in New York."

After the opening series of witty, seemingly unrelated aphorisms, there is an abrupt shift to a scene at the grave of Jackson Pollock. (In an earlier version, the poem was called "Ode at the Grave of Jackson Pollock," and Donald Allen notes that lines 8–9, in which the little girl Maude shows the poet Pollock's grave, refer to its actual location at the Springs near Easthampton, Long Island [*CP*, 542]). The sight of the grave and the child's comment that " 'he isn't under there, he's out in the woods' " leads to a moment of transcendence as the poet prays for his own artistic powers:

> and like that child at your grave make me be distant and imaginative
> make my lines thin as ice, then swell like pythons
> the color of Aurora when she first brought fire to the Arctic in a sled
> a sexual bliss inscribe upon the page of whatever energy I burn for art
> and do not watch over my life, but read and read through copper earth
>
> not to fall at all, but disappear or burn! seizing a grave by throat
> which is the look of earth, its ambiguity of light and sound. . . .
>
>   (*CP*, 302)

After rejecting the usual trappings of funeral rites ("for Old Romance was draping dolors on a scarlet mound"), O'Hara concludes by celebrating the great painter in terms of his own art:

> let us walk in that nearby forest, staring into the growling trees
> in which an era of pompous frivolity or two is dangling /
>   its knobby knees
> and reaching for an audience
>   over the pillar of our deaths a cloud
> heaves
>   pushed, steaming and blasted
>   love-propelled and tangled /
>   glitteringly
>   has earned himself the title *Bird in Flight.*

The oracular, exclamatory mode of "Ode on Causality" and "Ode to Joy" ("make me be distant and imaginative / make my lines thin as ice, then swell like pythons") recalls neither Wordsworth nor Keats but the Shelley of "Ode to the West Wind" or perhaps the Collins of "Ode on the Poetical Character." But to be perfectly accurate, we would have to say that O'Hara's model is Shelley-cum-Dada, for the "Ode on Causality," like the "Ode to Joy," frequently injects comic burlesque elements like the following:

> sweet scripts to obfuscate the tender subjects of their future lays
> to be layed at all! romanticized, elaborated, fucked, sung, put to "rest"
> is worse than the mild apprehension of a Buddhist type caught halfway up
> the tea-rose trellis with his sickle banging on the Monk's lead window. . . .

Here the pun on "lays," the four-letter words, and the absurd image of the Buddhist and the Monk deflate the lyric intensity of the earlier passage. But in ending his ode with the rhapsodic reference to the painter's apotheosis (he becomes a work of art),[40] the poet recaptures his original ecstasy.

"Ode on Causality" thus provides us with an interesting example of the fusion between disparate modes and conventions. The basic structure of the ode is the "free Pindaric" of Cowley as adapted by Collins and Shelley, but such imagistic passages as "Maude lays down her doll" derive from quite different sources—in this case, Rimbaud's "Enfance, Part II," which begins: "That's she, the little dead girl, behind the rose bushes." At the same time, the aphorisms ("suddenly everyone's supposed to be veined, like marble" or "the rock is the least living of the forms man has fucked"), as well as the passage punning on *lays* which I cited above, introduce a Dada note; they recall Tzara or Apollinaire. The total effect of the poem is that of a Brahms or Schumann *lied,* interrupted at certain junctures by "noise" passages in the vein of Satie or Cage. Such conjunctions are wholly characteristic of O'Hara's lyricism.

4. Love Poems

Finally, I wish to say something about the remarkable series of love poems written for Vincent Warren between 1959 and 1961. O'Hara had been writing love poems ever since his Harvard days, but it was not until he fell in love with the beautiful dancer in 1959 that what he himself called "my delicate and caressing poems" (*CP*, 356) were perfected. These forty-odd erotic lyrics should be read in sequence, although they are not found that way in the chronologically arranged *Collected Poems*.[41] The range of moods from sexual excitement, joy, and hope, to loneliness, delusion, despair, and cynicism, and finally to the stoical acceptance of the way things are is extraordinary. Even such seemingly trivial little songs as "Did you see me walking by the Buick Repairs" (*CP*, 367) repay study. This particular short lyric, with its intricate repetition ("I was thinking of you") and foreshortened last line—"and right now"—recalls Yeats's famed "A Deep-sworn Vow."

The risk of the intimate erotic lyric is that the poet is too close to his own experience to objectify it; in O'Hara's words, "sentiment is always intruding on form" (*CP*, 276). And we do find cases in the Vincent Warren sequence where the sentiment is stated too flatly:

> When I am feeling depressed or anxious sullen
> all you have to do is take your clothes off
> and all is wiped away revealing life's tenderness. . . .
>
> when I am in your presence I feel life is strong
> and will defeat all its enemies and all of mine
> and all of yours and yours in you and mine in me. . . .
>
> (*CP*, 349)

Or again, the poem may succumb to triviality:

> I want some bourbon / you want some oranges / I love the leather
> jacket Norman gave me
> and the corduroy coat David
> gave you, it is more mysterious than spring. . . .   (*CP*, 356)

And occasionally, there is an irritating note of campy cuteness:

> everything
>
> seems slow suddenly and boring except
> for my insatiable thinking towards you
> as you lie asleep completely plotzed and
> gracious as a hillock in the mist. . . .   (*CP*, 354)

But for the most part, the Vincent Warren poems do work because O'Hara defines his sexual longing or sexual pleasure in terms of witty and fantastic hyperbole. He rarely resorts to that stock-in-trade of what I have elsewhere called "corn-porn" poetry[42]—that is, the elaborate metaphor in which the lover's penis is compared to a firehose on a burning deck, the vagina to a cave full of roses, and so on. Rather, his analogies are intentionally absurd; witness the following epigrammatic lyric:

> Some days I feel that I exude a fine dust
> like that attributed to Pylades in the famous
> *Chronica nera areopagitica* when it was found
>
> and it's because an excavationist has
> reached the inner chamber of my heart
> and rustled the paper bearing your name
>
> I don't like that stranger sneezing over our love   (*CP,* 366)

Here the pseudo-learned reference to the recently excavated Greek statue, still "exud[ing] a fine dust," provides the poet with a playful twist on a very familiar theme: the longing to keep one's love all to oneself.

Or again, "To You" (*CP,* 342), which begins as a very conventional love poem with the lines, "What is more beautiful than night / and someone in your arms," shifts ground in the third line to an entirely different frame of reference, the poet now burlesquing his romantic overture:

> that's what we love about art
> it seems to prefer us and stays
>
> if the moon or a gasping candle
> sheds a little light or even dark
> you become a landscape in a landscape
> with rocks and craggy mountains
>
> and valleys full of sweaty ferns
> breathing and lifting into the clouds. . . .

So the landscape of love is defamiliarized, becoming a valley "full of sweaty ferns."

The ability to transform ordinary experience in this way is nowhere more evident than in "You are Gorgeous and I'm Coming" (*CP*, 331), an acrostic poem in which the first letters of successive lines spell out the name Vincent Warren. Here is the first or "Vincent" half:

Vaguely I hear the purple roar of the torn-down Third Avenue El
it sways slightly but firmly like a hand or a golden-downed thigh
normally I don't think of sounds as colored unless I'm feeling corrupt
concrete Rimbaud obscurity of emotion which is simple and very definite
even lasting, yes it may be that dark and purifying wave, /
                           the death of boredom
nearing the heights themselves may destroy you in the pure air
to be further complicated, confused, empty but refilling, exposed to light

Here the love scene becomes a fantastic blend of real and imaginary objects, noises, colors, and movements; such images as "the purple roar of the torn-down Third Avenue El" which "sways lightly but firmly like a hand or a golden-downed thigh" have intensely erotic overtones, but the poet's orgasm is never described overtly. Rather, the long, unpunctuated, sinewy lines with their run-on clauses and condensed catalogues of nouns and adjectives ("corrupt / concrete Rimbaud obscurity of emotion") convey the lover's passion ("empty but refilling," "thundering and shaking") as it moves toward a final crescendo in the poem's last line, which is distinguished by its eleven monosyllables, its repetition of words and sounds (especially voiceless stops), and its internal rhyme (st*ar*s, *are*, f*or*, *our*), to create a stunning cadenza:

newly the heavens stars all out we are all for the captured time of our being

The same technique informs "Poem (Twin spheres full of fur and noise)," although this one begins with a graphic (and some would say, distasteful) description:

              Twin spheres full of fur and noise
              rolling softly up my belly beddening on my chest
              and then my mouth is full of suns
              that softness seems so anterior to that hardness. . . .   (*CP*, 405)

If the piece continued in this vein, it would be just another self-indulgent poem, elaborating unnecessarily on what the poet does in bed. But O'Hara rapidly transforms the "Twin spheres" into celestial bodies, and what began as a description of fellatio becomes a parody Sun God myth:

> jetting I commit the immortal spark jetting
> you give that form to my life the Ancients loved
> those suns are smiling as they move across the sky
> and as your chariot I soon become a myth
> which heaven is it that we inhabit for so long a time
> it must be discovered soon and disappear   (*CP*, 406)

The poet knows he is no Helios driving his golden chariot across the sky; he is not even the golden chariot. But it's nice to think that love confers immortality upon himself and Vincent, even if "the immortal spark" lasts only a moment.

The sense of tentativeness introduced in the poem's last line ("it must be discovered soon and disappear") is found again and again in these love poems, the ecstatic tone of "You are Gorgeous and I'm Coming" giving way, more often than not, to a rueful, self-deprecatory one. "Present," for example, is a kind of parody version of Donne's "The Good Morrow" or "The Extasie"; images of celestial spheres and heavenly bodies are again used as points of reference, but the poet knows he and Vincent are, at best, sublunary lovers, and even then, all too often their paths don't cross, although Frank likes to imagine that they can and do:

>   even now I can lean
> forward across the square and see
> your surprised grey look become greener
> as I wipe the city's moisture from
> your face
>   and you shake the snow
> off onto my shoulder, light as a breath. . . .   (*CP*, 353)

The longing to be with the beloved affords "some peculiar insight," but when the poet supplicates the heavens, he is greeted only by "the mixed-up air."

Perhaps the most moving of the Vincent Warren poems is "St. Paul

and All That" (*CP*, 406). It concerns the brief reunion of the lovers at a
time when Frank already knows that their love is doomed, that his love
is greater than Vincent's. The poem traces the graph of the poet's
shifting emotions as he unexpectedly finds Vincent in his room:

> Totally abashed and smiling
> > > I walk in
> > > sit down and
> > > face the frigidaire
>
> > it's April
> > no May
> > it's May
>
> such little things have to be established in morning
> after the big things of night
> > > do you want me to come?

"Totally abashed and smiling" (a phrase picked up later in the poem
in the line "full of anxious pleasures and pleasurable anxiety"), Frank
tries to act normal: "I walk in / sit down and / face the frigidaire" (the
reception is evidently cold!), but he is so excited that he can't remember "little things" like whether it's April or May. He goes over in his
mind all the meaningful statements he was going to make when this
longed-for moment finally occurred, statements like "life in Birming-
ham is hell" or "you will miss me / but that's good," or allusions to
"this various dream of living," but at the same time he understands the
futility of it all. O'Hara successfully distances himself from the
"Frank" who exists in the poem:

> when the tears of a whole generation are assembled
> they will only fill a coffee cup
> > > just because they evaporate
> doesn't mean life has heat. . . .

In the bittersweet passage that follows, the poet recognizes that his
love is now met with some measure of indifference:

> I am alive with you
> > > full of anxious pleasures and pleasurable anxiety
> hardness and softness
> > > listening while you talk and talking while you read

I read what you read
                 you do not read what I read
which is right, I am the one with the curiosity. . . .
                 when you're not here someone walks in and says

                                                    "hey,
there's no dancer in that bed"

Recognition of the truth is one thing. But now the poet suddenly recalls the heyday of love, exclaiming with the rapt lyricism of his beloved Rachmaninoff:

                 O the Polish summers! those drafts!
                 those black and white teeth!

But this bravura passage is punctuated immediately by the clear-headed acceptance of the fact that "you never come when you say you'll come but on the other hand you do come."

What role does the title of the poem play? Vincent Warren has noted that "St. Paul" is a play on his middle name.[43] But it is also a nice irony to bring St. Paul into the picture, for the allusion points up Vincent's delinquency. No faithful apostle, responding to the Call and always "coming" when he is needed, this "St. Paul" fails to bring his disciple a New Dispensation. And yet, the Pauline doctrine of Reversal, of a love that will turn the world upside down and which redeems suffering, is central to the poem, for the "I" who speaks still believes in it. When he finds the dancer in his room, he experiences such a moment of reversal. But the reversal is, of course, temporary and illusory, and the poet is shown as accepting the inevitable: "the sun doesn't necessarily set, sometimes it just disappears."

In the summer of 1961, the love poems to Vincent Warren come to an abrupt end, and the poetry written after this date is recognizably different. The center of O'Hara's world was shifting somewhat. As the Museum took up more of his energies, he spent more time uptown, away from Second Avenue. He was also meeting a whole group of younger poets, whose conversation and work influenced his style. The most notable of these was Bill Berkson ("Golden Bill," as Frank called him in a letter to John Ashbery),[44] who worked with O'Hara at the

Museum and became an especially close friend. The letters to Bill Berkson are full of intellectual excitement and discussion, and the "Bill Berkson" poems, written in the early sixties, are correspondingly less emotional and more abstract than those written for, say, Grace Hartigan or Joe LeSueur or Vincent Warren. But surely age also played a part in the increasing detachment of the "I do this, I do that" poems written for various occasions. For in June of 1961, Frank O'Hara turned thirty-five. And that month he began a poem with the lines:

> April is over is May too June
> and thundershowers tomorrow
> you wouldn't want those tears to
> stick to your cheeks long. . . .   (*CP*, 408)

5
THE
PILLAR OF
OUR DEATHS

—I don't think I want to win anything I think I want to die unadorned
("Biotherm," CP, 438)

THE LAST YEARS

DURING THE LAST five years of his short life, O'Hara wrote relatively little poetry.[1] After the enormous productivity of the late fifties, a lull was perhaps inevitable, and, in any case, the Museum now took up much of his time and energy. Between 1961 and 1963, the poet seems to have suffered periodic bouts of depression. Emptiness, despair, and death now become frequent themes:

> Darkness and white hair
> everything empty, nothing there,
> but thoughts how awful
> image is, image errrgh
> all day long to sit in a window
> and see nothing but the past
> the serpent is coiled thrice
> around her she is dead. . . .   (*CP*, 419)

The light presses down
in an empty head the trees
and bushes flop like
a little girl imitating
The Dying Swan the stone
is hot the church is a
Russian oven. . . .
it is all suffocating. . . .   (*CP*, 475)

A number of poems contain references to suicide, although O'Hara
usually treats this subject with self-deprecatory humor:

I see the cobwebs collecting already
and later those other webs, those awful predatory webs
if I stay right here I will eventually get into the newspapers
like Robert Frost
willow trees, willow trees they remind me of Desdemona
I'm so damned literary
and at the same time the waters rushing past me remind me of nothing
I'm so damned empty. . . .   (*CP*, 429)

can I borrow your forty-five
I only need one bullet preferably silver
if you can't be interesting at least you can be a legend. . . .
                                               (*CP*, 430)

where am I what is it
I can't even find a pond small enough
to drown in without being ostentatious. . . .   (*CP*, 434)

Soon I will fall drunken off the train into
the arms of Patsy and Mike and the greenish pain.
Obliterate everything, Neapolitan seventh!
It will be a long hard way to the railway station,

and Anna Karenina never wore dungarees.   (*CP*, 474)

Perhaps the most poignant of these "dark poems" is "The Clouds
Go Soft" (1963), which Jasper Johns used in his collage-painting *Skin
with O'Hara poem*. This meditative lyric, whose muted, subdued tone
immediately sets it apart from most of the poet's work, is surely
O'Hara's Dejection Ode. Change, motion, vitality, openness—these
had always been his lifeblood: recall "To Hell With It" (1957), with its

exclamation: "how I hate subject matter! melancholy intruding on the vigorous heart . . . and all things that don't change" (*CP*, 275). But now only the external landscape is capable of transformation, and even then, the movement is, in Wallace Stevens's phrase, "downward to darkness":

> The clouds go soft
>
>   change color and so many kinds
>   puff up, disperse
>   sink into the sea

It is the time of Sputnik, when the very heavens "go out of kilter" as "an insane remark greets / the monkey on the moon." But "here on earth," in the poet's mental landscape, all seems frozen, static:

>   at 16 you weigh 144 pounds and at 36
>
>   the shirts change, endless procession
>   but they are all neck 14 sleeve 33
>
>   and holes appear and are filled
>   the same holes   anonymous filler
>   no more conversion, no more conversation
>   the sand inevitably seeks the eye
>
>   and it is the same eye
>   (*CP*, 475)

O'Hara has rarely been so conscious of the inexorability of fate, the sense that he can escape neither his shirt size nor the sand that gets in his eye ("the same eye"). In the context, the "holes" are, of course, not armholes but graves. Even the verse form of "The Clouds Go Soft," with its ominous blank spaces and its lines that trail off, never quite meeting the next line, conveys the poet's sense of inner emptiness. Struggle, this particular poem tells us, is simply not worth it.

But one must be careful not to generalize about the later poems, for the same Frank O'Hara who wrote "The Clouds Go Soft" also wrote the wonderfully droll "Poem (Lana Turner has collapsed!)":

> Lana Turner has collapsed!
> I was trotting along and suddenly

it started raining and snowing
and you said it was hailing
but hailing hits you on the head
hard so it was really snowing and
raining and I was in such a hurry
to meet you but the traffic
was acting exactly like the sky
and suddenly I see a headline
LANA TURNER HAS COLLAPSED!
there is no snow in Hollywood
there is no rain in California
I have been to lots of parties
and acted perfectly disgraceful
but I never actually collapsed
oh Lana Turner we love you get up

(February 1962; *CP*, 449)

Certainly, O'Hara himself consistently rejected "collapse" as an easy way out. Indeed, during the five-year span under consideration, the variety of his accomplishments and the range of his activities continued to be as astonishing as ever. Collaboration became especially important in these years, as O'Hara worked on collages with Joe Brainard and Jasper Johns, and with Alfred Leslie on films. In 1961–62, he was art critic for *Kulchur;* the three important *Art Chronicles* date from this period, as do the NETA interviews with David Smith and Barnett Newman, and the Larry Rivers memoir. Within the next three years, he organized three major shows for the Museum: *Mother-well, Nakian,* and *Smith.* The catalogues for these exhibitions are now collector's items, the poet's introductions reflecting, once again, his uncanny ability to make the important discriminations about the art of his day. At the time of his death, O'Hara was working on a major retrospective of Jackson Pollock and had begun to make plans for the first major exhibition of de Kooning's painting at the museum.

As Associate Curator (he was to be named Curator in late 1966 when his death intervened), he now traveled abroad a good deal. In the fall of 1963, for example, he was in Europe for the opening of the Franz Kline exhibition at the Stedelijk Museum in Amsterdam and its second showing at the Museo Civico in Turin. On this particular trip, he also visited Rome, Milan, Paris, Antwerp, Copenhagen, Stockholm,

Zagreb, Belgrade, Prague, and Vienna. The letter from Belgrade to Joe LeSueur (quoted in Chapter 1) is full of wit, good humor, and high spirits; certainly the Frank who parties in Rome, visits nightclubs in Prague, and makes friends with local artists everywhere, does not sound like the despairing poet of "The Light Presses Down."

What is probably O'Hara's best play, *The General Returns from One Place to Another,* a parodistic fantasy about General MacArthur's return to the Pacific theater in peacetime—a general in search of a war—was produced at the Writer's Stage Theatre in 1964 and published the following year in *Art and Literature.* This comedy, evidently inspired by a production of Brecht's *In the Jungle of Cities,*[2] exploits some wonderfully absurd devices: in Scene 1, for example, the General enters "almost nude, but wearing galoshes and a toupee." In each subsequent scene, according to the stage directions, "he enters with one more article of clothing added, decorations, etc."[3] Since the General's power declines by a notch or two at each step of the way, we are finally confronted by a four-star general in full regalia—and no army to command—a general despised by the greedy natives and even by that predatory American camp follower, the cocktail-swilling Mrs. Forbes. Unlike some of the early plays like *Try! Try!,* which are merely silly, *The General Returns* has shrewd and funny things to say about East–West relations.

In this period, O'Hara was also teaching for the first time. In the spring of 1963, he gave a poetry workshop at the New School. Joe LeSueur recalls that it turned out to be a very *expensive* course, not for the class but for its instructor, because Frank invariably brought eager students round for drinks after class, and the liquor supply at 791 Broadway needed constant replenishment. Frank was, for that matter, now becoming something of an underground celebrity; young poets began to besiege him with letters and phone calls, and LeSueur remembers that when Ted Berrigan, one of O'Hara's most ardent disciples, first arrived in New York fresh from the Midwest, he would stand patiently on Avenue A near their apartment, hoping to catch a glimpse of his idol.[4] O'Hara, LeSueur notes, was "generous to a fault"; he couldn't turn down any of the writers who sought his help, always finding time for a long talk at the Cedar or a word of advice. The following excerpts from a letter (6 February 1963), written to the poet

Frank Lima at a time when the latter had a drug problem and couldn't bring himself to seek help, is typical:

> . . . no matter how much anyone likes you, you are the only one who can really do anything about things. . . . You've got to think of yourself first, because nobody else will. Everybody who likes and tries to help you is thinking of themselves first and you at least second: that's the way life is. . . .
>
> Think of your book with John Myers, think of going to Spain, think of going to France, think of the other books you'll write. All these things can happen, and each more easily than the last, if you can just get over these first difficulties. If it's not one psychiatrist it can be another, if not one job another, but you've got to want to, and right now you've got to want to very hard, in order to make it happen. And you do want to so come on. Rome wasn't built in a day and neither are individual lives or careers, you know that. The end.
>
> Boy, I bet this letter makes you mad.
>
> Love,
Frank[5]

O'Hara would have been happy to know that Lima *did* "make it happen"; he has since won a number of poetry awards and, at this writing, his new collection *Angel* is receiving enthusiastic reviews.[6]

Edwin Denby, whose poetry and dance criticism O'Hara consistently admired, sums up what many artist-friends felt about O'Hara's generosity: "Frank was so wonderful about the book [*In Public, In Private*[7]] and wrote a review in *Poetry* and had the marvelous gift of saying nice things. He would make compliments and then quote lines from the poems and in some instinctive way he managed to prepare the ear for what was interesting about the quotations." Yet there were all too many hangers-on ready to take advantage of Frank's "marvelous gift." "He had started giving parties at his loft on Broadway after he started making enough money working very hard at the Museum of Modern Art. No one was grateful for it. He was writing less and working hard. He really wanted to establish the painters he liked."[8]

One concludes that O'Hara wrote fewer poems during the sixties than he had in preceding years primarily because he was too busy doing other things. Indeed, it is a particularly bitter irony that the very summer O'Hara died was a time of special promise, both personal and literary. In his *Panjandrum* memoir of 1973, Vincent Warren recalls: "In the spring of 1966 Frank and I came together again. I decided to return to N.Y. We had one beautiful weekend at Patsy Southgate's on Long Island in June and Frank was planning to come to Montreal in August to see what would have been my last performance here when his life was interrupted."[9]

A new writing project was also under way: the collaboration with John Ashbery and Kenneth Koch on a play the three poets had begun in 1953. Ashbery remarks: "We wrote the second act in about June of 1966 and were planning to write a third act the following week, but Kenneth couldn't make it, and very shortly thereafter Frank was killed. His collaboration on Act II is therefore one of the last things he ever wrote, although unfortunately I am unable to recall now which of us wrote what."[10]

Throughout the sixties, even when he himself was writing little, O'Hara regarded poetry as his first love. In a long letter to Bill Berkson (12 August 1962), in which he contrasts the formal qualities of music to those of poetry, O'Hara urges his friend to make poetry—rather than fiction or any other kind of writing—his first priority, for "Poetry is the highest art, everything else, however gratifying . . . moving and grand, is less demanding, more indulgent, more casual, more gratuitous, more instantly apprehensible, which I assume is not exactly what we are after. . . ."[11]

This rejection of the "casual," the "gratuitous," the "instantly apprehensible" is nothing if not sound, but it is only fair to say that many of O'Hara's own poems written in the sixties suffer from precisely these faults. Take "The Lunch Hour FYI," written in the summer of 1961:

Plank plank   tons of it
                        plank plank
marching   the streets
                up and down
                                                and it's all ours
2
what we all want is a consistent musical development heh heh
                tappety-tap drrrrrrrrrrp!

Just as aloha means goodbye in Swahili

so it is 9:05

and I must go to work   roll OVER dammit

(see previous FYI)

hip? I haven't even coughed yet this morning

The poem goes on in this way for three more sections, ending with the lines:

coughcough

coughcoughcoughcough

good morning,

darling,

how do you like the first snow of summer?

your

plant in   your window

(*CP*, 421–22)

"The Lunch Hour" is one of a series of "For Your Information" poems written for Bill Berkson. Their background is related in the following letter from Berkson to Donald Allen (12 August 1970):

> The F.Y.I. works were written as correspondence between Frank & me & mostly by Frank—he would write the poems, like *Lunch Poems,* at his desk at the Museum of Modern Art. Together, they were supposed to form "The Collected Memorandums of Angelicus & Fidelio Fobb"—2 brothers (Frank was Angelicus, I was Fidelio) who wrote poems, letters, postcards (all "memorandums") to each other. The poems, however, don't seem to involve this brother-act too much—they have to do with what our lives in New York were like at the time (1960–61). "F.Y.I." comes from the typical heading for office memorandums—"For Your Information"—which was also the title of *Newsweek* magazine's "house organ," a little offset journal of employee gossip distributed weekly. I had worked at *Newsweek* the summers 1956–57 and told Frank about it & he picked up on "F.Y.I." He was also inspired to ring a lot of changes on the original in titles like "F.M.I." ("For My Information"), etc.   (*CP*, 551)

Since the "For Your Information" poems were written, like *Hymns of St. Bridget* (on which O'Hara and Berkson collaborated between 1960 and 1962) and "The Letters of Angelicus & Fidelio Fobb,"[12] mostly for the poets' own diversion, it may be unfair to judge them too stringently on aesthetic grounds. Nevertheless, I would argue that there *is* a falling off in the FYI poems, that "Lunch Hour" replaces the Personism of *Lunch Poems* with a somewhat self-conscious games-manship. Modulation now gives way to simple repetition ("Plank plank"); the language is usually that of ordinary talk ("roll OVER dammit") and simplistic sound imitation ("tappety-tap drrrrrrrrrrp!"). These new lyrics are much more loosely articulated: words tend to be spread all over the page, the blank space becoming an important prosodic element as a sort of musical rest. The three-step (or modified two-step) line of Williams's late poems is used frequently as is the device of placing verse paragraphs alternately on the left and right sides of the page as in "For a Dolphin" (*CP*, 407). Often, as in the case of "Lunch Hour," one is hard put to find a *raison d'être* for the particu-lar prosodic shape used; sheer randomness seems to be the rule. These are poems that can start or stop anywhere, that accommodate almost anything the poet happens to want to record. Their tone, moreover, is curiously detached; O'Hara's former emotional vibrancy—a vibrancy that linked him to Mayakovsky—is absent.

But perhaps these "For Your Information" poems are best consid-ered as bits of muscle flexing, exercises that prepare the way for that great Bill Berkson poem, "Biotherm." This long (464 lines) lyric se-quence was written over a five-month period (26 August 1961–23 Jan-uary 1962). In a letter to Donald Allen (20 September 1961), O'Hara provides an important background statement about the poem:

> I've been going on with a thing I started to be a little birthday poem for BB and then it went along a little and then I remembered that was how Mike's Ode [*Ode to Michael Goldberg ('s Birth and Other Births)*] got done so I kept on and I am still going day by day (middle of 8th page this morning). I don't know anything about what it is or will be but am enjoy-ing trying to keep going and seem to have something. Some days I feel very happy about it, because I seem to have been able to keep it "open" and so there are lots of possibilities, air and such. For example, it's been called *M.L.F.Y., Whereby Shall Seace* (from Wyatt), *Biotherm,* and back and forth, probably ending up as *M.L.F.Y.* The Wyatt passage is very beautiful: "This dedelie stroke, wherebye shall seace / The harborid sighis within my herte. . . ." *M.L.F.Y.,* I hasten to add, is not like that at all though, so don't get your hopes too high. . . . Biotherm is a marvelous sunburn preparation full of attar of roses, lanolin and plankton ($12 the

tube) which Bill's mother fortunately left around and it hurts terribly
when gotten into one's eyes. Plankton it says on it is practically the most
health-giving substance ever rubbed into one's skin.[13]

How much openness can a poem bear? This is a tricky question, of
course, and for a long time I regarded "Biotherm" as just another FYI
(or rather MLFY) poem—a witty improvisation, a transcript of the
charming if jumbled talk of a marvelous raconteur. Its endless puns,
in-jokes, phonetic games, allusions, cataloguing, journalistic parodies,
and irrelevant anecdotes may seem, on a first or even a later reading,
merely tiresome.[14] Interestingly, "Biotherm" also seems to have much
less relationship to painting than do the earlier poems. Film is now the
dominant sister art; the poem is full of references to movie stars, Hollywood films, and invented scenarios, and its structure often resembles
the film technique of crosscutting at accelerated speed, a technique
particularly common in the silent film comedies of the twenties, for
example those of Buster Keaton.

If we study O'Hara's crosscutting, we find that everything in this
seemingly wild talk-poem relates to everything else. The setting is the
beach: the first line of "Biotherm" invokes the magic suntan lotion
("The best thing in the world"); and twelve pages later, O'Hara concludes with the lines:

yes always though you said it first
you the quicksand and sand and grass
as I wave toward you freely
the ego-ridden sea
there is a light there that neither
of us will obscure
rubbing it all white
saving ships from fucking up on the rocks
on the infinite waves of skin smelly and crushed and light and absorbed
(*CP,* 448)

Although the beach setting is never formally introduced or presented
in realistic detail, sand, sea, and cloud images, as well as larger beach
scenes, fade in and out at fairly regular intervals:

or what's the use the sky
the endless clouds trailing we leading them by the bandanna, red
(*CP,* 436)

after "hitting" the beach at Endzoay we drank up the liebfraumilch
and pushed on up the Plata to the pampas   (*CP*, 437)

bent on his knees the Old Mariner said where the fuck
is that motel you told me about mister I aint come here for no clams
I want swimmingpool mudpacks the works carbonateddrugstorewater /
hiccups
from a nice sissy under me clean and whistling a donkey to ride rocks
(*CP*, 437)

the dulcet waves are
sweeping along in their purplish
way and a little girl is
beginning to cry and I know
her but I can't help because
she has just found her first brick
what can you do what   (*CP*, 438)

One day   you are posing in your checkerboard bathing trunks (*CP*, 440)

on the beach we stood on our heads
I held your legs it was summer and hot
the Bloody Marys were spilling on our trunks
but the crocodiles didn't pull them
it was a charmed life full of
innuendos and desirable hostilities   (*CP*, 444)

These brief flashes of real and fantastic beach locales provide a sense
of continuity rather like that of a Godard film; they are brief reminders that the poem's variations radiate from a center which is the loving
relationship between Frank and Bill, and which is epitomized by the
line "pretty rose preserved in biotherm" on the same page as the Wyatt
love poem (439). What the poet preserves in "biotherm" in order to
entertain his friend is a dazzling array of memories and inventions.
There are fantastically absurd menus, alluding to French dishes and
American friends:

Hors-d'oeuvre abstrait-expressionistes, américan-styles, bord-durs, etc.
Soupe Samedi Soir à la Strawberry-Blonde
Poisson Pas de Dix au style Patricia
Histoire de contrefilet, sauce Angelicus Fobb
La réunion des fins de thon à la boue
Chapon ouvert brûlé à l'Hoban, sauce Fidelio Fobb
Poèmes 1960–61 en salade   (*CP*, 445)

Or burlesque film scenarios:

"Practically Yours"
>   with June Vincent, Lionello Venturi and Casper Citron
>   a Universal-International release produced by G. Mennen Williams
>   directed by Florine Stettheimer
>   continuity by the Third Reich
>   (*CP*, 437)

Or comic word substitutions:

> you meet the Ambassador   "a year and a half of trying to make him"
>   he is dressed in red, he has a red ribbon down his chest he
>   has   7   gold decorations pinned to his gash   (*CP*, 436)

Or bastard foreign language, in this case German:

>   "vass hass der mensch geplooped
>   that there is sunk in the battlefield a stately grunt
>   and the idle fluice still playing on the hill
>   because of this this this this slunt"   (*CP*, 440)

Or bittersweet memories of actual events:

> then too, the other day I was walking through a train
> with my suitcase and I overheard someone say "speaking of faggots"
> now isn't life difficult enough without that
> and why am I always carrying something
> well it was a shitty looking person anyway
> better a faggot than a farthead   (*CP*, 441)

Or catalogues containing unexpected items:

> favorites: vichyssoise, capers, bandannas, fudge-nut-ice, collapsibility,
>   the bar of the Winslow, 5:30 and 12:30, leather sweaters, tuna fish,
>   cinzano and soda, Marjorie Rambeau in *Inspiration*
>   whatdoyoumeanandhowdoyoumeanit
>   (*CP*, 445)

> favorites: going to parties with you, being in corners with you,
>   being in gloomy pubs with you smiling, poking you at /
>   parties when

you're "down," coming on like South Pacific with you at them,
shrimping with you into the Russian dressing, leaving /

                                        parties with
you alone to go and eat a piece of cloud   (*CP*, 447)

Or literary parodies, in this case of Pound's famous *Usura* Canto:

> I am talking about the color of money
> the dime so red and the 100 dollar bill so orchid
> the sickly fuchsia of a 1 the optimistic
> orange of a 5 the useless penny like a seed
> the magnificent yellow zinnia of a 10
> especially a roll of them the airy blue of a
> 50 how pretty a house is when it's filled with them
> that's not a villa that's a bank
> where's the ocean
> now this is not a tract against usury it's just putting two and two together
> and getting five (thank you, Mae)
> (*CP*, 446)

Individually, such passages may seem to be pure slapstick, but the
remarkable thing about "Biotherm" is that, as in a sophisticated or-
chestral composition, everything mentioned casually is picked up
somewhere later in the poem in an altered context. Thus the "bandanna" of line 6 reappears nine pages later in the catalogue quoted
above. Or again, the reference to "Swan Lake Allegra Kent / those
Ten Steps of Patricia Wilde" reappears in the "(MENU) / Déjeuner
Bill Berkson," first as "Poisson Pas de Dix au Style Patricia" and then
as "Café ivesianien 'Plongez au fond du lac glacé'". One remembered
lunch dissolves into another; and the film-menu-poetry-party parodies
are regularly juxtaposed to sudden expressions of deep affection:

> we are alone no one is talking it feels good
> we have our usual contest about claustrophobia
> it doesn't matter much
> doing without each other is much more insane   (*CP*, 441)

or

> you were there I was here you were here I was there where are /
>   you I miss you. . . .

> when you went I stayed and then I went and we were both lost /
> and then I died
> (*CP,* 442)

Like Godard's *La Chinoise* or *Weekend,* "Biotherm" consistently plays off the intensities of personal emotion against the vagaries of everyday conversation. It is an extremely difficult poem because the reader enters the "frame" only gradually, overhearing snatches of conversation between Frank, Bill, Patsy, and John, and only gradually realizing that "Biotherm" is something of a rock opera, partly playful but also full of anxiety, alternating percussive passages with lyrical tunes, an extravaganza celebrating the poet's great love for his friend and memorializing their careless summer beach days of "infinite waves of skin smelly and crushed and absorbed." Another way of putting it is that O'Hara's long lyric sequence is an elegy for "Biotherm," that magic potion that preserves roses—a potion interchangeable with "kickapoo joyjuice halvah Canton cheese / in thimbles" (*CP,* 437) or "marinated duck saddle with foot sauce and a tumbler of vodka" (*CP,* 448). Food and liquor images are especially prominent in this poem because the poet's imagination transforms them into *Plankton,* the "health-giving substance" that makes Biotherm so special. Thus when the poet says in one expansive moment:

> I am sitting on top of Mauna Loa seeing thinking feeling
> the breeze rustles through the mountains gently trusts me
> I am guarding it from mess and measure   (*CP,* 444)

he is describing not only his guardianship of Mauna Loa but the creative act as well. "Biotherm" is a poem dangerous to imitate for it implies that anything goes, that all you have to do is "merely continue." But in fact O'Hara does succeed here in "guarding it from mess and measure"—that is, from total formlessness on one hand, and from a more traditional rhetorical and prosodic organization on the other. It is his last great poem and one of the important poems of the sixties.

THE DAY FRANK O'HARA DIED

By 1964 or so, O'Hara's style, especially the style of the "I do this, I do that" poems, was beginning to have a marked influence. Ted Berrigan wrote a series of "Sonnets," one of which, subtitled "After Frank O'Hara," begins:

> It's 8:54 in Brooklyn it's the 28th of July and
> it's probably 8:54 in Manhattan but I'm
> in Brooklyn I'm eating English muffins and drinking
> pepsi and I'm thinking of how Brooklyn is New
> York city too how odd I usually think of it as
> something all its own like Bellows Falls like Little
> Chute like Uijongbu. . . .[15]

And Ron Padgett wrote a poem called "16 November 1964," whose opening recalls O'Hara's "Personal Poem" ("Now when I walk around at lunchtime . . ."):

> As this morning seemed special when I woke up
> I decided as is my custom, to go for a refreshing walk
> in the street. Preparing myself for the unexpected, I
> Combed my hair and generally made ready. I was ready.
> In the hall outside my door the lady from down the hall
> Shouted my name to get my attention.[16]

Such early imitations were, of course, merely derivative; in these poems, Berrigan and Padgett capture the O'Hara manner without the substance. Their model is quite obviously the occasional mode of "A Step Away from Them," "Adieu to Norman, Bon Jour to Joan and Jean-Paul," and especially O'Hara's celebrated elegy for Billie Holiday:

> THE DAY LADY DIED
>
> It is 12:20 in New York a Friday
> three days after Bastille day, yes
> it is 1959 and I go get a shoeshine
> because I will get off the 4:19 in Easthampton
> at 7:15 and then go straight to dinner
> and I don't know the people who will feed me
>
> I walk up the muggy street beginning to sun
> and have a hamburger and a malted and buy
> an ugly NEW WORLD WRITING to see what the poets
> in Ghana are doing these days
>
> > I go on to the bank

and Miss Stillwagon (first name Linda I once heard)
doesn't even look up my balance for once in her life
and in the GOLDEN GRIFFIN I get a little Verlaine
for Patsy with drawings by Bonnard although I do
think of Hesiod, trans. Richmond Lattimore or
Brendan Behan's new play or *Le Balcon* or *Les Nègres*
of Genet, but I don't, I stick with Verlaine
after practically going to sleep with quandariness

and for Mike I just stroll into the PARK LANE
Liquor Store and ask for a bottle of Strega and
then I go back where I came from to 6th Avenue
and the tobacconist in the Ziegfield Theatre and
casually ask for a carton of Gauloises and a carton
of Picayunes, and a NEW YORK POST with her face on it

and I am sweating a lot by now and thinking of
leaning on the john door in the 5 SPOT
while she whispered a song along the keyboard
to Mal Waldron and everyone and I stopped breathing

(*CP,* 325)

"In one brief poem," Ted Berrigan said in his obituary essay on O'Hara, "he seemed to create a whole new kind of awareness of feeling, and by this a whole new kind of poetry, in which everything could be itself and still be poetry." [17] What Berrigan means here, I think, is that O'Hara dispenses with all the traditional props of elegy—the statement of lament, the consolation motif, the procession of mourners, the pathetic fallacy, and so on—and still manages to pay an intensely moving tribute to the great jazz singer. It is not an easy feat. In his own earlier elegies, for example the four poems prompted by the sudden tragic death of the young James Dean in 1955, [18] O'Hara often makes a straightforward statement of lament and complaint, thus risking sentimentality, much as William Carlos Williams does in his "Elegy for D. H. Lawrence," which begins:

Green points on the shrub
and poor Lawrence dead
the night damp and misty
and Lawrence no more in the world
to answer April's promise
with a fury of labor

> against waste, waste and life's
> coldness.

(*Collected Earlier Poems,* 361)

O'Hara avoids the bathos inherent in such a frontal attack by making no reference at all to Lady Day until the twenty-fifth line of his poem, and then only obliquely: the poet catches a glimpse of "a NEW YORK POST with her face on it." The title leads us to expect an elegy or at least an account of Billie Holiday's death; instead, O'Hara traces the *process* whereby he comes across the news of that death, a process so immediate, so authentic that when we come to the last four lines, we participate in his poignant memory of Lady Day's performance. Reading the last six words of the poem, "and everyone and I stopped breathing" (reminiscent of the arresting ending of Yeats's "In Memory of Major Robert Gregory": "but a thought / Of that late death took all my heart for speech"), we too stop breathing. For a moment, however brief, memory and art enable us to transcend the ordinary particulars of existence.

How does the poet accomplish this? If we look at the details that make up the first twenty-five lines of the poem, we see that they are not, after all, as random as they appear to be. As Charles Altieri has observed: "The actual particulars by which the poem captures the vitality of life at the same time constantly call attention to their own contingency and perpetual hovering on the brink of disconnection."[19] O'Hara knows exactly that he will get off the train at 7:15 and go to dinner, but he doesn't know the people who will feed him. He goes to the bank where the barely familiar teller "Miss Stillwagon (first name Linda I once heard)" disproves his expectations by not looking up his "balance for once in her life." He cannot decide what book to buy for Patsy Southgate and practically goes to sleep "with quandariness." This is a particularly odd detail: when one is in a quandary, one may well suffer from insomnia but hardly from sleepiness!

A similar disconnection characterizes the network of proper names and place references in the poem. On the one hand, the poet's consciousness is drawn to the foreign or exotic: Ghana, the Golden Griffin, Verlaine, Bonnard, Hesiod, trans. Richmond Lattimore, Brendan Behan, *Le Balcon, Les Négres,* Genet, Strega, Gauloises, Picayunes.[20] On the other, the poem contains a set of native American references:

"shoeshine," "the muggy street beginning to sun," "a hamburger and a malted," "an ugly NEW WORLD WRITING," "6th Avenue," "a NEW YORK POST," "the 5 SPOT," "the john door," and the reference to Billie's accompanist, Mal Waldron.

Why does O'Hara introduce Verlaine and Genet, Gauloises and the Golden Griffin into a poem about Billie Holiday? I think because he wants to make us see—and this is his great tribute to Lady Day—that she embodies both the foreign-exotic and the native American. As a person, Billie Holiday was, of course, quintessentially American: a southern Black who had experienced typical hardships on the road to success, a woman of great passions who finally succumbed to her terrible drug addiction, a victim of FBI agents and police raids. In this sense, hers is the world of muggy streets, hamburgers and malteds, the john door, the "5 SPOT." But her great voice transcends what she is in life, linking her to the poets, dramatists, and artists cited in the first part, to *Le Balcon* and *Les Nègres*, to Gauloises and Strega. Even the name Lady Day (ingeniously reversed in the elegy's title) reconciles these opposites.

Disconnections which turn out to be connections, isolated moments in time which lead to one moment transcending time—everything in the elegy works in this way. The syntax is particularly interesting in this regard. The paratactic structure (and ... and ... and), linking short declarative statements sequentially rather than causally, calls attention to what seems to be the meaningless flux of time. One moment is succeeded by another as Frank moves back and forth from street to street, from store to store. But then it seems as if he is virtually running out of steam. The conjunctions become increasingly insistent (eleven of the poem's nineteen *and*'s occur in the last ten lines), and the pace slows down until finally the sequence of meaningless moments is replaced by the *one* moment of memory when Lady Day enchanted her audience by the power of her art. Time suddenly stops.

O'Hara does not have to say here, as he did in "For James Dean," "For a young actor I am begging / peace, Gods. ... I speak as one whose filth / is like his own" (*CP*, 228), or as Williams says in the Lawrence elegy, "Sorrow for the young / that Lawrence has passed / unwanted from England." "The Day Lady Died" moves surely and swiftly to its understated climax; it establishes the singer as an authentic presence even though the poem never mentions her by name and seems to be "about" the poet's own activities, his trivial preweekend errands on a typical July Friday in muggy Manhattan.

In their imitations of O'Hara's mode, Berrigan and Padgett use the poet's particulars—the time signals, the place names, the random recounting of activities—but theirs tend to be simple empiricism, a cataloguing of "this is what happened to me today," in which the particulars don't add up. Comparing the model to its offshoots, one can appreciate, more than ever, O'Hara's exquisite modulations of tone, his split-second dissolves, his time shifts, syntactic displacements, and emotional resonances, especially when one realizes that, in the best poems, each small detail, like the bottle of Strega which Frank buys for Mike, plays its part in the larger network.

Yet, whatever the faults of their early versions of "Personism," young poets like Berrigan and Padgett played an important role; they were the first to recognize that O'Hara had struck a new chord, that a new poetry was in the making. And after his death in 1966, the literary response was astonishing. Almost immediately, elegies for O'Hara began to appear in the little magazines. If none of these elegies is as brilliant as "The Day Lady Died," many are poignant and arresting; indeed, a whole anthology could be compiled of poems written for Frank O'Hara in the five years or so following his death. A short list would begin with Allen Ginsberg's "City Midnight Junk Strains," written four days after the poet's death, and include, in order of publication: Patsy Southgate's "Nobody Operates Like an IBM Machine: For Frank O'Hara," George Montgomery's "The Death of Frank O'Hara," Tony Towle's "Sunrise: Ode to Frank O'Hara," James Schuyler's "Buried at Springs," David Shapiro's "Ode (Permit me to take this sleeping man . . .)," Gerard Malanga's "In Memory of the Poet Frank O'Hara 1926–1966," Ron Padgett's "Strawberries in Mexico," John Wieners's "After Reading *Second Avenue:* For Frank O'Hara," and Diane di Prima's "From Kerhonson, July 28, 1966" and "Inverness, Cape Breton Island."[21]

One should note that this list is not limited to the so-called New York poets. John Wieners, originally a student at Black Mountain College, later a resident of Boston and briefly of San Francisco, stands apart from the New York group, an important poet in his own right.

And Ginsberg, of course, was never considered primarily a New York poet, having much closer ties to the Beats—Kerouac, Corso, Snyder, Whalen—than to the poets and painters originally associated with the Eighth Street Club, although the two groups did overlap.

Ginsberg's elegy for O'Hara is not one of his important poems, but it is a fascinating literary document, defining the relationship between two of the leading poets of the postwar era, poets united by their dislike of the Academic Establishment, their allegiance to Rimbaud, Whitman, Pound, and Williams, their search for open forms, and their homosexuality, but separated by their very different sensibilities and poetic aims. "City Midnight Junk Strains" begins:

> Switch on lights yellow as the sun
> > in the bedroom . . .
> The gaudy poet dead
> > > *(Planet News,* 134)

The image of Frank as "gaudy poet" dominates the elegy. Ginsberg has much affection for him, but one senses that he doesn't take him quite seriously. O'Hara is repeatedly referred to as "chattering Frank," mourned by his "Faithful drunken adorers," as the "Chatty prophet / of yr own loves, personal / memory feeling fellow," as the poet who wanders down Fifth Avenue "with your tie / flopped over your shoulder in the wind . . . off to a date with Martinis & a blond." Ginsberg recalls his "broken roman nose," his "wet mouth-smell of martinis / & a big artistic tipsy kiss"; he regrets the loss of "so many fine parties and evenings' / interesting drinks together with one / faded friend or new / understanding social cat." He concludes:

> Elegant insistency
> > on the honking self-prophetic Personal
> > as Curator of funny emotions to the mob,
> Trembling One, whenever possible. I see New York thru your eyes
> > and hear of one funeral a year nowadays—
> > > From Billie Holiday's time
> > appreciated more and more
> a common ear
> > > for our deep gossip.   (p. 137)

This is essentially the mythologized poet discussed in Chapter 1, the "gay" (in both senses of the word) "Curator of funny emotions," the celebrant of New York and purveyor of "deep gossip." The Fire Island accident turns this connoisseur of art into a piece of modern sculpture:

> ... dear Edwin Denby serious as Herbert Read
> with silvery hair   announcing your dead gift
> to the grave crowd   whose historic op art   frisson was
> the new sculpture your big blue wounded body made in the
> Universe
> when you went away   to Fire Island for the weekend
> tipsy with a family of decade-olden friends   (p. 136)

The melodrama of these lines (O'Hara did not, for instance, have a "big" body) looks ahead to Alfred Leslie's painting *The Killing of Frank O'Hara*. A more individual note is struck in Ginsberg's peculiarly candid appraisal of O'Hara's sexuality:

> Who were you, black suited, hurrying to meet,
> Unsatisfied one?
> Unmistakable,
> Darling date
> for the charming solitary   young poet with a big cock
> who could fuck you all night long
> till you never came
> (p. 135)

His own sexual capacities, Ginsberg asserts, are very different:

> I tried   your boys and found them ready
> sweet and amiable
> collected gentlemen
> with large sofa apartments
> lonesome to please   for pure language

The self-congratulatory note of this passage is, I think, out of key with the demands of the elegy form; it is as if, even though Frank's "bones" are "under cemetery grass," Allen still wants to compete with him for the favors of young men. And this competitive, aggressive note gives us some measure of the enormous difference between the two poets: the prophetic, expansive, religious Ginsberg, who wants his poetry to *change* the world, can only partially penetrate the consciousness of the urbane, witty, sophisticated, skeptical, agnostic O'Hara. The scattered references to Ginsberg in the *Collected Poems* suggest that the reverse was equally true: consider the following comically petulant response to Ginsberg's projected journey to India in 1961:

> Now that the Charles Theatre has opened
> it looks like we're going to have some wonderful times
> Allen and Peter, why are you going away
> our country's black and white past spread out
> before us is no time to spread over India. . . .   (*CP*, 399)

In this context, Ginsberg's declaration in the elegy that "I see New York thru your eyes" is inadvertently funny, for in fact Ginsberg sees New York through the most different eyes possible. His New York is a kind of urban hell, the city of cops and drug raids, of crime and ugliness and injustice; it is the opposite of O'Hara's companionable, exciting, and eternally entertaining Manhattan. Witness the following lines from Ginsberg's "Waking in New York":

> The giant stacks burn thick grey
>   smoke, Chrysler is lit with green,
> down Wall street islands of skyscraper
>   black jagged in Sabbath quietness—
> Oh fathers, how I am alone in this
>   vast human wilderness
> Houses uplifted like hives off
>   the stone floor of the world—
> the city too vast to know, too
>   myriad windowed to govern
>   from ancient halls—
> "O edifice of gas!"   (*Planet News*, p. 72)

Surely Frank O'Hara could never have written these lines which recall the visionary fervor of Hart Crane's *The Bridge*. O'Hara never felt "alone in this / vast human wilderness"; on the contrary, he felt at home only when he was participating in the life of "this hairy city," for he was convinced that "the country is no good for us / there's nothing / to bump into / or fall apart glassily / there's not enough / poured concrete" (*CP*, 476–77).

Near the end of "City Midnight Junk Strains," Ginsberg introduces a facet of O'Hara's character that the other elegists stress with equal conviction and of which I have already spoken—the poet's incredible generosity, his ability to make anyone he was with feel better:

> You're in a bad mood?
> Take an Asprin.
> In the Dumps?
> I'm falling asleep
> safe in your thoughtful arms.
>
> (*Planet News,* p. 136)

It is O'Hara's marvelous capacity for friendship that Ginsberg most admires. As such, his portrait of the artist may be somewhat one-sided, but it is a testament of love. And we must remember that in 1966, when Ginsberg wrote this elegy, no one, not even Frank's closest friends, had an adequate idea of the magnitude of the poet's accomplishment, the number of still unknown poems whose publication would dispel the romantic image of O'Hara as "Chatty prophet" and "Curator of funny emotions."

It is interesting to turn from "City Midnight Junk Strains" to Patsy Southgate's elegy for O'Hara. Hers is a much more modest poem, the testimonial of a close friend:

> You said:
> "I love your house because my poems are always on the coffee table!"
> "I always have such fun with you!"
> "Oh really, don't be an ass!"
> "Just pull yourself together and sweep in!"
> "Now *stop* it!"
>
> An endless series of exclamation points
> has ended.
>
> Your voice
> ran across the lawn wearing nothing but a towel
> in the good old summertime.
> You always sounded so positive!
> What freedom!
> I'll get a flag! (I must!)

> I loved your house too
> with Grace Church looking in the window
> and your imposingly empty ice-box;
> all that work piled on the table
> and lavished love on the walls and everywhere.
> You would say, yacking away, shaving at the kitchen sink (*the* sink)
> that we were going to be late again, for shit's sake, but
> "You look perfectly gorgeous, /
> my dear, would you mind feeding the cats?"
> in those arrogant days
> before your grave.
>
> You said, during the intermissions, on the phones, at the lunches,
> in the cabs:
> "If you *want* to do it, just *do* it! What else is there?"
> "My heart your heart" you wrote.
> It all added up.
> How flawless you were!

In focusing on Frank's own words and gestures, Patsy Southgate has saved her elegy from sentimentality. The repetitions "You said," "Your voice," "You would say," "You always sounded" unify the poem, and the expressions chosen give us an image of strength rather than the weakness of Ginsberg's charming child-poet. Despite his childlike abandon ("Your voice / ran across the lawn wearing nothing but a towel"), his candor ("'I love your house because my poems are always on the coffee table!'"), his insouciance ("your imposingly empty ice-box," "shaving at the kitchen sink [*the* sink]"), Frank's most memorable quality, according to Patsy Southgate, is his resilience, both for himself and for others: "'If you *want* to do it, just *do* it! What else is there?'" It is this peculiar courage ("You always sounded so positive!"), this unsentimental optimism that makes Patsy Southgate exclaim, "How flawless you were!"

A third elegy of a very different kind is James Schuyler's "Buried at Springs." Unlike Ginsberg's, this poem makes no attempt to recapture the immediate particulars of O'Hara's life; unlike Southgate's, it does not invoke his typical phrases and gestures. A more traditional elegy in the Romantic tradition, it begins:

> There is a hornet in the room
> and one of us will have to go

out of the window into the late
August mid-afternoon sun. I
won.

In the course of the poem, it becomes apparent that the "one of us"
who "will have to go" is not just a hornet but Frank, and that the
speaker has "won" nothing at all. Watching from his window, he sees
"Rocks with rags / of shadow, washed dust clouts / that will never
bleach." But then he pulls back and says laconically "It is not like this
at all." The dust clouts *will* bleach for nothing remains the same:

> The rapid running of the
> lapping water a hollow knock
> of someone shipping oars:
> it's eleven years since
> Frank sat at this desk and
> saw and heard it all

This is not just the conventional opposition of the mortality of man to
the eternal renewal of nature. For Schuyler's "nature," like that of
such related painters as de Kooning, Motherwell, and Kline, is submitted to a series of "painterly" arrangements. He recomposes landscapes ("rock, trees, a stump") in various ways, finding new shapes and
patterns:

> Sandy
> billows, or so they look,
> of feathery ripe heads of grass,
> an acid-yellow kind of
> goldenrod glowing or glowering
> in shade.
>
> Boats are light lumps on the bay
> stretching past erased islands
> to ocean and the terrible tumble

But because of Frank's absence, none of these painterly compositions
is finally satisfying, and in the end, Schuyler gives it up. No more
billows looking like "feathery ripe heads of grass"; no more boats
resembling "light lumps on the bay," sailing past "erased islands." The

pastoral landscape now gives way to a harsher reality:

> a faint clammy day, like wet silk
> stained by one dead branch
> the harsh russet of dried blood.

Within the earlier context of pretty seascapes with "great gold lichen" on "granite boulders," this oblique deathnote is arresting. "Buried at Springs" is a poem O'Hara himself would surely have admired; its modest tone, its unexpected line breaks ("I / won") and halting rhythms ("the incessant water the / immutable crickets"), its abstraction from natural forms—all these are reminiscent of O'Hara's own poetry, although O'Hara never possessed Schuyler's intrinsic reverence for the world of nature.

One poet who did *not* write an elegy for Frank O'Hara, even though he wrote the beautiful introduction to the *Collected Poems,* was John Ashbery. I mention this not because I think Ashbery should have written one, but because it tells us something about the essential difference between these two poets, who have so frequently been paired in critical commentary.[22] The personal elegy has never been an Ashbery genre; his is a poetic mode that absorbs personality into larger metaphysical structures.

Ashbery and O'Hara first became friends at Harvard, and when O'Hara moved to Manhattan in 1951, the two poets met regularly. In an interview with Richard Kostelanetz, Ashbery recalls:

> Frank got me interested in contemporary music . . . before much of this music had been recorded. He used to play it to me on the piano. He was also reading Beckett and Jean Rhys and Flann O'Brien before anybody heard of them. . . . We were all young and ambitious then. American painting seemed the most exciting art around, American poetry was very traditional at that time, and there was no modern poetry in the sense that there was modern painting. So one got one's inspiration and ideas from watching the experiments of others. Much of my feeling for Rothko and Pollock came through Frank.[23]

When *Some Trees* appeared in 1956, O'Hara gave it a perceptive review in *Poetry.* "Everywhere in the poems," he declared, "there is the difficult attention to calling things and events by their true qualities.

He establishes a relation between perception and articulateness." And he concluded: "Mr. Ashbery has written the most beautiful first book to appear in America since *Harmonium*."[24] In thus comparing Ashbery to Stevens, O'Hara was obviously on the right track; since then, most commentators, especially Ashbery's most famous advocate, Harold Bloom, have been at pains to demonstrate the Stevens connection. By the same token, however, O'Hara was suggesting that Ashbery's inspiration was unlike his own, for Stevens was never a central influence on O'Hara's work, nor was he himself particularly interested in "calling things and events by their true qualities."

It is important to note that since Ashbery lived in Paris from 1954 to 1965, he was absent from the New York scene during O'Hara's productive years. But the two poets corresponded regularly and copied out each others' poems in letters to friends. Writing to Mike Goldberg on 26 August 1957, Frank announced with great excitement: "JOHN ASHBERY IS ARRIVING SEPTEMBER 2d. I got a letter from him Saturday with some wonderful new poems. . . ." He proceeds to quote the funnier parts of Ashbery's letter and then the complete text of " 'They Dream Only Of America,' " followed by the comment, "Pretty snappy, eh?"[25] Or again, in 1961, when Ashbery asked O'Hara to contribute to the Reverdy issue he was preparing for the *Mercure de France*, Frank responded with a long letter (1 February 1961) saying, among other things: "I am still enthralled (literally) with *Europe* and love *America* too. . . . If I get up the energy after sending you some of the things I think are related to Reverdy . . . I'll try to include a couple of new things which are footnotes to *Europe*, and should be collected under the title *Little Verses for the Admirers of Ashbery's Europe*."[26]

It is interesting that O'Hara was so enchanted by "Europe," that long disjointed poem made up of 111 fragments, which Ashbery himself now thinks of as a dead end.[27] Harold Bloom has called it "a fearful disaster," arguing that "The Ashbery of *The Tennis Court Oath* [the volume in which "Europe" appeared] may have been moved by de Kooning and Kline, Webern and Cage, but he was not moved to the writing of poems. . . . who can hope to find any necessity in this calculated incoherence?"[28] The point here is that Bloom, reading *The Tennis Court Oath* with the retrospective insight gained from his exposure to *The Double Dream of Spring* (1970) and *Three Poems* (1972), responds to Ashbery's early experimentation with Dada and Surrealist modes with "outrage and disbelief." O'Hara, on the other hand, was fascinated by these experiments because he himself was tapping the same springs, even if the results turned out to be very different. "Europe" is, in fact, an exercise in automatic writing; Ashbery recalls: "I'd get American magazines like *Esquire,* open the pages, get a phrase from it, and then start writing on my own. When I ran out, I'd go back to the magazine. It was pure experimentation." Several passages in the poem were taken intact from a British children's book, *Beryl of the Biplane* by William Le Queux, which Ashbery found in a Paris bookstall.[29] One is immediately reminded of Max Ernst's collage novels, currently being rediscovered.[30] In this context, Richard Kostelanetz calls "Europe" "one of the great long poems of recent years—a classic of coherent diffuseness." It can, he argues, "be characterized as 'acoherent,' much as certain early 20th-century music is called 'atonal'" (p. 23).

Ashbery's assimilation of French Surrealism complements O'Hara's, but it is remarkable how different their experiments are. Take "'They Dream Only of America'" (1957), which O'Hara cites so enthusiastically in his letter to Mike Goldberg. It begins:

> They dream only of America
> To be lost among the thirteen million pillars of grass:
> "This honey is delicious
> *Though it burns the throat.*"
>
> And hiding from darkness in barns
> They can be grownups now
> And the murderer's ash tray is more easily—
> The lake a lilac cube.[31]

Compare this to the opening of O'Hara's "Easter" (1952):

> The razzle dazzle maggots are summary
> tattooing my simplicity on the pitiable.
> The perforated mountains of my saliva leave cities awash
> more exclusively open and more pale than skirts.
> O the glassy towns are fucked by yaks
> slowly bleeding a quiet filigree on the leaves of that souvenir
> of a bird chastely crossing the boulevard of falling stars

cold in the dull heavens
drowned in flesh,
it's night like I love it all cruisy and nelly
fingered fan of boskage fronds the white smile of sleeps.

(CP, 96–97)

"'They Dream Only Of America'" is a much quieter, more reflective, more detached and abstract poem than "Easter," with its racy, slangy, concrete language, its nervous rhythms and purposely foolish alliteration, its exclamatory fervor and intimate, personal tone. Ashbery's language is more chaste, and his verse forms and sentence structure are more traditional than O'Hara's, the four-line stanzas providing an orderly frame for a series of complete sentences. But although a statement like "They dream only of America" offers no syntactic difficulties, semantically it is much more elusive than anything we find in "Easter." Who are the "They" of line 1 and line 6? The murderer of line 7? The link between one phrase and the next, between, say, the image of the "murderer's ash tray" and the "lake" as a "lilac cube," is even more tenuous than are O'Hara's typical connections. It is impossible to tell with any certainty what these two stanzas are saying; indeed Ashbery himself has always insisted that poems like this one aren't "saying" anything. By comparison, "Easter" is almost transparent; this first section, as I pointed out in Chapter 2, presents the poet's scatological vision of an unredeemed pre-Easter landscape with its absurd parade of bodily parts and other objects filing across the stage.

Interestingly, when both poets renounced "straight" Surrealism in the later fifties, the divergent stylistic traits I have just noted persisted—a situation that suggests to me that *The Tennis Court Oath* is not, as Bloom would have it, a total aberration from the Ashbery canon, a volume we can wish away in the interest of the later poetry. Here is a passage from "The Skaters," which is generally regarded as the finest poem in *Rivers and Mountains,* the volume Ashbery published in 1966, the year of O'Hara's death.

There was much to be said in favor of storms
But you seem to have abandoned them in favor of endless light.
I cannot say that I think the change much of an improvement.

There is something fearful in these summer nights that go on
    forever. . . .

We are nearing the Moorish coast, I think, in a *bateau*.
I wonder if I will have any friends there
Whether the future will be kinder to me than the past, for example,
And am all set to be put out, finding it to be not.

Still, I am prepared for this voyage, and for anything else you
    may care to mention.
Not that I am not afraid, but there is very little time left.
You have probably made travel arrangements, and know the feeling.
Suddenly, one morning, the little train arrives in the station, but
    oh, so big.
It is! Much bigger and faster than anyone told you.
A bewhiskered student in an old baggy overcoat is waiting to
    take it.
"Why do you want to go *there*," they all say. "It is better in the
    other direction."
And so it is. There people are free, at any rate. But where you
    are going no one is.[32]

This is one of the more accessible parts of Ashbery's complex meditative poem about selfhood. Certainly its quest motif—the poet em-
barks on some sort of spiritual journey—is a familiar Romantic topos.
Lines like "I cannot say that I think the change much of an improvement" or "But where you / are going no one is" recall the Eliot of *Four
Quartets;* others, like "There is something fearful in these summer
nights that go on / forever" recall the Stevens of "An Ordinary Evening in New Haven." The text as a whole has affinities to Rilke's *Duino
Elegies*.

But the nature of the journey is shrouded in mystery. It begins "in
these summer nights" as the unspecified "We" near "the Moorish
coast, I think, in a *bateau*"—an obvious allusion to Rimbaud. But then
the *"bateau"* is replaced by "the little train," and it must be winter for
"A bewhiskered student in an old baggy overcoat is waiting to take it."
We do not know what the poet fears or why "there is very little time
left." "They"—whoever "They" are—warn him not to go *"there,"* and
he agrees that "in the other direction . . . people are free, at any rate."
But since we have no idea where *"there"* is, we cannot discriminate
between it and its opposite. And Ashbery obviously wants it that way.

The "travel arrangements" depicted in "The Skaters" are thus

worlds apart from O'Hara's daily journeys through the streets of
Manhattan:

> It's my lunch hour, so I go
> for a walk among the hum-colored
> cabs. First, down the sidewalk
> where laborers feed their dirty
> glistening torsos sandwiches
> and Coca-Cola, with yellow helmets
> on. They protect them from falling
> bricks, I guess. Then onto the
> avenue where skirts are flipping
> above heels and blow up over
> grates. The sun is hot but the
> cabs stir up the air. I look
> at bargains in wristwatches. There
> are cats playing in sawdust   (*CP*, 257)

O'Hara's "voyage" is a perfectly ordinary lunchtime stroll, but the
poet's "phalanx of particulars" is carefully chosen to convey the peculiar animation that characterizes the city even on a hot day: the
"hum-colored cabs" "stir up the air," the laborers' "dirty . . . torsos"
are "glistening"; their "yellow helmets" "protect them from falling /
bricks"; "skirts are flipping / above heels and blow over grates."
Everything is moving, changing, shifting ground, for the poem deals
with the passage of time and eventually with death.[33] Ashbery's voyage "into the secret, vaporous night . . . the unknown that loves us"
(note the allusion to Baudelaire's "Le Voyage") is, by contrast, elusive,
shadowy, archetypal. If his poetry lacks O'Hara's immediacy, it has,
perhaps, a greater suggestiveness, a deeper resonance. If his voice is
less genial and engaging, it compensates by its astonishing self-aware-
ness, its fidelity to the mind's baffling encounter with the objects,
whether real or imaginary, that it contemplates.

But we need not prefer one mode or one poet to the other. I have
outlined some of the major differences between Ashbery and O'Hara
only to make clear that the label "New York School," always something of a misnomer,[34] is no longer meaningful. Edwin Denby has put
it beautifully:

Met these four boys Frank O'Hara, John Ashbery, Kenneth Koch, and
Jimmy Schuyler . . . at the Cedar Bar in '52 or '53. Met them through Bill

(de Kooning) who was a friend of theirs and they admired Kline and all those people. The painters who went to the Cedar had more or less coined the phrase "New York School" in opposition to the School of Paris (which also originated as a joke in opposition to the School of Florence and the School of Venice). Great things started to happen in the Fifties—the point was the great effort in the Eighth Street Club ... the brilliant discussions among painters which had broken through the provincialism of American painting. .... So the poets adopted the expression "New York School" out of homage to the people who had de-provincialized American painting. It's a complicated double-joke. ... So the New York School was a cluster of poets and it was through Frank O'Hara that the uptown poets and the downtown poets got together and eventually the West Coast too, plus the painters and Frank was at the center and joined them all together. After his death there was no center for that group.[35]

"After his death there was no center for that group." There we may, for the time being, let the matter rest. Today both Ashbery and O'Hara, like Allen Ginsberg, who was already famous in the early sixties, have an influence that transcends schools and geographic boundaries. Younger poets coming out of the O'Hara tradition no longer write direct imitations of his "personal poems" as did the first set of disciples who believed, in the words of Anne Waldman, that "Frank O'Hara gave a whole new generation of poets the freedom to put anything you want in a poem" and "showed that poems could be written on the run."[36]

It was, of course, never as simple as that. David Shapiro, a poet still under thirty, has observed that O'Hara's special forms of improvisation and speed must not be confused with "dashing things off" or putting anything you want in a poem. For at its best, "improvisation" becomes a way of discovering truth; in poems like "Memorial Day 1950," or "Joe's Jacket," or "The Day Lady Died," the fleeting "improvisatory" gestures ultimately become what Wallace Stevens called "Parts of a World." As in the great Abstract Expressionist paintings O'Hara loved, the "charged" poetic surface exemplifies the notion that "thinking *is* looking."[37]

"I remember," writes Joe Brainard, "Frank O'Hara's walk. Light and sassy. With a slight bounce and a slight twist. It was a beautiful walk. Confident. 'I don't care' and sometimes 'I know you are look-ing.'"[38] All his life, O'Hara refused to *care* in the conventional sense; he would not fight for publication or scramble for prizes. But perhaps he adopted this stance because he knew, all along, that sooner or later we would indeed be looking. As David Shapiro put it in the elegy he wrote for O'Hara when he was only twenty, we are now "lying against [the] cement to bring it back."[39]

NOTES

ABBREVIATIONS

CP   *The Collected Poems of Frank O'Hara.* Edited by Donald Allen. New York: Knopf, 1971.

PR   *Poems Retrieved.* Edited by Donald Allen. 240-page manuscript, in press. Bolinas, Calif.: Grey Fox Press. References are to typescript.

AC   *Art Chronicles 1954–1966.* New York: Braziller, 1975.

SS   *Standing Still and Walking in New York.* Edited by Donald Allen. Bolinas, Calif.: Grey Fox Press, 1975.

MS   All unpublished manuscripts, unless otherwise indicated, belong to the Frank O'Hara Estate. The numbers have been assigned by the executrix, Maureen Granville-Smith, and the literary editor, Donald Allen.

Chapter 1.: THE AESTHETIC OF ATTENTION

[1] Frank O'Hara speaking about David Smith in the NETA broadcast, "David Smith: Sculpting Master of Bolton Landing," *New York: The Continuity of Vision* series (New York: WNDT–TV, 1964).

[2] Alfred Leslie, preface to the catalogue of his solo exhibition, Allan Frumkin Gallery, 50 West 57th Street, New York (October 25–November 21, 1975). *The Killing of Frank O'Hara* is reproduced in the catalogue (Pl. 1) and in the following: *New York Times,* 9 November 1975, Section 2, p. 33; *Village Voice,* 10 November 1975, p. 112; and *Journal of Modern Literature,* 5, no. 3 (September 1976), 447.

[3] *Village Voice,* 10 November 1975, p. 113.

[4] *Soho Weekly News,* 13 November 1975, p. 24.

[5] Hilton Kramer comments: "It is a powerful painting, in which a great many pictorial tasks are handled with remarkable authority, and all of its dramatic effects serve to amplify a single, sustained idea. Yet I have to confess that I found something foolish in the notion, so clearly implied in the treatment here, that the poet's death, unbearably sad though it was for his friends and admirers, could legitimately be compared to Christ's descent from the cross. It is no disrespect to the memory of Frank O'Hara—quite the contrary, I think—to feel that the whole idea has been woefully misconceived." *New York Times,* 9 November 1975, Section 2, p. 33.

[6] The 1972 version was exhibited at the Whitney Biennial: see Jeanne Siegel, *Art News,* 72 (March 1973), 68–69. This version shows O'Hara lying flat on his back on the beach, while boys and girls in bathing suits are pushing the beach buggy away from the body. A young girl sits in front of the beach buggy, guarding the corpse. Stylistically, the 1972 version resembles the later one, but the death is not mythologized so thoroughly.

[7] Review of *CP* in *New York Times Book Review,* 28 November 1971, p. 7.

[8] Cf. O'Hara's "Ode on Causality" (*CP,* 302):
> make my lines thin as ice, then swell like pythons
> the color of Aurora when she first brought fire to the Arctic in a sled
> a sexual bliss inscribe upon the page of whatever energy I burn for art
> and do not watch over my life. . . .

[9] "Frank O'Hara Dead at 40," *East Village Other,* August 1966, p. 11.

[10] *Planet News* (San Francisco: City Lights Books, 1968), pp. 135–36.

[11] For a challenging but ultimately unconvincing presentation of the "myth" of the suicidal poet, see A. Alvarez, *The Savage God, A Study in Suicide* (New York: Random House, 1972).

[12] *The Advocate* (San Francisco), 2 June 1976, pp. 23–24, 31–33. Saslow draws much of his information from John Gruen's journalistic memoir, *The Party's Over Now, Reminiscences of the Fifties—New York's Artists, Writers, Musicians, and their Friends* (New York: Viking, 1972). Elaine de Kooning's comment, for example, is cited by Gruen on p. 212.

[13] See John Button, "Frank's Grace," *Panjandrum,* 2 & 3 (1973): Special Supplement, *Frank O'Hara (1926–1966),* edited by Bruce Boone, unpaginated. My sources for the information about the accident itself are: (1) the official transcript of the State of New York Department of Motor Vehicles hearing (Case No. 6-374190) held at Suffolk County Center, Riverhead, New York, February 15, 1967, before Roger Whelan, referee. Testifying were Kenneth L. Ruzicka, the driver of the jeep that hit O'Hara, and Patrolman Warren Chamberlain. (2) The deposition made on 15 January 1968 by J. J. Mitchell in the law offices of Sol Lefkowitz, 50 Broadway, New York, N.Y. I cite only those facts that are identical in both reports.

[14] "Frank O'Hara: Lost Times and Future Hopes," *Art in America,* 60 (March–April 1972), 53.

[15] *The New American Poetry,* ed. Donald Allen (New York: Grove, 1960). For an amusingly vituperative attack on *New American Poetry* and on O'Hara in particular, see Cecil Hemley, *Hudson Review,* 13 (Winter 1961), 626–30.

[16]*New York Review of Books,* 31 March 1966, p. 20. For similar response, see Galway Kinnell, review of *Meditations in an Emergency* (1957) in *Poetry,* 92 (June 1958), 179; Kenneth Rexroth, review of *Meditations in an Emergency* in *New York Times,* 6 October 1957, p. 43; Raymond Roseliep, review of *Lunch Poems* (1964) in *Poetry,* 107 (February 1966), 326; Francis Hope, review of *Lunch Poems* in *New Statesman,* 69 (30 April 1965), 688.

Those who praised these books include Kenneth Koch, review of *Second Avenue* (1960) in *Partisan Review,* 28 (January–February 1961), 130–32; Ted Berrigan, review of *Lunch Poems* in *Kulchur,* 5, no. 17 (Spring 1965), 91–94.

[17]*Hudson Review,* 25 (Summer 1972), 308. See also Pearl K. Bell, review of *CP* in *New Leader,* 55 (10 January 1972), 15–16. For more favorable reviews, see Ralph Mills, Jr., *Showcase/Chicago Sun-Times,* 13 February 1972, Section 16, p. 19; Walter Clemons, *Newsweek,* 20 December 1971, pp. 95–96.

[18]"The Virtues of the Alterable," *Parnassus: Poetry in Review,* I(Fall/Winter 1972), 5.

[19]*CP,* v. Since the publication of the *Collected Poems,* dozens of other O'Hara poems, especially from his earlier years, have surfaced and will fill two more volumes (see Bibliographical Note). We may, then, conceivably look forward to an even larger *Collected Poems* in the future.

[20]"All the Imagination Can Hold" (review of *CP*), *New Republic,* 1 & 8 January 1972, p. 24.

[21]Shapcott, *Poetry,* 122 (April 1973), 41; Rosenthal, *The New Poets, American and British Poetry Since World War II* (New York: Oxford, 1967). Cf. Monroe K. Spears, *Dionysus and the City, Modernism in Twentieth-Century Poetry* (New York: Oxford, 1970). Spears devotes twenty pages to Lowell, nine to James Dickey, two to Ginsberg, none to O'Hara.

[22]*Salmagundi,* ed. Robert Boyers, No. 22–23 (Spring–Summer 1973); *The Norton Introduction to Literature: Poetry,* ed. J. Paul Hunter (New York: Norton, 1973). The most notable exception among anthologies is *Contemporary American Poetry,* ed. A. Poulin Jr., 2d ed. (Boston: Houghton Mifflin, 1975). Poulin covers thirty poets, representing the various contemporary schools—O'Hara is given nine pages—about the same number devoted to Denise Levertov or W. S. Merwin. In *The Norton Anthology of Modern Poetry* (New York: Norton, 1973), editors Richard Ellmann and Robert O'Clair adopt a very inclusive policy (more than 150 poets appear!); O'Hara is represented by nine poems.

[23]The new interest in O'Hara among younger poet-critics may be exemplified by the following: Veronica Forrest-Thomson, "Dada, Unrealism and Contemporary Poetry," *20th Century Studies,* 12 (December 1974), 77–93; Charles Molesworth, "'The Clear Architecture of the Nerves': The Poetry of Frank O'Hara," *Iowa Review,* 6 (Summer–Fall 1975), 61–74; Anthony Libby, "O'Hara on the Silver Range," *Contemporary Literature,* 17 (Spring 1976), 240–62; Susan Holahan, "Frank O'Hara's Poetry," in *American Poetry Since 1960, Some Critical Perspectives,* ed. Robert B. Shaw (Cheadle Hulme: Carcanet Press, 1973), 109–22. A hopeful sign of things to come is the new edition of the well-known anthology, *Naked Poetry, Recent American Poetry in Open Forms* (New York: Bobbs–Merrill, 1976), edited by the poets Stephen Berg and Robert Mezey. The first edition (1969) did not include O'Hara among its nineteen poets. The new edition rectifies this omission.

[24] *The Poem in its Skin* (Chicago: Big Table, 1968), p. 204.

[25] See Fig. 3. This collaboration will be discussed fully in Chapter 3.

[26] Notes for a talk on "The Image in Poetry and Painting," The Club, 11 April 1952. Unpub. MS 467. In a second talk at The Club (14 May 1952), O'Hara criticizes younger poets like Richard Wilbur for creating an aesthetic "based on the memory of adolescent reading of Tennyson's *Idylls* and the dross of such important writers as T. S. Eliot." Even the California poets are criticized for "following the line Eliot discovered in his study of the English Metaphysical and French Symbolist poets. . . ." (unpub. MS 156).

[27] "The End of the Line: American Poetry, 1945-1955," Chapter 1 of a projected book; p. 23 of typescript.

In an unpublished letter to Mike Goldberg, 16 February 1956, O'Hara writes: "Did you read William Carlos Williams' autobiog? I love his poems, but the book is oddly crotchety and contentious and provincial. . . . I'm not sure that at the time things happened he didn't feel genuine admirations and thereby could advance and be stimulated, and then when he comes to right [*sic*] this book so many years later he forgets them. . . ." This comment would bear out Breslin's contention.

[28] See "T. S. Eliot as The International Hero," *Partisan Review*, 12 (Spring 1945); rpt. in *The Selected Essays of Delmore Schwartz*, eds. Donald A. Dike and David H. Zucker (Chicago: University of Chicago Press, 1970), pp. 120-28; "The Literary Dictatorship of T. S. Eliot," *Partisan Review*, 16 (February 1949); rpt. *Selected Essays*, pp. 312-31. On Williams's reputation, see Paul L. Mariani, *William Carlos Williams, the Poet and his Critics* (Chicago: American Library Association, 1975), esp. pp. 125-37.

[29] *Poetry and the Age* (New York: Knopf, 1953), p. 140.

[30] Phillip Cooper, *The Autobiographical Myth of Robert Lowell* (Chapel Hill: University of North Carolina Press, 1970), pp. 38-43.

[31] Breslin, "The End of the Line," p. 34.

[32] Frederick Seidel, "An Interview with Robert Lowell," *The Paris Review*, 25 (Winter-Spring 1961); rpt. in *Robert Lowell: A Portrait of the Artist in his Time*, eds. Michael London and Robert Boyers (New York: David Lewis, 1970), pp. 269-70.

[33] "A Poem's Becoming," *In Radical Pursuit* (New York: Harper & Row, 1975), p. 42.

[34] Boston: Little, Brown, 1964, p. 17.

[35] Paul Carroll's last chapter, "Faire, Foul and Full of Variations: The Generation of 1962," *Poem in its Skin*, pp. 202-59, is very helpful. See also Robert Creeley, *Contexts of Poetry: Interviews 1961-1971*, ed. Donald Allen (Bolinas: Four Seasons Foundation, 1973), especially Fred Wah's interview with Creeley and Ginsberg in Vancouver in 1963, pp. 29-43. Almost every essay in the special Charles Olson issue of *Boundary 2*, II (Fall 1973/Winter 1974) touches on the question of the Black Mountain revolt against tradition.

[36] "Frank O'Hara's Question," *Book Week*, 25 September 1966, p. 6.

[37] Edward Lucie-Smith, "An Interview with Frank O'Hara," *SS*, 13; first published in abbreviated form in *Studio International*, September 1966.

[38] Joseph LeSueur, "Four Apartments: A Memoir of Frank O'Hara," in *Another*

World, ed. Anne Waldman (New York: Bobbs-Merrill, 1971), p. 290. This important essay is hereafter cited as "Four Apartments." LeSueur added further detail to the anecdote and discussed O'Hara's reluctance to criticize other poets in an interview with the author on 30 July 1975, hereafter cited as "LeSueur Interview."

[39] In my opinion, O'Hara's judgment is less than fair here. "Skunk Hour," like the other poems in *Life Studies,* does represent a significant departure from neo-Symbolist poetics. See my *Poetic Art of Robert Lowell* (Ithaca, N.Y.: Cornell University Press, 1973), pp. 80–99.

[40] "Non-American Painting: Six Opinions of Abstract Art in Other Countries," *It is* (Winter–Spring 1959); rpt. as "American Art and Non-American Art" in *SS,* 98. In "Gregory Corso" (*SS,* 82–85), O'Hara talks of "the extraordinary beauties of Corso's poems."

[41] In an unpublished letter to Jasper Johns of 15 July 1959, O'Hara says, "Gary Snyder and Philip Whalen are both marvellous but you have to find them in EVERGREEN, MEASURE, BLACK MOUNTAIN, or YUGEN I think." He also praises Mike McClure.

[42] In the letter to Johns cited above, O'Hara writes: "Kerouac's DOCTOR SAX is his best work, I think, and after that the first sections of OLD ANGEL MIDNIGHT which are printed in the first issue of BIG TABLE." Joe LeSueur recalls an evening at the Cedar Bar in the Village, c. 1960, when Kerouac, very drunk, came up to O'Hara and said: "I thought you liked me." O'Hara replied: "It's not you I like, it's your work," a remark that pleased Kerouac very much.

[43] In the letter to Johns, Wieners heads O'Hara's list of poets that interest him.

[44] Letter to Johns. Of Robert Duncan, O'Hara writes to Johns: "I can't stand him myself, but he is their [the West Coast's] Charles Olson—to me he is quite flabby by comparison, but maybe because I'm on the East Coast."

[45] "Frank O'Hara and his Poems," *Art and Literature,* 12 (Spring 1967), 54.

[46] In the 1961 "Statement for Paterson Society" (*CP,* 510–11), O'Hara explains that "Personism" was intended for *New American Poetry,* but that "Allen thought it unwise to use it in relation to the earlier poems included, quite rightly, so I wrote another which he did use. This latter [*CP,* 500], it seems to me now, is even more mistaken, pompous, and quite untrue, as compared to the manifesto. But it is also, like the manifesto, a diary of a particular day." In "Four Apartments," Joe LeSueur describes the amusing genesis of "Personism," written in less than an hour (the zero hour because Don Allen was on his way over to pick it up!) to the tune of Rachmaninoff's Third blasting on the radio: Waldman, *Another World,* p. 296.

[47] O'Hara's familiarity with "Projective Verse" is made clear from the reference to "Charles Olson (whose theory of projective verse, among other things, recommends the use of the typewriter as an instrument, not just a recorder of thought)," in "Design Etc." (notes for a talk at The Club, 11 April 1952), *SS,* 34.

[48] *SS,* 33–34.

[49] See, for example, Bly, "On English and American Poetry," *The Fifties,* No. 2 (1959), pp. 45–47; and "The Dead World and the Live World," *The Sixties,* No. 8 (Spring 1966), pp. 2–7. LeRoi Jones attacks Bly's poetry and poetics in *Kulchur* 3 (Summer 1963), 83–84.

[50] L. S. Dembo, "George Oppen: An Interview," *Contemporary Literature,* 10 (Spring 1969), 161. Although this interview was made after O'Hara's death, it represents the kind of theorizing he disliked.

[51] Cited by John Ashbery in his review of *In Memory of My Feelings* in *Art News,* 66 (January 1968), 68.

[52] Unpub. letter to Bill Berkson, 12 August 1962.

[53] "Statement for *The New American Poetry* (1960)," *CP,* 500.

[54] "Art as Technique," in *Russian Formalist Criticism: Four Essays,* trans. and ed. Lee T. Lemon and Marion J. Reis (Lincoln, Neb.: University of Nebraska Press, 1965), pp. 12–13. For a fuller discussion of Shklovsky's aesthetic and a comparison of various translations of his key terms, see my "New Thresholds, Old Anatomies: Contemporary Poetry and the Limits of Exegesis," *Iowa Review,* 5 (Winter 1974), 88–89.

[55] "American Art and Non-American Art," *SS,* 98.

[56] There are a number of allusions to Rilke in the *Collected Poems,* for example: "Do you know young René Rilke?" in "Poem (To be idiomatic in a vacuum)," *CP,* 282; and "Aus Einem April" (*CP,* 186) is a loose adaptation of Rilke's poem. Albert Cook praises this poem for its ingenious way of "de-'poeticizing' the language" of the German poet. "His *Aus einem April,*" says Cook, "is a commentary on Rilke so full-throated that all the chaste ironies of Pound's commentaries on Propertius and Gautier, Waller or Homer, get lost in the Saturnalian shuffle . . . ," "Frank O'Hara, We Are Listening," *Audit/Poetry,* 4, no. 1 (1964): Frank O'Hara Issue, 34.

[57] The German text is:

> Ja, die Frühlinge brauchten dich wohl. Es muteten manche
> Sterne dir zu, dass du sie spürtest. Es hob
> sich eine Woge heran im Vergangenen, oder
> da du vorüberkamst am geöffneten Fenster,
> gab eine Geige sich hin. Das alles war Auftrag.

The text used is Rainer Maria Rilke, *Duino Elegies, with English Translations* by C. F. MacIntyre (Berkeley and Los Angeles: Univ. of California Press, 1968), p. 4. The translation is my own since I disagree with some of MacIntyre's readings, but it is a very difficult passage to translate accurately: "die Frühlinge," for example, when translated literally as "the springs," loses its effect. On the poet's duty to be "attentive," see also Rilke, *Letters to a Young Poet,* trans. M. D. Herter Norton (New York: Norton, 1962), p. 65.

[58] "Larry Rivers: A Memoir," *CP,* 515.

[59] Larry Rivers, *Collage with O'Hara Poem,* exhibited in "Frank O'Hara, A Poet Among Painters," *Whitney Museum of American Art,* 12 February–17 March 1974. In "Post the Lake Poets Ballad" (*CP,* 336–37), O'Hara refers to "a letter from Larry":

> it's so hot out
> and I read the letter which says
> in your poems your gorgeous self-pity
> how do you like that
>
> that is odd I think of myself
> as a cheerful type who pretends to

> be hurt to get a little depth into
> things that interest me. . . .

> no more self-pity than Gertrude
> Stein before Lucey Church or Savonarola
> in the pulpit Allen Ginsberg at the
> Soviet Exposition am I Joe

[60] According to Donald Allen, this essay was written in 1953 or later, apparently as a letter to an editor of a literary magazine (*CP*, 495).

[61] "The Search for the Real in the Visual Arts," in *Search for the Real and Other Essays,* eds. Sara T. Weeks and Bartlett H. Hayes, Jr. (Cambridge, Mass.: M.I.T. Press, 1967), pp. 44–45.

[62] *Jackson Pollock* (New York: Braziller, 1959); rpt. *AC,* 34–35.

[63] "Growth and Guston," *Art News* (May 1962); rpt. *AC,* 141.

[64] "Art Chronicle I," *Kulchur,* 2 (Summer 1962); rpt. *SS,* 132; *AC,* 11.

[65] "Art Chronicle I," *SS,* 130; *AC,* 9.

[66] "Art Chronicle III," *Kulchur* 3 (Spring 1963), 56; rpt. *SS,* 141.

[67] "David Smith: The Color of Steel," *Art News,* 60 (December 1961); rpt. *SS,* 123.

[68] "The Sorrows of the Youngman, John Rechy's *City of Night,*" *Kulchur* 3 (Winter 1963); rpt. *SS,* 162–63.

[69] In a letter to the author dated 13 July 1975, Donald Allen writes: "In conversation with me in 1958 and 1959 Frank spoke several times of WCW as being the only poet around that he could read in the late forties (when *Paterson* was appearing)." In the unpublished letter to Mike Goldberg of 16 February 1956 (see Note 27 above), O'Hara says: "If the long poem in his new book of poems JOURNEY TO LOVE isn't great, I'm going to take up knitting." The reference is to "Asphodel, that Greeney Flower." Williams's influence is discussed more fully in the next chapter.

[70] "About Zhivago and his Poems," commissioned by Donald Allen and first published in *Evergreen Review,* 2 (Winter 1959); rpt. *CP,* 503.

[71] "Abstraction in Poetry," *It Is,* 3 (Winter–Spring 1959), 75.

[72] On this point, see Charles Altieri, "The Significance of Frank O'Hara," *Iowa Review,* 4 (Winter 1973), 99. Altieri's essay is of central importance and I am indebted to it throughout this book.

[73] *Belgrade, November 19, 1963* (New York: Adventures in Poetry, n.d.), pp. 1–2.

[74] *CP,* 325–26. "515 is 'off' Madison on 53d; Frank would have passed it every day to and from the Museum. Its door facade is very beautiful" (Bill Berkson to Donald Allen, July 1969), *CP,* 543.

Chapter 2: THE EARLY YEARS (1946–53)

[1] Journal: October 8, 1948 to January 28, 1949. Unpub. MS 472, p. *n.* Hereafter cited as Harvard Journal.

[2] *A Portrait of the Artist as a Young Man* (New York: Viking/Compass, 1967), p. 168.

[3] "Lament and Chastisement: a Travelogue of War and Personality," Unpub. MS 631, pp. 7, 17–18.

[4] Unpub. Course Description, "Francis Russell O'Hara. Harvard College A.B. 1950," prepared by Marion C. Belliveau, Registrar, Harvard University, June 24, 1974.

[5] Notebook A, Unpub. MS, pp. 73–131.

[6] Harvard Journal, pp. *i–j*.

[7] "V. R. Lang: A Memoir," *Village Voice,* 23 October 1957; rpt. *SS,* 86.

[8] Dated 24 April 1947: Notebook A, p. 10.

[9] Unpub MS 146.

[10] In an interview conducted on 15 September 1975 in New York, John Ashbery told the author that he doubts O'Hara knew enough French to read these difficult texts. Donald Allen, in a letter to the author of 19 September 1975, writes: "Frank was not terribly confident of his French. He asked me to have John A. check his translations before publishing them because John had lived so long in France and perfected his knowledge. But Frank's knowledge must have been considerable; he read it with ease; and he did translate some very difficult French verse. He translates part of a Breton title in 'All that Gas,' another instance." Paul Schmidt, who says in the Preface to his translation of Rimbaud's *Complete Works* (New York: Harper & Row, 1975) that he owes a special debt "to the late Frank O'Hara, whose criticism and suggestions are reflected many times here" (p. xx), concurs with Allen's view in a letter to the author dated 16 September 1975.

[11] Lucie-Smith, "Interview with Frank O'Hara," *SS,* 10. Later in the interview, O'Hara tells Lucie-Smith, "There's a big gap in my thinking about English poetry, although for instance I admire very much Tomlinson and Thom Gunn" (p. 24).

[12] Notes for a talk on "The Image in Poetry and Painting," The Club, 11 April 1952, Unpub MS 467, p. 2.

[13] In the interview of 15 September 1975, Ashbery described how O'Hara tried to talk him into attending a Schoenberg concert at Harvard; Ashbery did not attend but later came round to O'Hara's high opinion of the composer.

[14] John Ciardi, undated letter to Donald Allen.

[15] Harvard Journal, pp. *g, t.*

[16] Aside from the Preface to the Collected Poems and the obituary essay in *Book Week,* 25 September 1966, p. 6, Ashbery wrote an important review of *In Memory of My Feelings* for *Art News,* 66 (January 1968), 50–51, 67–68.

[17] PR, 1.

[18] Dated 15 November 1946: Notebook A, pp. 1–4.

[19] *CP,* 12–13. O'Hara here weaves together lines and phrases from various poems by Baudelaire, especially "La Beauté," and Rimbaud's notorious prose poem, "H," which

is generally taken to be about masturbation or anal intercourse and ends with the enigmatic words, "trouvez Hortense." See Rimbaud, *Oeuvres,* ed. Suzanne Bernard (Paris: Garnier, 1960), pp. 531–32.

[20] Unpub. MS 296, "Pastorals," pp. *d–p.* Cf. *CP,* 519.

[21] One could make an interesting comparison between O'Hara's early poetry and that of Rimbaud. Both poets begin by trying to write—against the grain—conventional heterosexual love poems in keeping with the going convention and then later drop the mask. In both cases, the early poetry is full of blasphemous attacks on the Church and scatological imagery. See, for example, Rimbaud's "Les premières communions" and "Remembrances du vieillard idiot."

[22] Rilke's clearest statement about the doll as a death symbol is found in the essay "Puppen, Zu den Wachs-Puppen von Lotte Pritzel," *Sämtliche Werke,* Vol. 6 (Berlin: Insel Verlag, 1960, pp. 1063–73, and notes on pp. 1486–89).

[23] *Dada* (New York: Studio Vista/Dutton, 1970), pp. 37–38.

[24] Mary Ann Caws, *The Poetry of Dada and Surrealism* (Princeton: Princeton University Press, 1970), p. 14.

[25] In the First Manifesto (1924), Breton gives this definition: "SURREALISM, noun. Pure psychic automatism by means of which we propose to express either verbally, in writing, or in some other fashion what really goes on in the mind. Dictation by the mind, unhampered by conscious control and having no aesthetic or moral goals." Translation by Herbert S. Gershman, *The Surrealist Revolution in France* (Ann Arbor: University of Michigan Press, 1974), p. 35.

[26] *CP,* 10. Duchamp invented the word play "Rrose Sélavy" in 1920; Desnos then borrowed the name for his amusing series of poems of 1922–23. In the same poem O'Hara also refers to Duchamp's famous *Nude Descending a Staircase:*
> the next time I see you
> clattering down a flight of stairs like a
> ferris wheel jingling your earrings and feathers . . .

[27] *The Poetry of Surrealism, An Anthology* (Boston: Little, Brown, 1974). Hereafter cited as *Poetry of Surrealism.*

[28] Notes for a talk on "The Image in Poetry and Painting," The Club, 11 April 1952. Unpub. MS 467, p. 2.

[29] Notes for a talk on "The New Poets," The Club, 14 May 1952, Unpub MS 156, p. 3.

[30] Letter to Jasper Johns, 15 July 1959. O'Hara's allusion is to Williams's essay "Revelation," first published in *Yale Poetry Review* (1947) and reprinted in *Selected Essays of William Carlos Williams* (New York: New Directions, 1954), pp. 268–71. The essay begins: "The objective in writing is, to reveal. It is not to teach, not to advertise, not to sell, not even to communicate . . . but to reveal."

[31] Notes for a talk on "The New Poets," The Club, 14 May 1952, Unpub. MS 156, p. 3.

[32] *The Collected Earlier Poems of William Carlos Williams* (Norfolk, Conn.: New Directions, 1951), p. 105.

[33] John Ashbery, Joe LeSueur, and Donald Allen have all noted in conversation that O'Hara's selection of poems to be published tended to be arbitrary, and that he did not care to judge his own work.

[34] Ashbery, Preface to the *Collected Poems,* vii.

[35] It is interesting to compare O'Hara's reference to plane trees to Robert Lowell's well-known "As a Plane Tree by Water," in which Lowell alludes to Ecclesiastes 24:19: "As a plane tree by the water in the streets, I was exalted," implying that in the modern "Babel of Boston," "flies are on the plane trees"—nature is wholly corrupted. The plane tree, used as a central symbol by Lowell, is simply an item in the Cambridge landscape for O'Hara—another tree would do just as well.

[36] Again an allusion to Rilke; see Note 22 above.

[37] See Caws, *Poetry of Dada and Surrealism,* pp. 20, 47–48. The concept of *vertige* is particularly prominent in the poetry of Aragon, for whom "the term *vertige* implies both rapidity . . . and total involvement."

[38] John Ciardi, unpublished letter to Donald Allen, undated.

[39] Underneath the title, O'Hara wrote "A Pathetic Note to George Montgomery" and then crossed it out.

[40] *The Collected Poems of Dylan Thomas* (New York: New Directions, 1953), p. 142.

[41] "John Ashbery and Frank O'Hara: The Painterly Poets," *Journal of Modern Literature,* 5, no. 3 (September 1976), 442–43.

[42] *A Homemade World, The American Modernist Writers* (New York: Knopf, 1975), pp. 86, 59.

[43] *Williams, Collected Earlier Poems,* p. 173. For additional analogues, see "The Descent of Winter, 9/30" (p. 298), especially the last stanza: "there is no hope—if not a coral / island slowly forming / to wait for birds to drop / the seeds will make it habitable"; and "Night Rider," in *The Collected Later Poems of William Carlos Williams* (New York: New Directions, 1963), p. 71.

[44] Many other love poems from the Ann Arbor period are similarly written in the Williams mode. "A Proud Poem" (*CP,* 52–53), for example, recalls Williams's "Danse Russe" in its charming bravado: "I am hopelessly happily conceited / in all inventions / and divertissement. . . .and when I'm cornered at the final / minute by cries 'you've / murdered angels with toys' I'll go down / grinning into clever flames."

[45] "Frank O'Hara: A Poet Among Painters" (review of the Whitney show by that name), *Art News,* 73 (May 1974), 44–45.

[46] "The Club," *Artforum,* 4, no. 1 (September 1965) Special Issue: The New York School, 27–31.

[47] "Design Etc.," *SS,* 33–35.

[48] See Eliot, "Reflections on Vers Libre" (1917) in *To Criticize the Critic* (New York: Farrar, Straus & Giroux, 1965), p. 185.

[49] Notes for a talk on "The Image in Poetry and Painting," The Club, 11 April 1952, Unpub. MS 467, p. 4.

[50] *A Homemade World,* Chapter 3, *passim.*

[51] W. H. Auden, unpublished letter to Frank O'Hara, 3 June (1955?). The parody of Wyatt may be compared to the actual octave:

> My galley charged with forgetfulness
> Through sharp seas in winter nights doth pass
> 'Tween rock and rock and eke my foe, alas,
> That is my lord, steereth with cruelness.
> And every [oar] a thought in readiness.
> As though that death were light in such a case,
> An endless wind doth tear the sail apace
> of forced sighs and trusty fearfulness.

[52] Caws, *Poetry of Dada and Surrealism,* pp. 33–35.

[53] I owe this information to Donald Allen (letter to the author, 2 January 1976).

[54] *The Collected Poems of Wallace Stevens* (New York: Knopf, 1961), pp. 3, 76.

[55] Thomas Shapcott, *Poetry,* 122 (1973), 43–44. Charles Molesworth, in "'The Clear Architecture of the Nerves': The Poetry of Frank O'Hara," *Iowa Review,* 6 (Summer–Fall 1975), calls the mode of "Easter" that of "surreal serendipity. . . . It resembles very strongly the 'paranoical-critical' method enunciated by Salvador Dali, and in attributing occult and protean abilities to everyday objects, it has the same mixture of theatricalized terror and whimpering playfulness as Dali's paintings" (pp. 66–67).

[56] Rimbaud, *Complete Works,* trans. Paul Schmidt, pp. 108–13. Schmidt freely translates the title as "Remarks to a Poet on the Subject of Flowers."

[57] "A Note on Frank O'Hara in the Early Fifties," *Audit/Poetry,* 4, no. 1 (1964): Frank O'Hara Issue, 33; rpt. *CP,* 526.

[58] "Poetry Chronicles," *Partisan Review,* 28 (January–February 1961), 130–32.

[59] *CP,* 558.

[60] Interview with Grace Hartigan, conducted in Baltimore, 25 November 1975.

[61] In *Parnassus* (Fall/Winter 1972), Helen Vendler says: "The longest poems end up simply messy, endless secretions, with a nugget of poetry here and there, slices of life arbitrarily beginning, and ending for no particular reason. 'Dear Diary,' says O'Hara, and after that anything goes" (pp. 5–6). In his essay on O'Hara for *Alone with America* (New York: Atheneum, 1969), pp. 396–412, Richard Howard writes: "Each time I read *Second Avenue* I bear off a handful of glittering lines . . . but they are never the same lines, and never suggest anything converging, opposing or even subordinating in the kind of tension that makes for unity. . . ." (p. 404). Howard calls *Second Avenue* "a poem . . . of promiscuous agglomerations, a virtuoso *performance* in discourse without composition" (p. 403).

[62] For another example of O'Hara's incorporation of the names of friends into the poetry of this period, see "Day and Night in 1952," *CP,* 93–94.

Chapter 3: POET AMONG PAINTERS

[1] *Art in America,* 53 (October–November 1965), 24.

[2] Preface to *In Memory of My Feelings. A Selection of Poems by Frank O'Hara*, ed. Bill Berkson (New York: Museum of Modern Art, 1967), pages unnumbered.

[3] *Art News*, 66 (January 1968), 68. Cf. John Button, "Frank's Grace," *Panjandrum*, 2 & 3 (1973): "The job at MOMA gave him less and less leisure at precisely the time he could have been writing his best poetry."

[4] "Four Apartments," p. 291. Cf. James Schuyler, *Art News*, 73 (May 1974), 45: "Frank needed a job and he was in love with the museum and brooked no criticism of it. . . . And he was highly organized, with a phenomenal memory."

[5] In a letter to Bruce Boone, the editor of the special O'Hara supplement of *Panjandrum*, Grace Hartigan writes: "that Frank was a homosexual was very understandable to me—I love men, why shouldn't he? It never—what would?—interfered with our love for each other. I'm not the first person to say that sex isn't necessarily love and vice-versa." Grace Hartigan made the same point to the author in an interview conducted on 25 November 1975. Between 1951 and 1960, she and Frank saw each other or spoke on the phone almost every day. They frequently spent weeks—even months— together in the country. Thus they knew each other's projects intimately. In 1960, after a major quarrel with Frank, Grace left New York, married, and settled in Baltimore. She sent him a strongly worded letter breaking off all relations. They did not see each other again for five years, and then only briefly.

[6] *CP*, 486.

[7] In a letter to the author dated 10 February 1976, Grace Hartigan identifies the first painting as "Ocean Bathers" (1953), Collection of Mrs. Muriel Newman (Chicago), and the second as "Frank O'Hara and the Demons" (1952), Collection Grace Hartigan. Both paintings, Hartigan notes, seek to capture "Frank's body stance, his posture."

[8] In an unpublished letter of 8 April 1957, O'Hara wrote to Helen Frankenthaler:

I'm enclosing a poem I wrote recently to find out if I can use your title on it [*Blue Territory*]. Now, please, if you don't like it or if the association bothers you in the slightest . . . please tell me and I can change it to "Boo Titulary" or something. . . . I can always call it tersely, "Poem" as in the past.

In a poetry reading at Buffalo on 25 September 1964, taped by Donald Allen, O'Hara remarked before reading "Blue Territory" that seeing Helen Frankenthaler's large abstract painting by that name in the Whitney gave him the idea for the poem, though he didn't quite know why.

[9] *Dada, Surrealism, and Their Heritage* (New York: Museum of Modern Art, 1968), p. 148. See also Diane Waldman, *Joseph Cornell* (New York: Braziller, 1977).

[10] See, for example, "Design Etc.," *SS*, 33; and "Apollinaire's Pornographic Novels," *SS*, 156–59. Grace Hartigan told me in the interview of 25 November 1975 that Frank often said he didn't want to live any longer than Apollinaire. The French poet died at the age of 40; so, by uncanny coincidence, did O'Hara.

[11] *Apollinaire on Art, Essays and Reviews 1901–1918*, The Documents of 20th Century Art (New York: Viking, 1971), p. xxix.

[12] *Kulchur*, 3, no. 9 (Spring 1963); rpt. *SS*, 140.

[13]John Canaday was the *Times* art critic; Emily Genauer wrote for the *Herald Tribune*. O'Hara writes:

> ... each has devoted, at least one slack week in each season, a whole column to their difficulties in getting themselves physically to the galleries, Mr. Canaday notably in his lament over bus service on Madison Avenue column, and Miss Genauer in her candid appraisal of a safari as far south as Houston Street, with aid of cab driver and delicatessen clerk, in search of the Delancey Street Museum. Neither one of them has any better sense of geography of traffic than they do of art.
>
> Mr. Canaday's speciality along this line has been the wise-suspicion-of esthetic-hoax strategy, a strategy aimed exclusively at the abstract-expressionists with the equally simplistic belief, apparently, that no figurative artist has ever wanted to sell a painting. (*SS*, 144-45)

[14] "Watch Out for the Paint! The Salon des Indépendants. 6,000 Paintings are Exhibited" (1910), in *Apollinaire on Art*, pp. 64-65.

[15] See Amy Golden, *Art in America*, 63 (March-April 1975), 41; Eleonor Dickinson, *San Francisco Review of Books*, 1, no. 4 (August 1975), 6, 18-19. I take the opposite position in my review of *AC* in *The New Republic*, 1 March 1975, pp. 23-24.

[16] "Introduction," *New Spanish Painting and Sculpture* (New York: Museum of Modern Art, 1960), p. 10.

[17] *Art News*, 52 (December 1953), 42.

[18] *Art News*, 53 (January 1954), 64.

[19] *Art News*, 54 (February 1955), 53.

[20] *Art News*, 53 (April 1954), 47.

[21] See, for example, Allen Weller, *Art Journal*, 20 (Fall 1960), 52-56. Similar strictures can be made about O'Hara's short essay, "Jackson Pollock 1912-1956," in *New Images of Man*, ed. Peter Selz (New York: Museum of Modern Art, 1959), pp. 123-28. O'Hara calls Pollock's black-and-white paintings of 1951 "ideographs from a subjective world we do not know . . . the *Chants de Maldoror* of American art" (p. 123).

[22] *Horizon* (September 1959), rpt. *AC*, 106-20. Cf. O'Hara's television interview with David Smith (cited Chapter 1, Note 1). O'Hara calls Smith's life "the American tragedy in reverse," for Smith was "a Henry James hero who influenced Europe rather than being corrupted by it," a "Thomas Wolfe, whose dreams, strangely enough, came true." The interview suggests that Smith did not think of his sculptures as "abstract" at all. He calls them "females," saying, "I don't do males. I like the presence of these females." To which O'Hara responds: "They seem like friends who came to New York. They're relieved not to be in mid-air any more." O'Hara interviewed Barnett Newman for the same series.

[23] See Sam Hunter, *Larry Rivers*, with a Memoir by Frank O'Hara and a Statement by the Artist, Exhibition of the Poses Institute of Fine Arts, Brandeis University, Waltham, Mass., 1965. Hunter provides a brief chronology (pp. 45-46), and his introduction is very useful.

[24] Hunter, *Larry Rivers*, p. 20.

[25] Larry Rivers wrote: "His long marvelous poem *Second Avenue,* 1953, was written in my plaster garden studio overlooking that avenue. One night late I was working on a piece of sculpture of him. Between poses he was finishing his long poem. Three fat cops saw the light and made their way up to make the 'you call this art and what are you doing here' scene that every N.Y. artist must have experienced." "Life Among the Stones," *Location* (Spring 1963); rpt. *CP,* 529.

[26] See Roger Shattuck, *Guillaume Apollinaire* (New York: New Directions, 1971), pp. 18–20.

[27] Reproduced in Rubin, *Dada, Surrealism and their Heritage,* pp. 27–28.

[28] Motherwell, *The Dada Painters and Poets, An Anthology* (New York: Wittenborn, Schultz, Inc., 1951), p. 62. The translation is by Ralph Manheim.

[29] Ibid., pp. 56, 274. In "The Grand Manner of Motherwell" (1965), O'Hara writes: "I first met Motherwell in East Hampton in, probably, 1952. When we did talk later, it was almost always about poetry: Apollinaire, Baudelaire, Jacob, Reverdy, Rilke (not so much), and Lorca (lots), and we also got to Wallace Stevens and William Carlos Williams. I had been tremendously impressed by the Documents of Modern Art Series [*Dada Painters* was No. 8] which Motherwell had edited (indeed it was the Gospels for myself and many other poets)," *SS,* 176.

[30] Rubin, *Dada, Surrealism,* p. 96, Plate 129.

[31] "Max Ernst: Passed and Pressing Tensions," *Hudson Review,* 23 (Winter 1970–71); rpt. *Art Journal,* 33 (Fall 1973), 12.

[32] Quoted by Lippard, "Max Ernst," 12.

[33] Lippard, 14.

[34] *Location* (Spring 1963), 90–98.

[35] "The Skin of the Stone," *The Scene, Reports on Post-Modern Art* (New York: Viking, 1976), p. 58. Tompkins provides a very interesting biographical sketch of Tatyana Grossman and discusses *Stones* as well as the other collaborations made in her workshop. See also Cleve Gray, "Tatyana Grossman's Workshop," *Art in America,* 53 (December–January 1965–66), 83; Herbert Mitgang, "Tatyana Grossman, 'the inner light of 5 Skidmore Place,'" *Art News,* 73 (March 1974), 29–32.

[36] Quoted by Tompkins, *The Scene,* pp. 61–62.

[37] Rivers, *Location,* 92. Succeeding quotations from Rivers are from the same source.

[38] Sidney Tillin, *Arts Magazine,* 34 (December 1959), 62.

[39] See Gertrude Stein, *Everybody's Autobiography* (1937; rpt. New York: Vintage, 1973), p. 15.

[40] In the Lucie-Smith interview, O'Hara suggests that his only true collaboration was *Stones* (*SS,* 4–5). He quite rightly points out that his work with painters like Mike Goldberg and Grace Hartigan did not involve collaboration; rather they used his poems. But he seems to have forgotten *Poem-Paintings,* which was nothing if not a truly collaborative effort, the two artists working simultaneously throughout.

[41]Notes to Exhibition catalogue of *Poem-Paintings,* Loeb Student Center, New York University, January 9–February 5, 1967.

[42]*Art News,* 65 (February 1967), 11.

[43]Interview with Norman Bluhm, 2 December 1975, New York.

[44]*Art News,* 65 (February 1967), 11.

[45]The O'Hara–Brainard cartoons were originally made for *C Comics,* edited by Joe Brainard (New York, 1964–65). A series of these is reproduced in *Panjandrum,* 2 & 3 (1973).

[46]A related example may be found in the work of Franz Kline. Kline took O'Hara's "Poem (I will always love you . . .)," written in 1957, and incorporated it in O'Hara's own handwriting in an etching made for the portfolio *21 Etchings and Poems,* published by the Morris Gallery in 1960; see Notes to the *CP,* 539.

[47]"Poets and Painters and Painters and Poets," *New York Times,* 11 August 1968, Section II, 24.

[48]Berkson, Notes to catalogue of *Poem-Paintings.*

[49]Unpub. letter to Gregory Corso, 15 March 1968.

Chapter 4: IN FAVOR OF ONE'S TIME (1954–61)

[1]Unpub. letter to Fairfield Porter, 7 July 1955.

[2]The friendship with Grace Hartigan ended in 1960 when she left New York (see Chapter 3, Note 5). Patsy Southgate met O'Hara on Memorial Day 1958 when she gave a Bloody Mary party at Easthampton; Mike Kanemitsu, Donald Allen, and Mike Goldberg (later Patsy's husband) were also there. In an interview conducted in New York on 30 March 1976, Patsy Southgate told the author, "I was his closest woman friend during the last part of his life. We were in love."

[3]Unpub. letter to John Ashbery, 1 February 1961.

[4]LeSueur Interview, 30 July 1975.

[5]Lawrence Ferlinghetti, letter to Bruce Boone, 3 February 1973, in *Panjandrum,* 2 & 3 (1973), unpaginated.

[6]*Lunch Poems* (San Francisco: City Lights Books, 1964), back cover. Ferlinghetti estimates that seven years elapsed between his proposal that O'Hara "make a book" from the "poems he wrote on his lunch hour" and the publication of *Lunch Poems* (letter to Bruce Boone cited above). We know that the project was on O'Hara's mind in 1959, because when John Ashbery asked him for a group of poems possibly influenced by Reverdy, to be used in Ashbery's forthcoming essay on Reverdy's influence on American poets, O'Hara replied: "I had them [the poems] prepared to go into *Lunch Poems* which Ferlinghetti asked me for 2 years ago and has doubtless ceased to care about. But that's why I have copies to send," unpub. letter to John Ashbery, 1 February 1961.

[7]The others are "Now that I am in Madrid and Can Think," "Song (Did you see me walking by the Buick Repairs?)," "Cohasset," "Beer for Breakfast," "St. Paul and All

That," "Pistachio Tree at Château Noir," "Adventures in Living," and "Hôtel Particulier."

⁸Introduction to *The Floating Bear,* rpt. of the semimonthly newsletter 1961–69, eds. Diane di Prima and LeRoi Jones (New York: 1970), pp. viii–ix. Diane di Prima was quite right, as O'Hara's Harvard Notebook and the forthcoming *Poems Retrieved* make clear.

⁹Unpub. letter to Mike Goldberg, 16 February 1956. Courtesy Giorno Poetry Systems, The Archives, in which the letter is numbered 15,306. The story of the lost typewriter is told by Joe LeSueur in "Four Apartments," p. 290.

¹⁰In an interview conducted in New York on 30 March 1976, David Shapiro told the author that John Ashbery once expressed this feeling about using long lines. That O'Hara equated line length with strength and vitality is suggested by the prayer in "Ode on Causality": "make my lines thin as ice, then swell like pythons" (*CP,* 302).

¹¹In the interview of 30 July 1975, LeSueur told the author that he preferred O'Hara's realistic, documentary poems—the "I do this, I do that" poems—to all others.

¹²Shapiro interview, 30 March 1976.

¹³"Art as Technique," in *Russian Formalist Criticism, Four Essays,* trans. and ed. Lee T. Lemon and Marion J. Reis (Lincoln, Neb.: University of Nebraska Press, 1965), p. 13.

¹⁴"The Significance of Frank O'Hara," *Iowa Review,* 4 (Winter 1973), 91.

¹⁵The phrase is David Shapiro's; interview of 30 March 1976. For an excellent account of O'Hara's ability to transcend "pure facts" and empiricism, see Shapiro's article on O'Hara in *Contemporary Poets,* ed. James Vinson, 2d ed. (New York: St. Martin's, 1975), pp. 1778–81.

¹⁶*The Poem in its Skin* (Chicago: Big Table, 1968), p. 164.

¹⁷*The Dada Painters and Poets, An Anthology,* ed. Robert Motherwell (New York: Wittenborn, Schultz, 1951), pp. xxxv–vi. The translation is by Dollie Pierre Carreau. See also Carroll, *The Poem in its Skin,* pp. 164–68.

¹⁸*The Cantos of Ezra Pound* (New York: New Directions, 1971), pp. 508–09.

¹⁹*Iowa Review,* 4 (Winter 1973), 93–94.

²⁰Eric Sellin, "The Esthetics of Ambiguity: Reverdy's Use of Syntactic Simultaneity," in *About French Poetry from DADA to "Tel Quel," Text and Theory,* ed. Mary Ann Caws (Detroit, Mich.: Wayne State University Press, 1974), p. 117.

²¹*Art and Illusion: A Study of the Psychology of Pictorial Representation,* The A. W. Mellon Lectures in the Fine Arts, 1956 (New York: Pantheon, Bollingen Series XXXV.5, 1960), pp. 281–86.

²²*Selected Writings of Guillaume Apollinaire,* trans. and ed. Roger Shattuck (New York: New Directions, 1971), p. 121.

²³A whole essay could be written on O'Hara's allegiance to Reverdy, although the actual influence of the French poet is one of spirit rather than substance. In "A Step Away from Them," O'Hara writes: "My heart is in my / pocket, it is Poems by Pierre Reverdy" (*CP,* 258). When Ashbery asked O'Hara to contribute poems that might be

influenced by Reverdy for the special Reverdy issue of *Mercure de France,* O'Hara responded, half-jokingly: "I just couldn't stand the amount of work it [the Reverdy project] would seem to take, since the minute you mentioned it I decided that everything I've written except *In Memory of My Feelings* and *Dig my Grave with a Silver Spoon* has been under his influence." Later in the letter (1 Feb. 1961), he adds: "I think probably 'the eyelid has its storms' is somewhat influenced by *Une vague solitaire*" and then asks, "Do you think *Naphtha* is sort of Reverdian?" O'Hara did collaborate with Bill Berkson on a short prose-poem on Reverdy; see *Mercure de France,* 344 (1962), 97–98. Among other things, this piece contains the sentence: "In America there is only one other poet *beside* Reverdy: William Carlos Williams." The prose poem is reprinted in *The World,* Special Translations Issue (4 April 1973), 91–92. See also John Ashbery, "Reverdy en Amérique," *Mercure de France,* 344 (1962), 109–12.

24 Translation by Eric Sellin, in Caws, ed., *About French Poetry,* p. 119.

25 See Chapter 1. In the interview with Lucie-Smith, O'Hara says: "I think Lowell has . . . a confessional manner which lets him get away with things that are really just plain bad but you're supposed to be interested because he's supposed to be so upset" (*SS,* 13).

26 See "About Zhivago and his Poems" (1950); rpt. *CP,* 501.

27 "All the Imagination Can Hold," *New Republic,* January 1 & 8, 1972, 24; David Shapiro, in a letter to the author dated 20 July 1976, says: "The collected works is Frank O'Hara's best work and should be thought of (like Stevens) as the lyric as it attempts epic scale." Joe LeSueur, in a letter to the author dated 20 July 1976, mentions that James Merrill also read the *CP* cover to cover "as an autobiography."

28 See James Schuyler's note to the poem "Mayakovsky" (1954) in *CP,* 532–33.

29 *The Bedbug and Selected Poetry,* ed. Patricia Blake and trans. Max Hayward and George Reavey (Bloomington, Ind.: Midland Books, 1975), p. 159.

30 *The Bedbug and Selected Poetry,* pp. 137–43.

31 Another influence frequently cited is that of Rilke. My own view (see Chapter 1) is that Rilke had more influence on O'Hara's poetic than on his poetry, although O'Hara's "Aus Einem April" (*CP,* 186) is an important example of "Making it New" via parody-translation. There are also important thematic links—the treatment of the dolls in "Memorial Day 1950" (see Chapter 2) is a case in point. But O'Hara's style does not really resemble Rilke's.

32 I owe this information to Patsy Southgate, interview of 30 March 1976.

33 Unpub. letter to Bill Berkson, 12 August 1962.

34 *Larry Rivers* (New York: Abrams, 1971), p. 24.

35 Grace Hartigan, letter to the author dated 14 March 1976.

36 Rimbaud, *Complete Works, Selected Letters,* ed. and trans. Wallace Fowlie (Chicago: Phoenix Books, 1966), pp. 217–18.
I am the saint in prayer on the terrace like the peaceful animals that graze as far as the sea of Palestine.
I am the scholar in his dark armchair. Branches and rain beat against the library window.

I am the wanderer along the main road running through the dwarfish woods ...
I might be the child abandoned on the wharf. ...

[37] See Chapter 3, Note 7.

[38] Unpub. letter to Fairfield Porter, 7 July 1955.

[39] Poetry Reading, Buffalo, New York, 25 September 1964, taped by Donald Allen.

[40] I think O'Hara is referring to Pollock's early painting *Bird* (1941; Collection Lee Krasner, New York), reproduced in Alberto Busignani, *Pollock* (New York: Crown, 1970), p. 20. The painting has a birdlike shape emerging from a white cloud near the top center of the canvas. Others have suggested that O'Hara was thinking of Brancusi's famous sculpture *Bird in Space* in the Museum of Modern Art. In either case, the implication is that the dead artist is reborn as a work of art.

[41] The fifteen poems in *Love Poems* (*Tentative Title*) (New York: Tibor de Nagy Gallery, 1965) are roughly equivalent to what I call the "Vincent Warren" poems although there are some exceptions like "Post the Lake Poets Ballad" and "Poem (Now the violets are all gone ...)." In the *Collected Poems,* the Vincent Warren poems are found on the following pages: 331, 332, 338, 342, 345, 346, 349–56, 360–62, 366–69, 373–74, 376–78, 380, 382, 385, 387, 396, 400, 402, 405–06.

[42] "The Corn-Porn Lyric: Poetry 1972–73," *Contemporary Literature,* 16 (Winter 1975), 84–125.

[43] Vincent Warren, untitled memoir of Frank O'Hara (Montreal 1973) in *Panjandrum,* 2 & 3 (1973), unpaginated.

[44] Unpub. letter to John Ashbery, 1 February 1961.

Chapter 5: THE PILLAR OF OUR DEATHS

[1] In the *Collected Poems,* the period from July 1961 to June 1966 is covered by a scant 84 of the total 491 pages, and most of the poems in this section date from 1961–62. The year 1963 is represented by only eleven poems, 1964 by thirteen, 1965 by three. We have only one published poem for 1966: the "Little Elegy for Antonio Machado," written for the catalogue of John Bernard Myers's "Homage to Machado" Show (a benefit for refugees of the Spanish Civil War) at the Tibor de Nagy Gallery. *Poems Retrieved* adds eleven poems from 1961 (a number of which are "For Your Information" poems for Bill Berkson), nine for 1962, three for 1964, one for 1965. These are, on the whole, slight occasional poems.

[2] In an unpublished letter to John Ashbery, dated 1 February 1961, O'Hara writes: "I have been writing in desultory fashion a little play called THE GENERAL'S RETURN FROM ONE PLACE TO ANOTHER but am having quite a bit of trouble as to ending it (and how?) or letting it go on until it is the size of a Lope de Vega. ... I believe it was inspired by a wonderful production of Brecht's wonderful *In the Jungle of Cities* which the Living Theatre has in repertory now and my dislike for General MacArthur, if inspired at all can be mentioned in 'connection' with it."

[3] *Art and Literature,* 10 (1965); rpt. in *Eight Plays from OFF-OFF Broadway,* eds. Nick Orzell and Michael Smith (New York: Bobbs Merrill, 1966), p. 21.

[4]Joe LeSueur Interview, 20 July 1975.

[5]Unpub. letter to Frank Lima, 6 February 1963.

[6]In advance commentary, John Ashbery writes: "The poems in Frank Lima's marvelous new collection are bright, corrosive, funny, terrifying—reflections in a surreal eye focused outward on life in today's city;" and David Shapiro says: "Frank Lima's work has developed into something as steely, menacing and fine as the welder's art of David Smith. It is a species of American linguistic sculpture" (*New York Review of Books,* 24 June 1976, p. 13).

[7]*In Public, In Private* was originally published in 1948 by James A. Decker Co., Prairie City, Illinois. It is reprinted in Edwin Denby's *Collected Poems* (New York: Full Court Press, 1975).

[8]"Paraphrase of Edwin Denby speaking on 'The New York School'," as recorded by Anne Waldman, *The World* (April 1974), 73.

[9]*Panjandrum,* 2 & 3 (1973), unpaginated.

[10]John Ashbery, Note appended to "Play," by John Ashbery, Kenneth Koch, and Frank O'Hara, *ZZZ* [*Z,* no. 3], ed. Kenward Elmslie (Calais, Vt.: Z Press, 1974), 122.

[11]Unpub. letter to Bill Berkson, 12 August 1962.

[12]*Hymns of St. Bridget* has been published in pamphlet form (New York: Adventures in Poetry, 1974). Two of these "Hymns," which are still very much in the tradition of O'Hara's "I do this, I do that" poems, were published in *Evergreen Review,* 6, no. 24 (May–June 1960), 107–09. "Us Looking up at St. Bridget," for example, begins:

Let's see now where are we
it is dust in New York about to be
Christmas and next 1961 we are not
detectives are we so we don't care
what time it is

The "Letters of Angelicus & Fidelio Fobb" have recently been reprinted in *ZZZ* [*Z,* no. 4] (1975), 90–109. These letters seem to be modeled on the prose of Ronald Firbank or Evelyn Waugh. For example, one letter from Angelicus to Fidelio, dated 14 August 1961 from the "Alhambra Hotel, Secondary Bridge Road, Punselheim, Pa.," begins:

Upon lighting my first cigarette of this morning, I found that I was excruciatingly bored, not to say sick unto death. Even the permissions which Prussy has placed and arranged so delicately on my breakfast plate could not assuage this terrible feeling which must have had something to do with the night before and the day (or days) ahead. (p. 92)

This is a fair example of the humor of the Fobb Letters.

[13]*CP,* 553–54. *M.L.F.Y.* evidently means "My Love For You." "Biotherm" was the one O'Hara poem included in Paris Leary and Robert Kelly's anthology, *A Controversy of Poets* (New York: Doubleday/Anchor, 1965), which also contains a brief biographical and bibliographical note on O'Hara (p. 544).

[14]This is the view of Charles Molesworth, who calls "Biotherm" a "collage which seldom rewards lingering attention or compels an energized response. Somehow the poem manages to bring the marvelous and the humdrum together, not so much as

fragments of heterogeneous values jostling together, but as an aleatory set of transcriptions, the recording of many merely different things," "The Clear Architecture of the Nerves: The Poetry of Frank O'Hara," *Iowa Review,* 6 (Summer–Fall 1975), 64.

[15] Ted Berrigan, *The Sonnets* (New York: Grove, 1964), p. 32.

[16] Ron Padgett, *Great Balls of Fire* (New York: Holt, Rinehart and Winston, 1969), p. 9.

[17] "Frank O'Hara Dead at 40," *East Village Other,* August 1966, p. 11.

[18] The four elegies are "To an Actor Who Died" (*CP,* 226); "For James Dean" (*CP,* 228); "Thinking of James Dean" (*CP,* 230); and "Four Little Elegies" (*CP,* 248)—all written in 1955–56.

[19] "The Significance of Frank O'Hara," *Iowa Review,* 4 (Winter 1973), 103. See also Paul Carroll, *The Poem in its Skin* (Chicago: Big Table, 1968), pp. 155–68.

[20] On this point, see Norman Holland, *Poems in Persons, An Introduction to the Psychoanalysis of Literature* (New York: Norton, 1973), p. 122.

[21] See the following: Allen Ginsberg, "City Midnight Junk Strains," *Planet News* (San Francisco: City Lights Books, 1969), pp. 134–37; Patsy Southgate, "Nobody Operates like an IBM Machine: For Frank O'Hara," *Evergreen Review,* 45 (February 1967), 50; Tony Towle, "Sunrise: Ode to Frank O'Hara," *Paris Review,* 11 (Fall 1967), 117; James Schuyler, "Buried at Springs," *Freely Espousing* (New York: Doubleday, 1969), rpt. *An Anthology of New York Poets,* ed. Ron Padgett and David Shapiro (New York: Random House, 1970), pp. 15–17; David Shapiro, "Ode," *Poems From Deal* (New York: Dutton, 1969), pp. 59–60; Gerard Malanga, "In Memory of the Poet Frank O'Hara 1926–1966," *The World Anthology,* ed. Anne Waldman (New York: Bobbs-Merrill, 1969), pp. 134–36; Ron Padgett, "Strawberries in Mexico," *Great Balls of Fire,* pp. 83–85; John Wieners, "After Reading *Second Avenue:* For Frank O'Hara," *Paris Review,* 13 (Winter 1971), 60–61; Diane di Prima, "From Kerhonson, July 28, 1966" and "Inverness, Cape Breton Island," *Panjandrum* 2 & 3 (1973), unpaginated.

[22] The trend for such pairing was probably first established by John Bernard Myers in his anthology *The Poets of the New York School* (Philadelphia: Falcon Press, 1969), pp. 1–29. See also Fred Moramarco, "John Ashbery and Frank O'Hara: The Painterly Poets," *Journal of Modern Literature* 5, no. 3 (September 1976), 436–62. Stephen Koch, "The New York School of Poets: The Serious at Play," *New York Times Book Review,* 11 February 1968, pp. 4–5.

[23] Richard Kostelanetz, "How to be a Difficult Poet," *New York Times Magazine,* 23 May 1976, pp. 19–20.

[24] "Rare Modern," *Poetry,* 89 (February 1957); rpt. *SS,* 77–78.

[25] Unpub. letter to Mike Goldberg, 26 August 1957.

[26] Unpub. letter to John Ashbery, 1 February 1961.

[27] Kostelanetz, *New York Times Magazine,* p. 22.

[28] "The Charity of Hard Moments," *Salmagundi,* 22–23 (Spring–Summer 1973), 103–31; rpt. *American Poetry Since 1960, Some Critical Perspectives,* ed. Robert B. Shaw (Cheadle Hulme: Carcanet Press, 1973), pp. 83–108. For the comments cited, see Shaw,

pp. 85–86. "Europe" appeared in *The Tennis Court Oath* (Middletown, Conn.: Wesleyan University Press, 1962), pp. 64–85.

29 Kostelanetz, *New York Times Magazine,* p. 22.

30 See, for example, John Russell, review of *Une Semaine de Bonté, A Surrealistic Novel in Collage* (1934; rpt. New York: Dover, 1976), in the *New York Times Book Review,* 4 July 1976, pp. 6–7.

31 *The Tennis Court Oath,* p. 13.

32 *Rivers and Mountains* (New York: Holt, Rinehart and Winston, 1966), p. 43. "The Skaters" first appeared in *Art and Literature,* 3 (Autumn/Winter 1964); O'Hara undoubtedly read it there.

33 I discuss "A Step Away from Them" more fully in "Poetry Chronicle 1970–71," *Contemporary Literature,* 14 (Winter 1973), 99–102.

34 At the time Donald Allen used the term in his *The New American Poetry* (1960), it did, of course, have validity in distinguishing O'Hara, Ashbery, Koch, Schuyler, Barbara Guest, and Edward Field from the Black Mountain Poets, the Beats, and the poets of the "San Francisco Renaissance." But Allen himself insists that his divisions are "somewhat arbitrary and cannot be taken as rigid categories" (p. xii). Of the New York group, he writes quite simply: "John Ashbery, Kenneth Koch, and Frank O'Hara, of the fourth group, the New York Poets, first met at Harvard where they were associated with the Poets' Theatre. They migrated to New York in the early fifties where they met Edward Field, Barbara Guest, and James Schuyler, and worked with the Living Theatre and the Artists' Theatre" (p. xiii).

35 *World,* 29 (April 1974), 73.

36 Lita Hornick, "Anne Waldman: A Myriad Woman," *The Poetry Project Newsletter,* 36 (1 June 1976), 1.

37 David Shapiro, letter to the author, 20 July 1976.

38 *I Remember* (New York: Full Court Press, 1975), p. 14.

39 "Ode," *Poems from Deal* (New York: Dutton, 1969), p. 60.

BIBLIOGRAPHICAL
NOTE

PRIMARY SOURCES

Poetry

The Collected Poems of Frank O'Hara, edited by Donald Allen (New York: Knopf, 1971), is the definitive critical edition. Aside from the poems, it contains selected essays and statements by the poet as well as excellent notes by Donald Allen. The volume thus supercedes the following earlier collections: *A City Winter, and Other Poems* (New York: Tibor de Nagy Gallery, 1952); *Meditations in an Emergency* (New York: Grove Press, 1957; 2nd ed., 1967); *Second Avenue* (New York: Totem Press-Corinth Books, 1960); *Odes* (New York: Tiber Press, 1960); *Lunch Poems* (San Francisco: City Lights Books, 1964); *Love Poems* (*Tentative Title*) (New York: Tibor de Nagy Gallery, 1965).

In 1974, Alfred A. Knopf published *The Selected Poems of Frank O'Hara,* edited by Donald Allen. This generous selection contains 216 pages of poems. Allen is currently preparing for publication two more volumes to include those poems that have come to light since 1971 as well as juvenilia. They will be called *Early Writing* and *Poems Retrieved,* both to be published by Grey Fox Press, Bolinas, California.

With the appearance of these two volumes, publication of the poems will be largely complete.

In Memory of My Feelings, A Selection of Poems by Frank O'Hara, edited by Bill Berkson, with "original decorations" by thirty artists, a Preface by René d'Harnoncourt and an Afterword by Bill Berkson, is an important collector's item containing illustrations by Willem de Kooning, Jasper Johns, Grace Hartigan, Alfred Leslie, and others.

The following of O'Hara's collaborations have been published: *Hymns of St. Bridget,* with Bill Berkson (New York: Adventures in Poetry, 1974); "Letters of Angelicus and Fidelio Fobb," with Bill Berkson, *ZZZZ,* ed. Kenward Elmslie (Calais, Vt.: Z Press, 1975), pp. 90–109; "The Purest Heart in the Whole Wide World" and "Sam" (1964) with Tony Towle, *Panjandrum,* 2 & 3 (San Francisco, 1973): Special Supplement, *Frank O'Hara (1926–1966),* ed. Bruce Boone.

The World, 27 (April 1973; Special Translations Issue), 92–98, contains O'Hara's translations of poems by Hoelderlin, Rilke, Rimbaud, Mallarmé, and Char. O'Hara was very modest about these translations; Ron Padgett, editor of the special issue, points out that "the versions selected and presented in this issue must not be considered final ones," since the poet would have wished to check them. But some, like the translation of Rimbaud's "Le Coeur Volé," are remarkable, constituting a valuable adjunct to the *Collected Poems.*

Miscellaneous Prose

O'Hara published more than a hundred essays, reviews, notes, and introductions to books and catalogues. The most important of these are collected in *Art Chronicles 1954–1966* (New York: Braziller, 1975) and *Standing Still and Walking in New York,* ed. Donald Allen (Bolinas, Calif.: Grey Fox Press, 1975). Others—art criticism, literary criticism, reviews of friends' books, etc.—are cited in the Notes above. The bibliography at the back of *Art Chronicles* is helpful for the uncollected art criticism.

Plays

The following plays have been published: "Try! Try!," in *Artist's Theatre,* ed. Herbert Machiz (New York: Grove Press, 1960); "The General Returns from One Place to Another," in *Art and Literature,* 10

(1965), rpt. in *Eight Plays from OFF-OFF Broadway,* eds. Nick Orzell and Michael Smith (New York: Bobbs Merrill, 1966), pp. 21–52; "Surprising J.A.," with Larry Rivers, in *Tracks,* 1 (November 1974), 59–62.

Unpublished Manuscripts

The Frank O'Hara Estate has an important group of unpublished essays, journals, and miscellaneous papers. Notebook A, dating from the Harvard years, contains, aside from the poems to be published by Donald Allen in *Early Writing,* a Commonplace Book, outlining O'Hara's literary interests. This, together with MS 146, a French reading list, help the reader to track down O'Hara's sources. MS 296, "Pastorals," a group of nineteen poems, is the first version of the early sequences of "Oranges."

MS 472 ("Journal, October 8, 1948 to November 30, 1948, with an appendix, January 21, 1949 to January 28, 1949") is an important autobiographical source, providing background on the Harvard years. MS 656 ("False Positions"), MS 631 ("Lament and Chastisement: a Travelogue of War and Personality"), and MS 638 ("Eye at Argos") are undergraduate essays. MS 467 ("Notes for a talk on 'The Image in Poetry and Painting,' The Club, 11 April 1952") and MS 156 ("Notes for a talk on 'The New Poets,' The Club, 14 May 1952") provide invaluable information about O'Hara's aesthetic. These two lectures should be read in conjunction with "Design Etc.," in *Standing Still and Walking in New York,* pp. 33–36.

Manuscripts of unpublished plays include: "Change Your Bedding," produced by the Poets' Theatre in Cambridge, Mass., in 1951; "Love's Labor: An Eclogue" and "Awake in Spain," both produced by the American Theatre for Poets in New York in 1960; "The Moon Also Rises" (MS 245), 1957, unproduced.

Forthcoming Publications

Donald Allen's edition of *Early Writing* will include the following: "Notebook Poems, 1946–1949"; a second group of poems written between 1946 and 1950, some of which were included in the manuscript of *Poems Retrieved,* which is my source throughout; "Pastorals" (MS 296)"; and prose pieces MSS 472, 631, 638, 656.

Full Court Press in New York is currently preparing an edition of the *Selected Plays of Frank O'Hara*, with a Preface by Joe LeSueur. The Museum of Modern Art is planning to reissue the Frank O'Hara-Larry Rivers lithographs *Stones* in a portfolio. Twenty-two of the O'Hara-Norman Bluhm *Poem-Paintings* were included in the Autumn 1976 show of the Grey Art Gallery, New York University, where they are available for viewing.

Donald Allen is editing the *Collected Letters of Frank O'Hara.* This is a formidable undertaking: O'Hara was a brilliant and prolific correspondent, and his letters will provide an invaluable document on the art world of the fifties and sixties.

Alex Smith is now at work on a comprehensive bibliography of Frank O'Hara for Garland Publishing Company.

SECONDARY SOURCES

The following short list includes only the most important items, both biographical and critical. All but the most minor articles, reviews, and memoirs of O'Hara are included in the Notes above.

Altieri, Charles. "The Significance of Frank O'Hara," *Iowa Review,* 4 (Winter 1973), 90–104.

Ashbery, John. "Frank O'Hara's Question," *Book Week,* 25 September 1966, p. 6.

———. Review of *In Memory of My Feelings, Art News,* 66 (January 1968), 50–51, 67–68.

———. Preface to *The Collected Poems of Frank O'Hara.*

Berkson, Bill. "Frank O'Hara and his Poems," *Art and Literature,* 12 (Spring 1967), 50–64.

———. Afterword to *In Memory of My Feelings* by Frank O'Hara.

Carroll, Paul. *The Poem in Its Skin* (Chicago: Big Table, 1968).

Feldman, Morton. "Frank O'Hara: Lost Times and Future Hopes," *Art in America,* 60 (March–April 1972), 52–55.

Forrest-Thompson, Veronica. "Dada, Unrealism and Contemporary Poetry," *20th Century Studies,* 12 (December 1974), 77–93.

Holahan, Susan. "Frank O'Hara's Poetry," *American Poetry Since 1960, Some Critical Perspectives,* ed. Robert B. Shaw (Cheadle Hulme: Carcanet Press, 1973), pp. 109–22.

Koch, Kenneth. "All the Imagination Can Hold" (review of the *Collected Poems*), *New Republic,* 1 & 8 (January 1972), 23–24.

LeSueur, Joseph. "Four Apartments: A Memoir of Frank O'Hara," *Another World,* ed. Anne Waldman (New York: Bobbs-Merrill, 1971), pp. 287–300.

Libby, Anthony. "O'Hara on the Silver Range," *Contemporary Literature,* 17 (Spring 1976), 140–62.

Lucie-Smith, Edward. "An Interview with Frank O'Hara" (1965), *Standing Still and Walking in New York,* ed. Donald Allen (Bolinas, Calif.: Grey Fox Press, 1975), pp. 3–26.

Molesworth, Charles. "'The Clear Architecture of the Nerves': The Poetry of Frank O'Hara," *Iowa Review,* 6 (Summer–Fall 1975), 61–73.

Myers, John Bernard. *The Poets of the New York School,* selected and edited by John Bernard Myers (Philadelphia: Falcon Press, 1969).

Perloff, Marjorie. "Poetry Chronicle 1970–71," *Contemporary Literature,* 14 (Winter 1973), 99–102.

———. "New Thresholds, Old Anatomies: Contemporary Poetry and the Limits of Exegesis," *Iowa Review,* 5 (Winter 1974), 83–99.

Rivers, Larry. "Life Among the Stones," *Location* (Spring 1963), 90–98.

Schuyler, James. "Frank O'Hara: Poet among Painters," *Art News,* 73 (May 1974), 44–45.

Shapiro, David. "Frank O'Hara," *Contemporary Poets,* ed. James Vinson, 2d. ed. (New York: St. Martin's, 1975), pp. 1778–81.

Vendler, Helen. "The Virtues of the Alterable," *Parnassus: Poetry in Review,* 1 (Fall/Winter 1972), 5–20.

Special Journal Issues Devoted to O'Hara

Audit/Poetry, 4, no. 1 (Buffalo, 1964): "Featuring Frank O'Hara," eds. Michael Anania and Charles Doria. Contains essays by Kenneth Koch and Albert Cook.

Panjandrum, 2 & 3 (San Francisco, 1973): "Special Supplement, Frank O'Hara (1926–1966)," ed. Bruce Boone. Contains memoirs and essays by Virgil Thompson, Vincent Warren, Joe Brainard, and John Button.

GENERAL INDEX

INDEX
THE WRITINGS OF
FRANK O'HARA

THE CRITIC

I cannot possibly think of you
other than you are: the assassin

of my orchards. You lurk there
in the shadows, meting out

conversation like Eve's first
confusion between penises and

snakes. Oh be droll, be jolly
and be temperate! Do not

frighten me more than you
have to! I must live forever.

—FRANK O'HARA
(1951)

CONTENTS

ACKNOWLEDGEMENTS

For permission to include material published by them, grateful acknowledgement is made to the following:

Alfred A. Knopf, Inc., for permission to quote from *The Collected Poems of Frank O'Hara,* edited by Donald Allen. Copyright © 1971 by Maureen Granville-Smith, Administratrix of the Estate of Frank O'Hara.

City Lights Books, for permission to quote from *Lunch Poems* by Frank O'Hara. Copyright © 1964 by Frank O'Hara; for permission to quote from *Planet News* by Allen Ginsberg. Copyright © 1968 by Allen Ginsberg.

Corinth Books, Inc., for Permission to quote from *Second Avenue* by Frank O'Hara. Copyright © 1960 by Frank O'Hara.

Grove Press, Inc., for permission to quote from *Meditations in an Emergency* by Frank O'Hara. Copyright © 1957 by Frank O'Hara; for permission to quote from *The Sonnets* by Ted Berrigan. Copyright © 1964 by Ted Berrigan and "*C*," a Journal of Poetry.

Donald Allen and Grey Fox Press, for permission to quote from *Standing Still* and *Walking in New York* by Frank O'Hara. Copyright © 1975 by Maureen Granville-Smith, Adminstratrix of the Estate of Frank O'Hara.

New Directions Publishing Corporation, for permission to quote from *Collected Earlier Poems* by William Carlos Williams. Copyright © 1938 by New Directions Publishing Corporation; Copyright © 1951 by William Carlos Williams; and to Faber and Faber Ltd, for permission to quote from *The Cantos* by Ezra Pound. Copyright © 1948 by Ezra Pound; for permission to quote from *Selected Writings* by Guillaume Apollinaire. Copyright © 1971 by Roger Shattuck. All Rights Reserved.

Harper & Row, Publishers, and to Weidenfeld & Nicholson, Publishers, for permission to quote from *The Bedbug and Selected Poetry* by Vladimir Mayakovsky. Copyright © 1960 by Patricia Blake and Max Hayward. Originally published by World Publishing Company.

Doubleday and Company, Inc., for permission to quote from *Freely Espousing* by James Schuyler. Copyright © 1969 by James Schuyler.

Ron Padgett, for permission to quote from *Great Balls of Fire.* Copyright © 1965, 1967, 1968, 1969 by Ron Padgett.

George Wittenborn, Inc. for permission to quote from *Dada Painters and Poets,* edited by Robert Motherwell. Copyright © 1951 by Robert Motherwell.

Wesleyan University Press, for permission to quote from *The Tennis Court Oath* by John Ashbery. Copyright © 1959 by John Ashbery.

Georges Borchardt, Inc., for permission to quote from *Rivers and Mountains.* Copyright © 1962, 1963, 1964, 1966, 1977 by John Ashbery.

Anne Waldman, for permission to quote from *Another World* (New York: Bobbs-Merrill Co., Inc. 1971). Copyright © 1971 by Anne Waldman.